WITH AMERICANS OF
PAST AND PRESENT DAYS

WITH AMERICANS OF
PAST AND PRESENT DAYS

BY

JEAN J. JUSSERAND

Essay Index Reprint Series

BOOKS FOR LIBRARIES PRESS
FREEPORT, NEW YORK

First Published 1916
Reprinted 1972

Library of Congress Cataloging in Publication Data

Jusserand, Jean Adrien Antoine Jules, 1855-1932.
    With Americans of past and present days.

    (Essay index reprint series)
    Reprint of the 1916 ed.
    1. U. S.--Bibliography. 2. U. S.--Relations
(general) with France. 3. France--Relations (general)
with the United States. 4. U. S.--History--Revolution
--French participation. 5. Rochambeau, Jean Baptiste
Donatien de Vimeur, comte de, 1725-1807. 6. L'Enfant,
Pierre Charles, 1755-1825. 7. Washington, George,
Pres. U. S., 1732-1799. I. Title.
E176.J96 1972   973'.099   73-156669
ISBN 0-8369-2555-6

PRINTED IN THE UNITED STATES OF AMERICA
BY
NEW WORLD BOOK MANUFACTURING CO., INC.
HALLANDALE, FLORIDA 33009

DEDICATION

This day, thirteen years ago, a new French ambassador presented his credentials. The ambassador was not very old for an ambassador. The President was very young for a president, the youngest, in fact, the United States ever had. Both, according to custom, read set speeches, and there followed a first conversation, which had a great many successors, touching on a variety of subjects not connected, all of them, with diplomacy. In which talk took part the genial, learned, and warm-hearted author of the "Pike County Ballads" and of the Life of Lincoln, present at the meeting as Secretary of State of the United States.

This was the first direct impression the newcomer had of broad-minded, strenuous America, his earliest ones, as a child, having been derived from the illustrated weekly paper received by his family, and which

v

*offered to view fancy pictures of the battles between
the bearded soldiers of Grant and Lee, the "poilus" of
those days; another impression was from Cooper's
tales, Deerslayer sharing with Ivanhoe the enthusiasm of the young people at the family hearth.
Another American impression was received by them
a little later, when, the Republic having been proclaimed, the street where the family had their winter
home ceased to be called "Rue de la Reine" and became "Rue Franklin."*

*Thirteen years is a long space of time in an
ambassador's life; it is not an insignificant one
in the life of such a youthful nation as the United
States; I have now witnessed the eleventh part of
that life. Something like one-fourth or one-fifth of
the population has been added since I began service
here. There were forty-five States then instead of
forty-eight; the commercial intercourse with France
was half of what it is now; the tonnage of the
American navy was less than half what it is at
present; the Panama Canal was not yet American;
the aeroplane was unknown; the automobile prac-*

tically unused. Among artists, thinkers, humorists, critics, scientists, shone La Farge, McKim, Saint-Gaudens, William James, Mark Twain, Furness, Newcomb, Weir Mitchell, who, leaving a lasting fame, have all passed away.

The speech at the White House was followed by many others. Little enough accustomed, up to then, to addressing any assembly at any time, I did not expect to have much to do in that line; but I had. I soon found that it was not a question of taste and personal disposition, but one of courtesy and friend-liness. The quick-witted, kindly-disposed, warm-hearted audiences of America, ever ready to show appreciation for any effort, greatly facilitated mat-ters.

I was thus led by degrees to address gatherings of many kinds, in many places, on many subjects, from the origins of the War of Independence to refores-tation in America, and from the Civil War to in-fantile mortality. Many such speeches had to be delivered impromptu; others, luckily for both orator and listeners, were on subjects which the former had studied with as much care as the fulfilling of a variety of tasks and duties had allowed him.

An examination of the development of the two countries will, I believe, lead any impartial mind to the conclusion that, with so many peculiar ties between them in the past, a similar goal ahead of them, and, to a great extent, similar hard problems to solve, it cannot but be of advantage to themselves and to the liberal world that the two Republics facing each other across the broad ocean, one nearly half a century old, the other three times as much, should ever live on terms of amity, not to say intimacy, comparing experiences, of help to one another whenever circumstances allow: this they have been on more than one occasion, and will doubtless be again in the future. During our present trials the active generosity of American men and women has exerted itself in a way that can never be forgotten.

The dean now, not only of the diplomatic corps in Washington, but of all my predecessors from the early days, when, on a raised platform in Independence Hall, my diplomatic ancestor, Gérard de

Rayneval, presented to Congress the first credentials brought here from abroad (and Gérard was then, he alone, the whole diplomatic body), I have presumed to gather together a few studies on some of the men or events of most interest from the point of view of Franco-American relations. Three addresses are added, just as they were delivered. May these pages find among readers the same indulgent reception their author found among listeners.

And so, having now lived in America thirteen years, offering good wishes to the forty-eight of to-day, I dedicate, in memory of former times, the following pages

TO

THE THIRTEEN ORIGINAL STATES.

J. J. JUSSERAND.

WASHINGTON, February 7, 1916.

CONTENTS

I

ROCHAMBEAU AND THE FRENCH IN AMERICA

FROM UNPUBLISHED DOCUMENTS

ROCHAMBEAU AND THE FRENCH IN AMERICA

FROM UNPUBLISHED DOCUMENTS

THE American war had been for five years in progress; for two years a treaty of alliance, having as sole object "to maintain effectually the liberty, sovereignty, and independence, absolute and unlimited, of the United States," bound us French to the "insurgents"; successes and reverses followed each other in turn: Brooklyn, Trenton, Brandywine, Saratoga. Quite recently the news had come of the double victory at sea and on land of d'Estaing at Grenada, and Paris had been illuminated. The lights were scarcely out when news arrived of the disaster of the same d'Estaing at Savannah. All France felt anxious concerning the issue of a war which had lasted so long and whose end continued to be doubtful.

When, in the first months of 1780, the report went about that a great definitive effort was to be attempted, that it was not this time a question of sending ships to the Americans, but of sending an army, and that the termination of the great drama was near, the enthusiasm was unbounded.

All wanted to take part. There was a prospect of crossing the seas, of succoring a people fighting for a sacred cause, a people of whom all our volunteers praised the virtues; the people led by Washington, and represented in Paris by Franklin. An ardor as of crusaders inflamed the hearts of French youths, and the intended expedition'was, in fact, the most important that France had launched beyond the seas since the distant time of the crusades. The cause was a truly sacred one, the cause of liberty, a magical word which then stirred the hearts of the many. "Why is liberty so rare?" Voltaire had said—"Because the most valuable of possessions."

All those who were so lucky as to be allowed to take part in the expedition were convinced that they would witness memorable, perhaps unique, events, and it turned out, indeed, that they were to witness a campaign which, with the battle of Hastings, where the fate of England was decided in 1066, and that of Bouvines, which made of France in 1214 a great nation, was to be one of the three military actions with greatest consequences in which for the last thousand years the French had participated.

A striking result of this state of mind is that an extraordinary number of those who went noted down their impressions, kept journals, drew sketches. Never perhaps during a military campaign was so much writing done, nor were so many albums filled with drawings.

Notes, letters, journals, sketches have come down to us in large quantities, and from all manner of men, for the passion of observing and narrating was common to all kinds of people: journals and memoirs of army chiefs like Rochambeau, or chiefs of staff like Chastellux, a member of the French Academy, adapter of Shakespeare, and author of a *Félicité Publique*, which, Franklin said, showed him to be "a real friend of humanity"; narratives of a regimental chaplain, like Abbé Robin, of a sceptical rake like the Duke de Lauzun, the new Don Juan, whose battle stories alternate with his love reminiscences, handsome, impertinent, licentious, an excellent soldier withal, bold and tenacious, marked, like several of his companions, to mount the revolutionary scaffold; journals of officers of various ranks, like Count de Deux-Ponts, Prince de Broglie, he, too, marked for the scaffold; Count de Ségur, son of the marshal, himself afterward an Academician and an ambassador; Mathieu-Dumas, future minister of war of a future King of Naples, who bore the then unknown name of Joseph Bonaparte; the Swedish Count Axel de Fersen, one of Rochambeau's aides, who was to organize the French royal family's flight to Varennes, and to die massacred by the mob in his own country; notes, map, and sketches

of Baron Cromot-Dubourg, another of Rochambeau's aides; journal, too, among many others, of a
modest quartermaster like Blanchard, who gives a
note quite apart, observes what others do not,
and whose tone, as that of a subordinate, is in
contrast with the superb ways of the "seigneurs"
his companions.

From page to page, turning the leaves, one sees
appear, without speaking of Lafayette, Kosciusko,
and the first enthusiasts, many names just emerg-
ing from obscurity, never to sink into it again:
Berthier, La Pérouse, La Touche-Tréville, the
Lameth brothers, Bougainville, Custine, the
Bouillé of the flight to Varennes, the La Cloche-
terie of the fight of *La Belle Poule*, the Duportail
who was to be minister of war under the Constit-
uent Assembly, young Talleyrand, brother of the
future statesman, young Mirabeau, brother of
the orator, himself usually known for his portly
dimensions as *Mirabeau-tonneau*, ever ready with
the cup or the sword, young Saint-Simon, not yet
a pacifist, and not yet a Saint-Simonian,[1] Suffren, in whose squadron had embarked the future
Director Barras, an officer then in the regiment of
Pondichéry. All France was really represented,

[1] Concerning his American campaign, in which he greatly distinguished himself, he wrote later: "In itself, war did not interest me,
but its object interested me keenly, and I willingly took part in its
labors. I said to myself: ' I want the end; I must adopt the means.' "
Œuvres, 1865, I, 11. He was wounded and promoted.

to some extent that of the past, to a larger one that of the future.

Many of those journals have been published (Cromot-Dubourg's only in an English version printed in America[1]); others have been lost; others remain unpublished, so that after all that has been said, and well said, it still remains possible, with the help of new guides and new documents, to follow Washington and Rochambeau once more, and in a different company, during the momentous journey which led them from the Hudson to the York River. The Washington papers and the Rochambeau papers, used only in part, are preserved in the Library of Congress. A juvenile note, in contrast with the quiet dignity of the official reports by the heads of the army, is given by the unprinted journal, a copy of which is also preserved in the same library, kept by one more of Rochambeau's aides, Louis Baron de Closen, an excellent observer, gay, warm-hearted, who took seriously all that pertained to duty, and merrily all the rest, especially mishaps. Useful information is also given by some unprinted letters of George Washington, some with the superscription still preserved: "On public service —to his Excellency, Count de Rochambeau, Williamsburg, Virginia," the whole text often in the great chief's characteristic handwriting, clear and

[1] *Magazine of American History*, March, 1880, ff.

steady, neither slow nor hasty, with nothing
blurred and nothing omitted, with no trepidation,
no abbreviation, the writing of a man with a
clear conscience and clear views, superior to fortune, and the convinced partisan, in every circumstance throughout life, of the straight line.

The British Government has, moreover, most
liberally opened its archives, so that, both through
the recriminatory pamphlets printed in London
after the disaster and the despatches now accessible, one can know what was said day by day in
New York and out of New York, in the redoubts
at Yorktown, and in the French and American
trenches around the place.

I

Lieutenant-General Jean-Baptiste Donatien de Vimeur, Comte de Rochambeau, aged then fifty-five, and Washington's senior by seven years, was in his house, still in existence, Rue du Cherche-Midi, Paris,[1] at the beginning of March, 1780; he was ill and about to leave for his castle of Rochambeau in Vendomois; post-horses were in readiness when, in the middle of the night, he received, he says in his memoirs,[2] a "courrier bringing him the order to go to Versailles and receive the instructions of his Majesty." For some time rumors had been afloat that the great attempt would soon be made. He was informed that the news was true, and that he would be placed at the head of the army sent to the assistance of the Americans.

The task was an extraordinary one. He would have to reach the New World with a body of troops packed on slow transports, to avoid the English fleets, to fight in a country practically un-

[1] A quite handsome house, now the offices of the Ministry of Labor. The gardens no longer exist.

[2] *Mémoires militaires, historiques et politiques de Rochambeau, ancien maréchal de France et grand officier de la Légion d'honneur*, Paris, 1809, 2 vols., I, 235.

known, by the side of men not less so, and whom we had been accustomed to fight rather than be-friend, and for a cause which had never before elicited enthusiasm at Versailles, the cause of re-publican liberty.

This last point was the strangest of all, so strange that even Indians, friends of the French in former days, asked Rochambeau, when they saw him in America, how it was that his King could think fit to help other people against "their own father," their King. Rochambeau replied that the latter had been too hard on his subjects, that they were right, therefore, in shaking off the yoke, and we in helping them to secure "that natural liberty which God has conferred on man."

This answer to "Messieurs les Sauvages," is an enlightening one; it shows what was the latent force that surmounted all obstacles and caused the French nation to stand as a whole, from be-ginning to end, in favor of the Americans, to ap-plaud a treaty of alliance which, while entailing the gravest risks, forbade us all conquest, and to rejoice enthusiastically at a peace which after a victorious war added nothing to our possessions. This force was the increasing passion among the French for precisely "that natural liberty which God has conferred on man."

Hatred of England, quickened though it had been by the harsh conditions of the treaty of

Paris bereaving us of Canada, in 1763, had much less to do with it than is sometimes alleged. Such a feeling existed, it is true, in the hearts of some of the leaders, but not of all; it did in the minds also of some of the officers, but again not of all. What predominated in the mass of the nation, irrespective of any other consideration, was sympathy for men who wanted to fight injustice and to be free. The cause of the insurgents was popular because it was associated with the notion of liberty; people did not look beyond.[1]

It is often forgotten that this time was not in France a period of Anglophobia, but of Anglomania. Necker, so influential, and who then held the purse-strings, was an Anglophile; so was Prince de Montbarey, minister of war; so was that Duke de Lauzun who put an end for a time to his love-affairs and came to America at the head of his famous legion. All that was English was admired and, when possible, imitated: manners, philosophy, sports, clothes, parliamentary institutions, Shakespeare, just translated by Le Tourneur, with the King and Queen as patrons of the

[1] "On a soutenu," said Pontgibaud, later Comte de Moré, one of Lafayette's aides, in a conversation with Alexander Hamilton, "que l'intérêt bien entendu de la France était de rester neutre et de profiter de l'embarras de l'Angleterre pour se faire restituer le Canada." But this would have been going against the general trend of public opinion, and a contrary course was followed. *Mémoires du Comte de Moré*, Paris, 1898, p. 169.

undertaking; but, above all, wrote Count de Ségur, "we were all dreaming of the liberty, at once calm and lofty, enjoyed by the entire body of citizens of Great Britain."[1]

Such is the ever-recurring word. Liberty, philanthropy, natural rights, these were the magic syllables to conjure with. "All France," read we in Grimm and Diderot's correspondence, "was filled with an unbounded love for humanity," and felt a passion for "those exaggerated general maxims which raise the enthusiasm of young men and which would cause them to run to the world's end to help a Laplander or a Hottentot." The ideas of Montesquieu, whose *Esprit des Lois* had had twenty-two editions in one year, of Voltaire, of d'Alembert were in the ascendant, and liberal thinkers saw in the Americans propagandists for their doctrine. General Howe having occupied New York in 1776, Voltaire wrote to d'Alembert: "The troops of Doctor Franklin have been beaten by those of the King of England. Alas! philosophers are being beaten everywhere. Reason and liberty are unwelcome in this world."

Another of the master minds of the day, the economist, thinker, and reformer Turgot, the one whose advice, if followed, would have possibly secured for us a bloodless revolution, was of the

---

[1] *Mémoires, souvenirs et anecdotes*, Paris, 1824, 3 vols., I, 140. English translation, London, 1825.

same opinion. In the famous letter written by
him on the 22d of March, 1778, to his English
friend, Doctor Price, Turgot showed himself, just
as the French nation was, ardently pro-American,
but not anti-English. He deplored the impending war, which ought to have been avoided by
England's acknowledging in time "the folly of its
absurd project to subjugate the Americans. . . .
It is a strange thing that it be not yet a commonplace truth to say that no nation can ever have
the right to govern another nation; that such a
government has no other foundation than force,
which is also the foundation of brigandage and
tyranny; that a people's tyranny is, of all tyran-
nies, the most cruel, the most intolerable, and
the one which leaves the least resources to the
oppressed . . . for a multitude does not calculate,
does not feel remorse, and it bestows on itself
glory when all that it deserves is shame."

The Americans, according to Turgot, must be
free, not only for their own sake, but for the sake
of humanity; an experiment of the utmost import
is about to begin, and should succeed. He added
this, the worthy forecast of a generous mind: "It
is impossible not to form wishes for that people to
reach the utmost prosperity it is capable of.
That people is the hope of mankind. It must
show to the world by its example, that men can
be free and tranquil, and can do without the chains

that tyrants and cheats of all garb have tried to lay on them under pretense of public good. It must give the example of political liberty, religious liberty, commercial and industrial liberty. The shelter which it is going to offer to the oppressed of all nations will console the earth. The ease with which men will be able to avail themselves of it and escape the effects of a bad government will oblige governments to open their eyes and to be just. The rest of the world will perceive by degrees the emptiness of the illusions on which politicians have festered." Toward England Turgot has a feeling of regret on account of its policies, but no trace of animosity; and, on the contrary, the belief that, in spite of what some people of note were alleging, the absolutely certain loss of her American colonies would not result in a diminution of her power. "This revolution will prove, maybe, as profitable to you as to America."[1]

Not less characteristic of the times and of the same thinker's turn of mind is a brief memorial written by him for the King shortly after, when Captain Cook was making his third voyage of discovery, the one from which he never returned. "Captain Cook," Turgot said, "is probably on his way back to Europe. His expedition having no other object than the progress of human knowledge, and interesting, therefore, all nations, it

[1] *Œuvres*, vol. IX, Paris, 1810, pp. 377 ff.

would be worthy of the King's magnanimity not to allow that the result be jeopardized by the chances of war." Orders should be given to all French naval officers "to abstain from any hostile act against him or his ship, and allow him to freely continue his navigation, and to treat him in every respect as the custom is to treat the officers and ships of neutral and friendly countries."[1] The King assented, and had our cruisers notified of the sort of sacred character which they would have to recognize in that ship of the enemy: a small fact in itself, but showing the difference between the wars in those days and in ours, when we have had to witness the wanton destruction of the Louvain library, the shelling of the Reims cathedral, and the Arras town hall.

An immense aspiration was growing in France for more equality, fewer privileges, simpler lives among the great, less hard ones among the lowly, more accessible knowledge, the free discussion by all of the common interests of all. A fact of deepest import struck the least attentive: French masses were becoming more and more thinking masses. One should not forget that between the end of the American Revolution and the beginning of the French one only six years elapsed, between the American and the French Constitutions but four years. At the very time of the

[1] Œuvres, IX, 417.

Yorktown campaign Necker was issuing his celebrated *Compte Rendu*, which he addressed, "pro
forma" to the King, and in reality to the nation.[1]
This famous account of the condition of France,
the piece of printed matter which was most widely
read in those days, began, "Sire," but ended:
"In writing this I have proudly counted on that
public opinion which evil-minded persons may try
to crush or to distort, but which, in spite of their
efforts, Truth and Justice carry along in their
wake."

To which may be added as another token of
the same state of mind that the then famous
Count de Guibert had some time before printed
his *Essay on Tactics*, so full of advanced ideas,
notably on the necessary limitation of the power
of kings, that it had been suppressed by the authorities; and he had dedicated it not to a prince
nor to any man, but to his mother country: "A
ma Patrie." [2]

Six years after the end of the American war, on
January 24, 1789, the King of France ordered
the drawing up of the famous *Cahiers*, desiring,

---

[1] January, 1781.
[2] He ends his dedication stating that he may fail and may have
dreamed a mere dream, but he should not be blamed: "Le délire d'un
citoyen qui rêve au bonheur de sa patrie a quelque chose de respectable." *Essai Général de Tactique précédé d'un Discours sur l'état
actuel de la politique et de la science militaire en Europe*, London,
1772 ; Liége, 1775.

he said, that "from the extremities of his kingdom and the most unknown habitations every one should be assured of a means of conveying to him his wishes and complaints." And the *Cahiers*, requesting liberties very similar to those of the Americans, came indeed from the remotest parts of France, the work of everybody, of quasi-peasants sometimes, who would offer excuses for their wild orthography and grammar. The notes and letters of the volunteers of our Revolution, sons of peasants or artisans, surprise us by the mass of general ideas and views which abound in them. It was not, therefore, a statement of small import that Franklin had conveyed to Congress when he wrote from France: "The united bent of the nation is manifestly in our favor." And he deplored elsewhere that some could think that an appeal to France's own interest was good policy: "Telling them their commerce will be advantaged by our success and that it is their *interest* to help us, seems as much as to say: 'Help us and we shall not be obliged to you.' Such indiscreet and improper language has been sometimes held here by some of our people and produced no good effect." The truth is, he said also, that "this nation is fond of glory, particularly that of protecting the oppressed." [1]

The treaty of commerce, accompanying the

[1] *Writings*, Smythe, VIII, 390, 391.

treaty of alliance of 1778,[1] had been in itself a justification of this judgment. Help from abroad was so pressingly needed in America that almost any advantages requested by France as a condition would have been granted; but that strange sight was seen: advantages being offered, unasked, by one party, and declined by the other. France decided at once not to accept anything as a recompense, not even Canada, if that were wrested from the English, in spite of Canada's having been French from the first, and having but recently ceased to be such. The fight was not for recompense but for liberty, and Franklin could write to Congress that the treaty of commerce was one to which all the rest of the world, in accordance with France's own wishes, was free to accede, when it chose, on the same footing as herself, England included.[2]

This was so peculiar that many had doubts; John Adams never lost his; Washington himself had some, and when plans were submitted to him for an action in Canada he wondered, as he wrote, whether there was not in them "more than the

[1] Both signed at Paris on the same day, February 6, 1778.

[2] Vergennes had written in the same way to the Marquis de Noailles, French ambassador in London: "Our engagements are simple; they are aggressive toward nobody; we have desired to secure for ourselves no advantage of which other nations might be jealous, and which the Americans themselves might regret, in the course of time, to have granted us." Doniol, *Participation de la France à l'établissement des Etats Unis*, II, 822.

disinterested zeal of allies."[1] What would take place at the peace, if the allies were victorious? Would not France require, in one form or another, some advantages for herself? But she did not; her peace was to be like her war, pro-American rather than anti-English.

Another striking trait in the numerous French accounts which have come down to us of this campaign against the English is the small space that the English, as a nation, occupy in them. The note that predominates is enthusiasm for the Americans, not hatred for their enemies. "In France," wrote Ségur in his memoirs, "in spite of the habit of a long obedience to arbitrary power, the cause of the American insurgents fixed the attention and excited the interest of all. From every side public opinion was pressing the royal government to declare itself in favor of republican liberty, and seemed to reproach it for its slowness and timidity." Of any revenge to be taken on the enemy, not a word. "No one among us," he said further, "thought of a revolution in France, but it was rapidly taking place in our minds. Montesquieu had brought to light again the long-buried title-deeds consecrating the rights of the people. Mature men were studying and envying the laws of England."

Summing up the motives of the new crusaders,

[1] November 11, 1778.

who were "starting off to the war in the name of philanthropy," he found two: "One quite reasonable and conscientious, the desire to well serve King and country . . . another more unique, a veritable enthusiasm for the cause of American liberty." Ministers hesitated, on account of the greatness of the risk, "but they were, little by little, carried away by the torrent." During the sea voyage only the chiefs knew exactly whither they were going; some officers thought at one time they might have to fight elsewhere than in America. One of Rochambeau's officers, the aforementioned Mathieu-Dumas, confided his misgivings to his journal: "Above all," he wrote, "I had heartily espoused the cause of the independence of the Americans, and I should have felt extreme regret at losing the honor of combating for their liberty."[1] Of the English, again, not a word; what he longed for, like so many others, was less to fight against the English than for the Americans.

More striking, perhaps, than all the rest: shortly after we had decided to take part in the war, the question of our motives and of a possible annihilation of England as a great power was plainly put, in the course of a familiar conversation, by the president of Yale University to the

[1] *Souvenirs du Lieutenant Général Comte Mathieu-Dumas, de 1770 à 1836*, Paris, 3 vols., I, 36.

future signer of the Louisiana Treaty, Barbé-Marbois, then secretary of our legation in the United States. "Mons. Marbois," Ezra Stiles confided to his diary, on the occasion of the French minister, La Luzerne, and his secretary's visit to Yale, "is a learned civilian, a councillor of the Parliament of Metz, æt. 35, as I judge; speaks English very tolerably, much better than his Excellency the minister. He was very inquisitive for books and American histories. . . . Among other things I asked Mons. Marbois whether the Powers of Europe would contentedly see Great Britain annihilated.

"He said, no; it would be for the interest of Europe that Britain should have weight in the balances of power. . . . France did not want to enlarge her dominions by conquest or otherwise."[1]

For the French diplomat, a man of great ability and well informed, addressing, as he was, one to whom a "yes" instead of a "no" would have caused no pain, far from it, the motive of our actions was neither a prospective loss by England of her rank nor the increase of our own possessions, but simply American independence.

[1] *Literary Diary*, September 11, 1779; New York, 1901, 3 vols.

II

Aware of the importance and difficulty of the move it had decided upon, the French Government had looked for a trained soldier, a man of decision and of sense, one who would understand Washington and be understood by him, would keep in hand the enthusiasts under his orders, and would avoid ill-prepared, risky ventures. The time of the d'Estaings was gone; definitive results were to be sought. The government considered it could do no better than to select Rochambeau. It could, indeed, do no better.

The future marshal of France had been first destined to priesthood for no other reason than that he was a second son, and he was about to receive the tonsure when his elder brother died, and Bishop de Crussol, who had been supervising Donatien's ecclesiastical studies, came one day to him and said: "You must forget all I have told you up to now; you have become the eldest of your family and you must now serve your country with as much zeal as you would have served God in the ecclesiastical state."

Rochambeau did so. He was appointed an officer and served on his first campaign in Germany at sixteen, fought under Marshal de Saxe, was a colonel at twenty-two (Washington was to become one also at twenty-two), received at Laufeldt his two first wounds, of which he nearly died. At the head of the famous Auvergne regiment, "Auvergne sans tache" (Auvergne the spotless), as it was called, he took part in the chief battles of the Seven Years' War, notably in the victory of Klostercamp, where spotless Auvergne had 58 officers and 800 soldiers killed or wounded, the battle made memorable by the episode of the Chevalier d'Assas, who went to his heroic death in the fulfilment of an order given by Rochambeau. The latter was again severely wounded, but, leaning on two soldiers, he could remain at his post till the day was won.

On the opposite side of the same battle-fields were fighting many destined, like Rochambeau himself, to take part in the American war; it was like a preliminary rehearsal of the drama that was to be. At the second battle of Minden, in 1759, where the father of Lafayette was killed, Rochambeau covered the retreat, while in the English ranks Lord Cornwallis was learning his trade, as was too, but less brilliantly, Lord George Germain, the future colonial secretary of the Yorktown period. At Johannisberg, in the same war, Clinton, future commander-in-chief at New York, was wounded, while here and there in the

French army such officers distinguished themselves as Bougainville, back from Ticonderoga,
and not yet a sailor, Chastellux, already a colonel,
no longer a secretary of embassy, not yet an Academician, and my predecessor, La Luzerne, an officer of cavalry, not yet a diplomat, who was to
be the second minister ever accredited to America,
where his name is not forgotten.

When still very young Rochambeau had con-
tracted one of those marriages so numerous in
the eighteenth, as in every other century, of
which nothing is said in the memoirs and letters
of the period, because they were what they should
be, happy ones. Every right-minded and right-
hearted man will find less pleasure in the sauciest
anecdote told by Lauzun than in the simple and
brief lines written in his old age by Rochambeau:
"My good star gave me such a wife as I could
desire; she has been for me a cause of constant
happiness throughout life, and I hope, on my
side, to have made her happy by the tenderest
amity, which has never varied an instant during
nearly sixty years." The issue of that union,
Viscount Rochambeau, from his youth the companion in arms of his father, an officer at fourteen, accompanied him to the States, and was,
after a career of devotion to his country, to die a
general at Leipzig, in the " Battle of Nations."

Informed at Versailles of the task he would

have to perform, the exact nature of which was
kept a secret from the troops themselves now
gathered at Brest, Rochambeau hastened to forget his "rhumatisme inflammatoire" and set to
work to get everything in readiness, collecting information, talking with those who knew America,
and noting down in his green-garbed registers,
which were to accompany him in his campaign,
the chief data thus secured. He also addressed
to himself, as a reminder, a number of useful
recommendations such as these: "To take with
us a quantity of flints, . . . much flour and bis-
cuit; have bricks as ballast for the ships, to be
used for ovens; to try to bring with us all we
want and not to have to ask from the Americans
who are themselves in want . . . to have a copy
of the Atlas brought from Philadelphia by Mr.
de Lafayette . . . to have a portable printing-
press, like that of Mr. d'Estaing, handy for proc-
lamations . . . siege artillery is indispensable."
Some of the notes are of grave import and were
not lost sight of throughout the campaign: "Nothing without naval supremacy."

To those intrusted with the care of loading the
vessels he recommends that all articles of the
same kind be not placed on the same ship, "so
that in case of mishap to any ship the whole supply of any kind of provisions be not totally lost."

As to the pay for himself and his officers, he

writes to the minister that he leaves that to him:
"Neither I nor mine desire anything extravagant;
we should like to be able to go to this war at our
own expense." But the government did not
want him to be hampered by any lack of funds,
and allotted him the then considerable sum of
twelve thousand francs a month, and four thousand a month the generals under him.

At Brest, where he now repaired, Rochambeau
found that the ships were not so numerous as
expected, so that only the first division of his
army could embark under Admiral Chevalier
de Ternay: a sad blow for the commander-in-
chief. He prescribed that care be at least taken
to select for the passage the most robust men,
and, in order to save space, that all horses be left
behind, himself giving the example. "I have,"
Rochambeau writes to Prince de Montbarey, the
minister of war, "to part company with two battle-
horses that I can never replace. I do so with the
greatest sorrow, but I do not want to have to reproach myself with their having taken up the
room of twenty men who could have embarked
in their stead." Officers, soldiers, ammunition,
artillery, spare clothing for the troops, and even
the printing-press go on board at last. Men and
things are close-packed, but end by shaking down
into place; all will go well, Rochambeau writes to
the minister, "without any overcrowding of the

troops; the rule for long journeys having been observed, namely one soldier for every two tons
burden."

When all were there, however, forming a total
of 5,000 men, the maximum was so truly reached
that a number of young men, some belonging to
the best-known French families, who were arriving at Brest from day to day, in the hope of being
added to the expedition, had to be sent back.
The fleet was already on the high seas when a
cutter brought the government's last instructions
to Rochambeau. On the boat were two brothers
called Berthier, who besought to be allowed to
volunteer. "They have joined us yesterday," the
general writes to the minister, "and have handed
us your letters. . . . They were dressed in linen
vests and breeches, asking to be admitted as mere
sailors." But there was really no place to put
them. "Those poor young men are interesting
and in despair." They had, nevertheless, to be
sent back, but managed to join the army later,
and so it was that Alexander Berthier began in
the Yorktown campaign a military career which
he was to end as marshal of France, and Prince
of Wagram and Neufchâtel.

The departure, which it was necessary to hasten
while the English were not yet ready, was beset
with difficulties. Tempests, contrary winds and
other mishaps had caused vexatious delay; the

Comtesse de Noailles and the *Conquérant* had come into collision and had had to be repaired. "Luckily," wrote Rochambeau to Montbarey, with his usual good humor, "it rains also on Portsmouth." At last, on the 2d of May, 1780, the fleet of seven ships of the line and two frigates conveying thirty-six transports, weighed anchor for good. "We shall have the start of Graves," the general wrote again, "for he will have to use the same wind to leave Portsmouth," and he added, with a touch of emotion at this solemn moment: "I recommend this expedition to the friendship of my dear old comrade, and to his zeal for the good of the state."

At sea now for a long voyage, two or three months, perhaps, with the prospect of calms, of storms, of untoward encounters, of scurvy for the troops. On board the big *Duc de Bourgogne*, of eighty guns, with Admiral de Ternay, Rochambeau adds now and then paragraphs to a long report which is a kind of journal, assuring the minister, after the first fortnight, that all is well on board: "We have no men sick other than those which the sea makes so, among whom the Marquis de Laval and my son play the most conspicuous part." He prepares his general instructions to the troops.

On board the smaller craft life was harder and numerous unflattering descriptions have come down to us in the journals kept by so many

officers of the army, especially in that of the aforementioned young captain, Louis Baron de Closen,
later one of the aides of Rochambeau.

He confesses, but with no undue sentimentalism,
that he was saddened at first to some extent at
the prospect of an absence that might be a long
one, particularly when thinking "of a charming
young fiancée, full of wit and grace. . . . My
profession, however, does not allow me to yield
too much to sensibility; so I am now perfectly
resigned." He was assigned to the *Comtesse de
Noailles*, of three hundred tons (the *Ecureuil*,
that kept her company, was of only one hundred
and eighty). Each officer had received fifty
francs for extra purchases; they found it was
little, but when they had made their purchases
they found that it had been much, so great was
the difficulty in stowing their possessions on the
ship. At last, "after much trouble and many
words—a few crowns here and there—each of us
succeeded in squeezing himself and his belong-
ings in those so-detested *sabots*."[1] Closen, for
his part, had provisioned himself with "sugar,
lemons, and syrups in quantity."

The crew consisted of forty-five men, "half of
them Bretons, half Provençals," speaking their
own dialect, "and who, little accustomed to the
language used by their naval officers when giving

---

[1] Wooden shoes, a nickname for a ship of mean estate.

their orders," were apt to misunderstand them, hence the bad manœuvring which sent the *Comtesse de Noailles* right across the *Conquérant*. A sad case; would they be left behind, and miss taking part in the expedition? By great luck "there were but the bowsprit, the spritsails, and the figure of the charming countess which were broken to pieces." Repairs are begun with all speed. Mr. de Deux-Ponts promises fifteen louis to the workmen if the ship is ready the next day at noon. "One more reassuring circumstance was that Mr. de Kersabiec, a very expert naval officer, was intrusted with the care of looking after the workmen." He never left them, and "encouraged them by extra distributions. I was intimate with all the family, having spent the winter at Saint-Pol-de-Léon; the souvenir of which still gives me pleasure." The next day all was right once more: "After eleven, the amiable countess was taken again—with no head, it is true, like so many other countesses—beyond the harbor chain." It was possible to start with the rest of the fleet: the high fortifications overlooking the harbor, the villages along the coast, so many sails curved by a wind "joli-frais," the clear sky, "all united to form the most beautiful picture at the time of our start. . . . So many vessels under way offered a truly imposing sight."

Every-day life now begins on the small craft;

it is hard at first to get accustomed, so tight-packed is the ship, but one gets inured to it, in spite of the "buzzing of so numerous a company," of the lack of breathing-space, and of what people breathe being made unpleasant by all sorts of "exhalations" from the ship, the masses of humanity on board, "and a few dogs." Closen has the good luck not to be inconvenienced by the sea, settles in his corner, and from that moment till the end takes pleasure in watching life around him. He learns how to make nautical observations, describes his companions in his journal, and especially the captain, a typical old tar who has an equal faith in the efficacy of hymns and of oaths. "Prayer is said twice a day on the deck, which does not prevent there being much irreligion among seamen. I have often heard our captain swear and curse and freely use the worst sailors' language, while he was praying and chanting:

> Je mets ma confiance,
> Vierge, en votre secours,
> Et quand ma dernière heure
> Viendra, guidez mon sort;
> Obtenez que je meure
> De la plus sainte mort."

Various incidents break the monotony of the journey. On the 18th of June the *Surveillante*

captures an English corsair, which is a joy, but
they learn from her the fall of Charleston and
the surrender of Lincoln, which gives food for
thought. Nothing better shows the difference
between old-time and present-time navigation
than the small fact that while on the way they
indulge in fishing. On board the *Comtesse de
Noailles* they capture flying-fishes, which are
"very tender and delicious to eat, fried in fresh
butter, like gudgeons."

An occasion offers to open fight, with the advantage of numerical superiority, on six English
vessels; some shots are exchanged, but with great
wisdom, and, in spite of the grumblings of all his
people, Ternay refuses to really engage them, and
continues his voyage. "He had his convoy too
much at heart," says Closen, "and he knew too
well the importance of our expedition, his positive
orders being that he must make our army arrive
as quickly as possible, for him not to set aside
all the entreaties of the young naval officers
who, I was told, were very outspoken on that
score, as well as most of the land officers, who
know nothing of naval matters."

The event fully justified Ternay, for Graves,
whose mission it had been to intercept him and
his slow and heavy convoy, missed his opportunity by twenty-four hours only, reaching New
York, where he joined forces with Arbuthnot

just as our own ships were safe at Newport.   The
slightest delay on Ternay's part might have been
fatal.

The more so since, when nearing the coast our
fleet had fallen into fogs.   "Nothing so sad and
dangerous at sea as fogs," Closen sententiously
writes; "besides the difficulty of avoiding col-
lisions in so numerous a fleet, each vessel, in order
to shun them, tries to gain space; thus one may
chance to get too far from the centre.   The standing orders for our convoy were, in view of avoiding those inconveniences, to beat the drums every
quarter of an hour or fire petards.   The men-of-
war fired their guns or sent rockets.   The speed-
limit was three knots during the fog, so that each
vessel might, as far as possible, continue keeping
company with its neighbor."   In spite of all
which the *Ile de France* was lost, and there was
great anxiety; she was not seen again during the
rest of the journey, but she appeared later, quite
safe, at Boston.

The landing orders of Rochambeau, making
known now to all concerned the intentions of the
government, were clear and peremptory.   Drawn
up by him on board the *Duc de Bourgogne*, he had
caused copies to be carried to the chiefs of the
several corps on board the other ships:

"The troops which his Majesty is sending to
America are auxiliary to those of the United

States, his allies, and placed under the orders of
General Washington, to whom the honors of a
marshal of France will be rendered. The same
with the President of Congress," which avoided
the possibility of any trouble as to precedence,
no one in the French army having such a rank.
"In case of an equality of rank and duration of
service, the American officer will take command.
. . . The troops of the King will yield the right
side to the allies; French troops will add black to
their cockades, black being the color of the United
States," and some such hats, with black and
white cockades, are still preserved at Fraunces'
Tavern,[1] New York. "The intention of his
Majesty," the general continues, "is that there
be perfect concert and harmony between the generals and officers of the two nations. The severest
discipline will be observed. . . . It is forbidden
to take a bit of wood, a sheaf of straw, any kind
of vegetables, except amicably and in paying. . . .
All faults of unruliness, disobedience, insubordina-
tion, ill-will, brutal and sonorous drunkenness
. . . will be punished, according to ordinances
with strokes of the flat of the sword." Even
"light faults of lack of cleanliness or attention"
will be punished. "To make the punishment the

[1] So called after its owner, Samuel Fraunces (Francis or François),
from the French West Indies, nicknamed "Black Sam" for the
color of his skin.

harder for the French soldier, he will be barred
from military service during his detention."

The army, but not the fleet, had been placed
under the orders of Washington. Ternay's instructions specified, however, that while his
squadron had no other commander than himself,
it was expected that he would "proffer all assistance that might facilitate the operations of the
United States," and that he would allow the use
of our ships "on every occasion when their help
might be requested." Good-will was obviously
the leading sentiment, and the desire of all was
to give as little trouble and bring as much useful
help as possible.

III

On the 11th day of July the fleet reached Newport, after seventy days at sea, which was longer
than Columbus had taken on his first voyage, but
which was nothing extraordinary. Abbé Robin,
a chaplain of the army, arrived later, after a journey of eighty-five days, none the less filled with
admiration for those "enormous machines with
which men master the waves"[1]—a very minute enormity from our modern point of view.
"There were among the land troops," says Closen,
"endless shouts of joy" at the prospect of being
on terra firma again. The troops, owing to their
having been fed on salt meat and dry vegetables,
with little water to drink (on board the *Comtesse
de Noailles* water had become corrupt; it was
now and then replaced by wine, "but that heats
one very much"), had greatly suffered. Scurvy
had caused its usual ravages; 600 or 700 soldiers
and 1,000 sailors were suffering from it; some had
died.

They were now confronted by the unknown.
What would that unknown be? Rochambeau

[1] *Nouveau Voyage dans l'Amérique Septentrionale en l'année 1781
et campagne de l'armée de M. le comte de Rochambeau*, Philadelphia,
1782.

had only his first division with him; would he be attacked at once by the English, who disposed of superior naval and land forces about New York? And what would be the attitude of the Americans themselves? Everybody was for them in France, but few people had a real knowledge of them. Lafayette had, but he was young and enthusiastic. Would the inhabitants, would their leader, Washington, would their army answer his description? On the arrival of the fleet Newport had fired "thirteen grand rockets" and illuminated its windows, but that might be a mere matter of course: of these illuminations the then president of Yale, Ezra Stiles, has left a noteworthy record: "The bell rang at Newport till after midnight, and the evening of the 12th Newport illuminated; the Whigs put thirteen lights in the windows, the Tories or doubtfuls four or six. The Quakers did not choose their lights should shine before men, and their windows were broken."[1]

The game was, moreover, a difficult one, and had to be played on an immense chess-board, including North and South—Boston, New York, Charleston, and the Chesapeake—including even "the Isles," that is, the West Indies; and what took place there, which might have so much importance for continental operations, had constantly to be guessed or imagined, for lack of news.

[1] *Literary Diary*, New York, 1901, II, 454.

Worse than all, the reputation of the French was,
up to then, in America such as hostile English
books and caricatures, and inconsiderate French
ones, had made it. We knew it, and so well,
too; that the appropriateness of having our troops
winter in our colonies of the West Indies was, at
one time, considered. Our minister, Gérard, was
of that opinion: "The Americans are little accustomed to live with French people, for whom they
cannot have as yet a very marked inclination."[1]
"The old-time prejudice kept up by the English,"
wrote Mathieu-Dumas in his *Souvenirs*, "about
the French character was so strong that, at the
beginning of the Revolution, the most ardent
minds and several among those who most desired
independence, rejected the idea of an alliance
with France." "It is difficult to imagine," said
Abbé Robin, "the idea Americans entertained
about the French before the war. They considered them as groaning under the yoke of despotism, a prey to superstition and prejudices, almost
idolatrous in their religion,[2] and as a kind of light,

[1] To Rochambeau; n. d., but 1780. (Rochambeau papers.)

[2] Writing to the president of Yale, July 29, 1778, Silas Deane,
just about to return to France, recommended the creation of a chair
of French: "This language is not only spoke in all the courts, but
daily becomes more and more universal among people of business
as well as men of letters, in all the principal towns and cities of
Europe." Ezra Stiles consulted a number of friends; the majority
were against or in doubt, "Mr. C——— violently against, because
of popery." *Literary Diary*, August 24, 1778, New York, 1901, II,

brittle, queer-shapen mechanisms, only busy frizzling their hair and painting their faces, without faith or morals." How would thousands of such mechanisms be received?

With his usual clear-headedness, Rochambeau did the necessary thing on each point. To begin with, in case of an English attack, which was at first expected every day, he lost no time in fortifying the position he occupied, "having," wrote Mathieu-Dumas, "personally selected the chief points to be defended, and having batteries of heavy artillery and mortars erected along the channel, with furnaces to heat the balls." During "the first six days," says Closen, "we were not quite at our ease, but, luckily, Messieurs les Anglais showed us great consideration, and we suffered from nothing worse than grave anxieties." After the second week, Rochambeau could write home that, if Clinton appeared, he would be well received. Shortly after, he feels sorry the visit is delayed; later, when his own second division, so ardently desired, did not appear, he writes to the war minister: "In two words, sir Henry Clinton and I are very punctilious, and the question is between us who will first call on the other. If we do not get up earlier in the morning than the English and the reinforcements they expect from

297. See also, concerning the prevalent impressions about the French the *Mémoires du Comte de Moré*, 1898, p. 69.

Europe reach them before our second division ar-
rives, they will pay us a visit here that I should
prefer to pay them in New York."

Concerning the reputation of the French, Rochambeau and his officers were in perfect accord:
it would change if exemplary discipline were maintained throughout the campaign. There is nothing the chief paid more attention to than this,
nor with more complete success. Writing to
Prince de Montbarey a month after the landing,
Rochambeau says: "I can answer for the discipline of the army; not a man has left his camp,
not a cabbage has been stolen, not a complaint
has been heard."[1] To the President of Congress
he had written a few days before: "I hope that
account will have been rendered to your Excellency of the discipline observed by the French
troops; there has not been one complaint; not a
man has missed a roll-call. We are your brothers
and we shall act as such with you; we shall fight
your enemies by your side as if we were one and
the same nation."[2] Mentioning in his memoirs
the visit of those "savages" who had been formerly under French rule and persisted in remaining
friendly to us, he adds: "The sight of guns, troops,
and military exercises caused them no surprise;
but they were greatly astonished to see apple-

[1] August 8, 1780. (Rochambeau papers.)
[2] August 3, 1780. (*Ibid.*)

trees with their apples upon them overhanging
the soldiers' tents." "This result," he concludes,
"was due not only to the zeal of officers, but more
than anything else to the good disposition of the
soldiers, which never failed."

Another fact which proved to our advantage
was that the French could then be seen in numbers and at close quarters. The difference between the portrait and the original was too glaring
to escape notice. William Channing, father of
the philanthropist, confides to the same Ezra
Stiles, in a letter of August 6, 1780, his delighted
surprise: "The French are a fine body of men, and
appear to be well officered. Neither the officers
nor men are the effeminate beings we were here-
tofore taught to believe them. They are as large
and likely men as can be produced by any nation."[1] So much for the brittle, queer-shaped
mechanisms.

With the French officers in the West Indies,
most of them former companions in arms and
personal friends, Rochambeau, as soon as he had
landed, began to correspond. The letters thus
exchanged, generally unpublished, give a vivid
picture of the life then led in the Isles. Cut off
from the world most of the time, not knowing
what was taking place in France, in America, on
the sea, or even sometimes on the neighboring

[1] Stiles's *Literary Diary*, II, 458.

island, unaware of the whereabouts of Rodney, having to guess which place he might try to storm and which they should therefore garrison, these men, suffering from fevers, having now and then their ships scattered by cyclones, played to their credit and with perfect good humor their difficult game of hide and seek.[1] They send their letters in duplicate and triplicate, by chance boats, give news of the French court when they have any, and learn after a year's delay that their letters of October, 1780, have been duly received by Rochambeau in June, 1781. The Marquis de Bouillé, who was to cover himself with glory at Brimstone Hill, and is now chiefly remembered for the part he played in Louis XVI's flight to Varennes, writes most affectionately, and does not forget to convey the compliments of his brave wife, who had accompanied him to Martinique. The Mar-

---

[1] Rodney "has left here two months ago without our being able to guess whither he was going. . . . Maybe you know better than I do where he may presently be. . . .

"We have just suffered from a terrible tornado, which has been felt in all the Windward Islands; it has caused cruel havoc. A convoy of fifty-two sails, arrived the day before in the roadstead of Saint-Pierre, Martinique, has been driven out to sea, and has disappeared for now a fortnight; five ships only returned here, the others may have reached San Domingo or must have perished. An English ship of the line of 44 guns, the *Endymion*, and two frigates, the *Laurel* and the *Andromeda*, of the same nationality, have perished on our coasts; we have saved some of their sailors." Marquis de Bouillé to Rochambeau, Fort Royal (Fort de France), October 27, 1780. (Rochambeau papers.)

quis de Saint-Simon[1] writes from Santo Domingo
to say how much he would like to go and fight
under Rochambeau on the continent: "I would
be delighted to be under your orders, and to give
up for that the command in chief I enjoy here."
And he supplies him, in the same unpublished
letter, with a most interesting account of Cuba,
just visited by him: "This colony has an air of
importance far superior to any of ours, inhabited
as it is by all the owners of the land, so that the
city (Havana) looks rather a European than a
colonial one; society is numerous and seems opu-
lent. If Spain would extend and facilitate the
trade of Cuba the island would become exceed-
ingly rich in little time. But prohibitory laws are
so harsh and penalties so rigorous that they cramp
industry everywhere."

A postscript in the same letter shows better
than anything else what was the common feeling
among officers toward Rochambeau: "Mont-
brun," writes Saint-Simon, "who has been suffering from the fever for a long time, asks me to assure you of his respectful attachment, and says
that he has written you twice, that your silence

---

[1] Three Saint-Simons took part in the American War of Independence, all relatives of the famous duke, the author of the memoirs:
the Marquis Claude Anne (1740–1819), the Baron Claude (retired,
1806), and the Count Claude Henri (1760–1825), then a very young
officer, the future founder of the Saint-Simonian sect, and first
philosophical master of Auguste Comte,

afflicts him very much, and that a token of friendship and remembrance from you would be for him
the best of febrifuges. All your former subordinates of Auvergne think the same, and have
the same attachment for you, in which respect I
yield to none."[1]

The stanch devotion of Rochambeau to his
duties as a soldier, his personal disinterestedness,
his cool-headedness and energy as a leader, his
good humor in the midst of troubles had secured
for him the devotion of many, while his brusquery,
his peremptoriness, the severity which veiled his
real warmth of heart whenever the service was at
stake, won him a goodly number of enemies, the
latter very generally of less worth as men than
the former. In the affectionate letter by which
he made up early differences with "his son Lafayette," shortly after his arrival, he observes,
concerning his own military career: "If I have
been lucky enough to preserve, up to now, the
confidence of the French soldiers . . . the reason
is that out of 15,000 men or thereabout, who have
been killed or wounded under my orders, of different rank and in the most deadly actions, I
have not to reproach myself with having caused
a single one to be killed for the sake of my own
fame." He seemed, Ségur said in his memoirs,
"to have been purposely created to understand

[1] January 7, 1781. (Rochambeau papers.)

Washington, and be understood by him, and to serve with republicans. A friend of order, of laws, and of liberty, his example more even than his authority obliged us scrupulously to respect the rights, properties, and customs of our allies."

IV

Nothing without my second division, Rochambeau thought. He had urged the government in his last letters before leaving France to send it not later than a fortnight after he himself had sailed: "The convoy will cross much more safely now under the guard of two warships," he had written to Montbarey, "than it will in a month with an escort of thirty, when the English are ready." And again, after having embarked on the *Duc de Bourgogne:* "For Heaven's sake, sir, hasten that second division. . . . We are just now weighing anchor." But weeks and months went by, and no news came of the second division. Washington with his ardent patriotism, Lafayette with his youthful enthusiasm, were pressing Rochambeau to risk all, in order to capture New York, the stronghold of the enemy and chief centre of their power. "I am confident," Rochambeau answered, "that our general (Washington) does not want us to give here a second edition of Savannah," and he felt the more anxious that, with the coming of recruits and going of veterans, and the short-term enlistments, "Washington would command now 15,000 men, now 5,000."

46

Rochambeau decided in October to send to
France his son, then colonel of the regiment of
Bourbonnais, to remonstrate. As capture was
possible and the envoy might have to throw his
despatches overboard, young Rochambeau, being blessed with youth and a good memory, had
learned their contents by heart. One of the best
sailors of the fleet had been selected to convey him,
on the frigate *Amazone*. On account of superior
forces mounting guard outside, the captain waited
for the first night storm that should arise, when
the watch was sure to be less strict, started in the
midst of one, after having waited for eight days,
was recognized, but too late, was chased, had his
masts broken, repaired them, and reached Brest
safely. The sailor who did so well on this occasion, and who was to meet a tragical death
at Vanikoro. bore the name, famous since, of La
Pérouse.

Time wore on, a sad time for the American
cause. One day the news was that one of the
most trusted generals, famous for his services on
land and water, Benedict Arnold, had turned
traitor; another day that Gates had been routed
at Camden and Kalb killed. In December Ternay died. In January, worse than all, the soldiers of the Pennsylvania line mutinied; unpaid,
underfed, kept under the flag long after the time
for which they had enlisted, "they went," Closen

writes in his journal, "to extremities.   In Europe
they would not have waited so long."

There was no doubt, in fact, that the life they
had to lead did not closely resemble that which,
in accordance with the uses then prevailing in
every country, the posters urging enlistment depicted to them.   One such poster, preserved in
Philadelphia, announces "to all brave, healthy,
able-bodied, and well-disposed young men in this
neighborhood who have any inclination to join the
troops now raising, under General Washington,
for the defense of the liberties and independence
of the United States," a "truly liberal and generous [encouragement], namely, a bounty of twelve
dollars, an annual and fully sufficient supply of
good and handsome clothing, a daily allowance
of a large and ample ration of provisions, together
with sixty dollars a year in gold and silver money
on account of pay."   The appeal vaunted, by
way of conclusion, "the great advantages which
these brave men will have who shall embrace this
opportunity of spending a few happy years in
viewing the different parts of this beautiful continent, in the honorable and truly respectable
character of a soldier, after which he may, if he
pleases, return home to his friends with his pockets
full of money and his head covered with laurels.
God save the United States!"   Pretty engravings
showed handsome soldiers, elegantly dressed, prac-
tising an easy kind of military drill.

The danger was great, but brief; tempted by the enemy to change sides and receive full pay, the Pennsylvania line refused indignantly. "We are honest soldiers, asking justice from our compatriots," they answered, "we are not traitors." On the margin of a French account of those events, published in Paris in 1787, Clinton scribbled a number of observations hitherto unprinted.[1] They are in French, or something like it. Opposite this statement the British general wrote: "*Est bien dit et c'est dommage qu'il n'est pas vrai.*" We cannot tell, but one thing is sure, namely, that in accordance with those words, spoken or not, the rebellious soldiers acted. Owing to Washington's influence, order soon reigned again, but the alarm had been very great, as shown by the instructions which he handed to Colonel Laurens, now sent by him to Versailles with a mission similar to that of young Rochambeau. The emotion caused by the last events is reflected in them: "The patience of the American army is almost exhausted. . . . The great majority of the inhabitants is still firmly attached to the cause of independence," but that cause may be wrecked if more money, more men, and more ships are not immediately supplied by the French ally. [2]

While the presence of the American and French

---

[1] *Histoire des Troubles de l'Amérique Anglaise*, by Soulès; Clinton's copy, in the Library of Congress, p. 360.

[2] January 15, 1781.

troops in the North kept Clinton and his powerful New York garrison immobile where they were,
the situation in the South was becoming worse
and worse, with Cornwallis at the head of superior forces, Lord Rawdon holding Charleston, and
the hated Arnold ravaging Virginia.

Against them the American forces under Greene,
Lafayette, and Morgan (who had partly destroyed Tarleton's cavalry at Cowpens, January
17) were doing their utmost, facing fearful odds.
With a handful of men, knowing that the slightest
error might be his destruction, young Lafayette,
aged twenty-four, far from help and advice, was
conducting a campaign in which his pluck, wisdom,
and tenacity won him the admiration of veterans.
Irritated ever to find him on his path, Cornwallis
was writing a little later to Clinton: "If I can
get an opportunity to strike a blow at him without loss of time, I will certainly try it." But Lafayette would not let his adversary thus employ
his leisure.

To arrest the progress of Arnold two French
expeditions were sent, taking advantage of moments when access to the sea was not blocked by
the English fleet before Newport, one in February, under Tilly, who pursued Arnold's convoy
up the Elizabeth River as high as the draft of
his ships permitted, but had to stop and come
home, having only captured the *Romulus*, of 44

guns, some smaller ships, a quantity of supplies
destined for Arnold, and made 550 prisoners; another of more importance under the Chevalier Destouches, in March, with part of Rochambeau's
army on board, in case a landing were possible.
In spite of all precautions, Destouches's intentions
were discovered; the English fleet engaged ours;
the fight, in which 72 French lost their lives and
112 were wounded, was a creditable one and
might easily have ended in disaster, for the enemy
had more guns, and several of our ships, on account of their not being copper-lined, were slow;
but clever manœuvring, however, compensated
those defects. Congress voted thanks, but the
situation remained the same. "And now," Closen
noted down in his journal, "we have Arnold free
to act as he pleases, Virginia desolated by his in-
cursions, and M. de Lafayette too weak to do
anything but keep on the defensive."

V

One day, however, something would have to be done, and, in order to be ready, Rochambeau kept his army busy with manœuvres, military exercises, sham warfare ("le simulacre de la petite guerre"), and the building of fortifications. As for his officers, he encouraged them to travel, for a large part of the land was free of enemies, and to become better acquainted with these "American brothers," whom they had come to fight for. French officers were thus seen at Boston, Albany, West Point, Philadelphia. It was at this period that Chastellux went about the country with some of his companions, and gathered the material for his well-known *Voyages dans l'Amérique du Nord*, the first edition of which, in a much abbreviated form, was issued by that printing-press of the fleet which Rochambeau had recommended to himself not to forget: "De l'Imprimerie Royale de l'Escadre," one reads on the title-page. Only twenty-three copies were struck off; the "Imprimerie Royale" of the fleet had obviously no superabundance of type nor of paper.

Closen, who, to his joy and surprise, had been made a member of Rochambeau's "family," that is, had been appointed one of his aides, as soon

as his new duties left him some leisure, began,
with his methodical mind, to study, he tells us,
"the Constitution of the thirteen States and of
the Congress of America," meaning, of course, at
that date, their several constitutions, which organization, "as time has shown, is well adapted
to the national character and has made the happiness of that people so respectable from every
point of view." He began after this to examine
the products of the soil of Rhode Island, "perhaps one of the prettiest islands on the globe."

The stay being prolonged, the officers began to
make acquaintances, to learn English, to gain
access to American society. It was at first very
difficult; neither French nor American understood
each other's language; so recourse was bravely
had to Latin, better known then than to-day.
*"Quid de meo, mi carissime Drowne, cogitas si-
lentio?"* A long letter follows, in affectionate
terms addressed to Doctor Drowne, a Newport
physician, and signed: "Silly, officier au régiment
de Bourbonnois," September 9, 1780. Sublieutenant de Silly announced, however, his intention to
learn English during the winter season: *"Inglicam
linguam noscere conabor."* His letters of an after-
date are, in fact, written in English, but a be-
ginner's English.[1]

[1] Specimens exhibited by the doctor's descendant in the Fraunces's
Tavern Museum.

For the use of Latin the commander-in-chief of
the French army was able to set the example, and
Ezra Stiles could talk at a dinner in that language
with Rochambeau, still reminiscent of what he
had learned when studying for priesthood. The
president of Yale notes in his journal:

"5 [October, 1780]. Introduced to the commander-in-chief of the French allied army, the
Count de Rochambeau. . . .

"7. Dined at the General de Rochambeau's,
in a splendid manner. There were, perhaps, thirty
at table. I conversed with the general in Latin.
He speaks it tolerably."

Beginning to know something of the language,
our officers risk paying visits and go to teas and
dinners. Closen notes with curiosity all he sees:
"It is good behavior each time people meet to
accost each other, mutually offering the hand and
shaking it, English fashion. Arriving in a company of men, one thus goes around, but must remember that it belongs to the one of higher rank
to extend his hand first."

Unspeakable quantities of tea are drunk. "To
crave mercy, when one has taken half a dozen
cups, one must put the spoon across the cup; for
so long as you do not place it so, your cup is always taken, rinsed, filled again, and placed before you. After the first, the custom is for the
pretty pourer (*verseuse*)—most of them are so—

to ask you: *Is the tea suitable?*"[1]—"An insipid drink," grumbles Chaplain Robin, over whom the prettiness of the pourers was powerless.

The toasts are also a very surprising custom, sometimes an uncomfortable one. "One is terribly fatigued by the quantity of healths which are being drunk (*toasts*). From one end of the table to the other a gentleman pledges you, sometimes with only a glance, which means that you should drink a glass of wine with him, a compliment which cannot be politely ignored."

In the course of an excursion to Boston the young captain visits an assembly of Quakers, "where, unluckily, no one was inspired, and ennui seemed consequently to reign."

But what strikes him more than anything else is the beauty of those young ladies who made him drink so much tea: "Nature has endowed the ladies of Rhode Island with the handsomest, finest features one can imagine; their complexion is clear and white; their hands and feet usually small." But let not the ladies of other States be tempted to resent this preference. One sees later that in each city he visits young Closen is similarly struck, and that, more considerate than the shepherd Paris, he somehow manages to refuse the apple to none. On the Boston ladies he is quite enthusiastic, on the Philadelphia ones not

[1] In English in the original.

less; he finds, however, the latter a little too
serious, which he attributes to the presence of
Congress in that city.

But, above all, the object of my compatriots'
curiosity was the great man, the one of whom
they had heard so much on the other side, the
personification of the new-born ideas of liberty
and popular government, George Washington.
All wanted to see him, and as soon as permission
to travel was granted several managed to reach
his camp.   For all of them, different as they might
be in rank and character, the impression was the
same and fulfilled expectation, beginning with
Rochambeau, who saw him for the first time at the
Hartford conferences, in September, 1780, when
they tried to draw a first plan for a combined
action.   A friendship then commenced between
the two that was long to survive those eventful
years.   "From the moment we began to correspond with one another," Rochambeau wrote in
his memoirs, "I never ceased to enjoy the sound-
ness of his judgment and the amenity of his style
in a very long correspondence, which is likely
not to end before the death of one of us."

Chastellux, who saw him at his camp, where the
band of the American army played for him the
"March of the Huron," could draw from life his
well-known description of him, ending: "Northern America, from Boston to Charleston, is a

great book every page of which tells his praise."[1]
Count de Ségur says that he apprehended his ex-
pectations could not be equalled by reality, but
they were. "His exterior almost told his story.
Simplicity, grandeur, dignity, calm, kindness,
firmness shone in his physiognomy as well as in
his character. He was of a noble and high sta-
ture, his expression was gentle and kindly, his
smile pleasing, his manners simple without famili-
arity. . . . All in him announced the hero of a
republic." "I have seen Washington," says Abbé
Robin, "the soul and support of one of the greatest revolutions that ever happened. . . . In a
country where every individual has a part in supreme authority . . . he has been able to maintain his troops in absolute subordination, render
them jealous of his praise, make them fear his
very silence." Closen was one day sent with despatches to the great man and, like all the others,
began to worship him.

As a consequence of this mission Washington
came, on the 6th of March, 1781, to visit the
French camp and fleet. He was received with
the honors due to a marshal of France, the ships
were dressed, the troops, in their best uniforms,
"dans la plus grande tenue," lined the streets from

[1] *Voyages de M. le Marquis de Chastellux dans l'Amérique Septentrionale, dans les années 1780, 1781 et 1782*, Paris, 1786, 2 vols., I,
118.

Rochambeau's house (the fine Vernon house, still in existence[1]) to the harbor; the roar and smoke of the guns rose in honor of the "hero of liberty." Washington saw Destouches's fleet sail for its Southern expedition and wished it Godspeed; and after a six days' stay, enlivened by "illuminations, dinners, and balls," he left on the 13th. "I can say," we read in Closen's journal, "that he carried away with him the regrets, the attachment, the respect, and the veneration of all our army." Summing up his impression, he adds: "All in him betokens a great man with an excellent heart. Enough good will never be said of him."

[1] Now the property of the Charity Organization Society. See *A History of the Vernon House*, by Maud Lyman Stevens, Newport, R. I., 1915. Illustrated.

VI

On the 8th of May, 1781, the *Concorde* arrived at Boston, having on board Count de Barras, "a commodore with the red ribbon," of the same family as the future member of the "Directoire," and who was to replace Ternay. With him was Viscount Rochambeau, bringing to his father the unwelcome news that no second division was to be expected. "My son has returned very solitary," was the only remonstrance the general sent to the minister. But the young colonel was able to give, at the same time, news of great importance. A new fleet under Count de Grasse had been got together, and at the time of the *Concorde's* departure had just sailed for the West Indies, so that a temporary domination of the sea might become a possibility. "Nothing without naval supremacy," Rochambeau had written, as we know, in his note-book before starting.

In spite, moreover, of "hard times," wrote Vergennes to La Luzerne, and of the already disquieting state of our finances, a new "gratuitous subsidy of six million livres tournois" was granted to the Americans. Some funds had already been sent to Rochambeau, one million and a half in

February, with a letter of Necker saying: "Be assured, sir, that all that will be asked from the Finance Department for your army will be made ready on the instant." Seven millions arrived a little later, brought by the *Astrée*, which had crossed the ocean in sixty-seven days, without mishap. As for troops, only 600 recruits arrived at Boston, in June, with the *Sagittaire*.

Since nothing more was to be expected, the hour had come for definitive decisions. A great effort must now be made, *the* great effort in view of which all the rest had been done, the one which might bring about peace and American liberty or end in lasting failure. All felt the importance and solemnity of the hour. The great question was what should be attempted—the storming of New York or the relief of the South?

The terms of the problem had been amply discussed in letters and conferences between the chiefs, and the discussion still continued. The one who first made up his mind and ceased to hesitate between the respective advantages or disadvantages of the two projects, and who plainly declared that there was but one good plan, which was to reconquer the South, that one, strange to say, was neither Washington nor Rochambeau, and was not in the United States either as a sailor or a soldier, but as a diplomat, and in drawing attention to the fact I am only performing the most agreeable duty toward a justly admired predecessor. This wise adviser was La Luzerne. In an unpublished memoir, drawn up by him on the 20th of April and sent to Rochambeau on May 19 with an explanatory letter in which he asked that his statement (a copy of which he also sent to Barras) be placed under the eyes of Washington, he insisted on the necessity of immediate action, and action in the Chesapeake: "It is in the Chesapeake Bay that it seems urgent to convey all the naval forces of the King, with such land forces as the generals will consider appropriate. This change cannot fail to have the most advantageous consequences for the continuation of the campaign," which consequences he points out with singular clear-sightedness, adding: "If the English follow us and can reach the bay only after us, their situation will prove very different from ours; all the coasts and the inland parts of the country are full of their enemies. They have neither the means nor the time to raise, as at New York, the necessary works to protect themselves against the inroads of the American troops and to save themselves from the danger to which the arrival of superior forces would expose them." If the plan submitted by him offers difficulties, others should be formed, but he maintains that "all those which have for their object the relief of the Southern States must be preferred, and that no time should be lost to put them in execution."

At the Weathersfield conference, near Hartford, Conn., between the Americans and French, on the 23d of May (in the Webb house, still in existence), Washington still evinced, and not without some weighty reasons, his preference for an attack on New York. He spoke of the advanced season, of "the great waste of men which we have found from experience in long marches in the Southern States," of the "difficulty of transports by land"; all those reasons and some others, "too well known to Count de Rochambeau to need repeating, show that an operation against New York should be preferred, in the present circumstances, to the effort of a sending of troops to the South." On the same day he was writing to La Luzerne: "I should be wanting in respect and confidence were I not to add that our object is New York."

La Luzerne, however, kept on insisting. To Rochambeau he wrote on the 1st of June: "The situation of the Southern States becomes every moment more critical; it has even become very dangerous, and every measure that could be taken for their relief would be of infinite advantage. . . . The situation of the Marquis de Lafayette and that of General Greene is most embarrassing, since Lord Cornwallis has joined the English divi-

sion of the Chesapeake.   If Virginia is not helped
in time, the English will have reached the goal
which they have assigned to themselves in the
bold movements attempted by them in the South:
they will soon have really conquered the Southern
States. . . .   I am going to write to M. de Grasse
as you want me to do; on your side, seize every
occasion to write to him, and multiply the copies
of the letters you send him," that is, in duplicate
and triplicate, for fear of loss or capture.   "His
coming to the rescue of the oppressed States is
not simply desirable; the thing seems to be now
of the most pressing necessity."   He must not
only come, but bring with him all he can find of
French troops in our isles: thus would be compensated, to a certain extent, the absence of the
second division.

Rochambeau soon agreed, and, with his usual
wisdom, Washington was not long in doing the
same.   On the 28th of May the French general
had already written to de Grasse, beseeching him
to come with every means at his disposal, to bring
his whole fleet, and not only his fleet, but a supply of money, to be borrowed in our colonies,
and also all the French land forces from our gar-
risons which he could muster.   The desire of Saint-
Simon to come and help had, of course, not been
forgotten by Rochambeau, and he counted on
his good-will.   After having described the ex-

treme importance of the effort to be attempted, he concluded: "The crisis through which America is passing at this moment is of the severest. The coming of Count de Grasse may be salvation."

Events had so shaped themselves that the fate of the United States and the destinies of more than one nation would be, for a few weeks, in the hands of one man, and one greatly hampered by imperative instructions obliging him, at a time when there was no steam to command the wind and waves, to be at a fixed date in the West Indies, owing to certain arrangements with Spain. Would he take the risk, and what would be the answer of that temporary arbiter of future events, François Joseph Paul Comte de Grasse, a sailor from the age of twelve, now a lieutenant-general and "chef d'escadre," who had seen already much service on every sea, in the East and West Indies, with d'Orvilliers at Ushant, with Guichen against Rodney in the Caribbean Sea, a haughty man, it was said, with some friends and many enemies, the one quality of his acknowledged by friend and foe being valor? "Our admiral," his sailors were wont to say, "is six foot tall on ordinary days, and six foot six on battle days."

What would he do and say? People in those times had to take their chance and act in accordance with probabilities. This Washington and Rochambeau did. By the beginning of June all

was astir in the northern camp. Soldiers did not
know what was contemplated, but obviously it
was something great. Young officers exulted.
What joy to have at last the prospect of an
"active campaign," wrote Closen in his journal,
"and to have an occasion to visit other provinces
and see the differences in manners, customs, products, and trade of our good Americans!"

The camp is raised and the armies are on the
move toward New York and the South; they are
in the best dispositions, ready, according to circumstances, to fight or admire all that turns up.
"The country between Providence and Bristol,"
says Closen, "is charming. We thought we had
been transported into Paradise, all the roads being
lined with acacias in full bloom, filling the air with
a delicious, almost too strong fragrance." Steeples
are climbed, and "the sight is one of the finest
possible." Snakes are somewhat troublesome, but
such things will happen, even in Paradise. The
heat becomes very great, and night marches are
arranged, beginning at two o'clock in the morning; roads at times become muddy paths, where
wagons, artillery, carts conveying boats for the
crossing of rivers cause great trouble and delay.
Poor Abbé Robin, ill-prepared for martyrdom,
becomes pathetic, talking of his own fate, fearful
of being captured by the English and of becoming
"the victim of those anti-republicans." He sleeps

on the ground, under a torrential rain, "in front
of a great fire, roasted on one side, drenched on the
other." He finds, however, that "French gayety
remains ever present in these hard marches.
The Americans whom curiosity brings by the
thousand to our camps are received," he writes,
"with lively joy; we cause our military instruments
to play for them, of which they are passionately
fond. Officers and soldiers, then, American men
and women mix and dance together; it is the
Feast of Equality, the first-fruits of the alliance
which must prevail between those nations. . . .
These people are still in the happy period when
distinctions of rank and birth are ignored; they
treat alike the soldier and the officer, and often
ask the latter what is his profession in his country,
unable as they are to imagine that that of a warrior may be a fixed and permanent one."

Washington writes to recommend precautions
against spies, who will be sent to the French
camp, dressed as peasants, bringing fruit and
other provisions, and who "will be attentive to
every word which they may hear drop."[1]

Several officers, for the sake of example, dis-
card their horses and walk, indifferent to mud
and heat; some of them, like the Viscount de
Noailles, performing on foot the whole distance
of seven hundred and fifty-six miles between

[1] To Rochambeau, June 30, 1781.

Newport and Yorktown. Cases of sickness were rare. "The attention of the superior officers," says Abbé Robin, "very much contributed to this, by the care they took in obliging the soldiers to drink no water without rum in it to remove its noisome qualities." It is not reported that superior officers had to use violence to be obeyed. This precaution, up to a recent date, was still considered a wise one; in the long journeys on foot that we used to take in my youth across the Alps, our tutor was convinced that no water microbe could resist the addition of a little kirsch. Anyway, we resisted the microbes.

On the 6th of July the junction of the two armies took place at Phillipsburg, "three leagues," Rochambeau writes, "from Kingsbridge, the first post of the enemy in the island of New York,"[1] the American army having followed the left bank of the Hudson in order to reach the place of meeting. On the receipt of the news, Lord Germain, the British colonial secretary, wrote to Clinton, who commanded in chief at New York: "The junction of the French troops with the

[1] This island's aspect fifteen years later is thus described by Duke de La Rochefoucauld-Liancourt: "Enfin nous sommes arrivés à King's Bridge dans l'île de New York, où le terrain, généralement mauvais, est encore en mauvais bois dans les parties les plus éloignées de la ville, et où il est cependant couvert de fermes et surtout de maisons de campagne dans les six ou sept milles qui s'en approchent davantage et dans les parties qui avoisinent la rivière du Nord et le bras de mer qui sépare cette île de Long Island." *Voyage*, V, 300.

Americans will, I am persuaded, soon produce
disagreements and discontents, and Mr. Washington will find it necessary to separate them very
speedily, either by detaching the Americans to
the southward or suffering the French to return
to Rhode Island. . . . But I trust, before that
can happen, Lord Cornwallis will have given the
loyal inhabitants on both sides of the Chesapeake
the opportunity they have so long ago earnestly
desired of avowing their principles and standing
forth in support of the King's measures." Similar
proofs of my lord's acumen abound in his partly
unpublished correspondence. He goes on rejoicing
and deducting all the happy consequences which
were sure to result from the meeting of the French
and American troops, so blandly elated at the
prospect as to remind any one familiar with La
Fontaine's fables, of Perrette and her milk-pot.

Washington, in the meantime, was reviewing
the French troops (July 9), and Rochambeau
the American ones, and—a fact which would
have greatly surprised Lord Germain—the worse
equipped the latter were, the greater the sympathy and admiration among the French for
their endurance. "Those brave people," wrote
Closen, "it really pained us to see, almost naked,
with mere linen vests and trousers, most of them
without stockings; but, would you believe it?
looking very healthy and in the best of spirits."

And further on: "I am full of admiration for the American troops. It is unbelievable that troops composed of men of all ages, even of children of fifteen, of blacks and whites, all nearly naked, without money, poorly fed, should walk so well and stand the enemy's fire with such firmness. The calmness of mind and the clever combinations of General Washington, in whom I discover every day new eminent qualities, are already enough known, and the whole universe respects and admires him. Certain it is that he is admirable at the head of his army, every member of which considers him as his friend and father." These sentiments, which were unanimous in the French army, assuredly did not betoken the clash counted upon by the English colonial secretary, and more than one of our officers who had, a few years later, to take part in another Revolution must have been reminded of the Continental soldiers of '81 as they led to battle, fighting for a similar cause, our volunteers of '92.

No real hatred, any more than before, appeared among the French troops for those enemies whom they were now nearing, and with whom they had already had some sanguinary skirmishes. During the intervals between military operations relations were courteous, and at times amicable. The English gave to the French news of Europe, even when the news was good for the latter, and passed to them newspapers. "We learned that news" (Necker's resignation), writes Blanchard, "through the English, who often sent trumpeters and passed gazettes to us. We learned from the same papers that Mr. de La Motte-Picquet had captured a rich convoy.[1] These exchanges between the English and us did not please the Americans, nor even General Washington, who were unaccustomed to this kind of warfare." The fight was really for an idea, but, what might have dispelled any misgivings, with no possibility of a change of idea.

[1] The convoy was carrying to England the enormous booty taken by Rodney at St. Eustatius. Eighteen of its ships were captured by La Motte-Picquet (May 2, 1781) and thus reached France instead of England.

Toward the Hessians, however, the feeling was different. Some had deserted to enlist in Lauzun's legion, but they almost immediately counterdeserted, upon which Rochambeau wrote to Lauzun: "You have done the best in deciding never to pester yourself again with Hessian deserters, of whom, you know, I never had a good opinion." Newport, December 22, 1780.

VII

Two unknown factors now were for the generals the cause of deep concern. What would de Grasse do? What would Clinton do? The wounded officer of Johannisberg, the winner of Charleston, Sir Henry Clinton, a lieutenant-general and former member of Parliament, enjoying great repute, was holding New York, not yet the second city of the world nor even the first of the United States, covering only with its modest houses, churches, and gardens the lower part of Manhattan, and reduced, owing to the war, to 10,000 inhabitants. But, posted there, the English commander threatened the road on which the combined armies had to move. He had at his disposal immense stores, strong fortifications, a powerful fleet to second his movements, and troops equal in number and training to ours.

There are periods in the history of nations when, after a continuous series of misfortunes, when despair would have seemed excusable, suddenly the sky clears and everything turns their way. In the War of American Independence, such a period had begun. The armies of Washington and Rochambeau, encumbered with their

carts, wagons, and artillery, had to pass rivers,
to cross hilly regions, to follow muddy tracks;
any serious attempt against them might have
proved fatal, but nothing was tried. It was of
the greatest importance that Clinton should, as
long as possible, have no intimation of the real
plans of the Franco-Americans; everything helped
to mislead him: his natural dispositions as well
as circumstances. He had an unshakable conviction that the key to the whole situation was
New York, and that the royal power in America,
and he, too, Lieutenant-General Sir Henry Clinton, would stand or fall with that city. Hence
his disinclination to leave it and to attempt anything outside. His instructions ordered him to
help Cornwallis to his utmost, the plan of the
British court being to conquer the Southern
States first and then continue the conquest northward. But he, on the contrary, was day after
day asking Cornwallis to send back some of his
troops. And while, as he never ceased to point
out afterward, he was careful to add, "if you
could spare them," he also remarked in the same
letter: "I confess I could not conceive you would
require above 4,000 in a station where General
Arnold has represented to me, upon report of
Colonel Simcoe, that 2,000 men would be amply
sufficient." [1]

[1] July 8, 1781.

A great source of light, and, as it turned out, of darkness also, was the intercepting of letters. This constantly happened in those days, to the benefit or bewilderment of both parties, on land or at sea. But luck had decidedly turned, and the stars shone propitious for the allies. We captured valuable letters, and Clinton misleading ones. It was something of a retribution after he had so often used or tried to use such captures to his advantage, as when, having seized an intimate letter of Washington, a passage of which might have given umbrage to Rochambeau, he had it printed in the newspapers. But the two commanders were not to be ruffled so easily, and all that took place was a frank explanation. Spontaneously acting in the same spirit, La Luzerne had written to Rochambeau concerning Washington and this incident: "I have told all those that have spoken to me of it that I saw nothing in it but the zeal of a good patriot, and a citizen must be very virtuous for his enemies not to find other crimes to reproach him with."[1]

More treasures had now fallen into the hands of Clinton: a letter of Chastellux to La Luzerne, speaking very superciliously of his unmanageable chief, Rochambeau, and of his "bourrasques." In it he congratulated himself, as Rochambeau narrates, on having "cleverly managed to cause

[1] April 13, 1781. (Rochambeau papers.)

me to agree with General Washington," the result being that "a siege of the island of New York
had at last been determined upon. . . . He
added complaints about the small chance a man
of parts had to influence the imperiousness of a
general always wanting to command." Clinton
caused that letter to be sent to Rochambeau, "obviously with no view," writes the latter, "to the
preservation of peace in my military family."
Rochambeau showed it to Chastellux, who blush-
ingly acknowledged its authorship; the general
thereupon threw it into the fire and left the unfortunate Academician "a prey to his remorse,"
—and to his ignorance, for he was careful not to
undeceive him as to the real plans of the combined army.

A text of the conclusions reached at the Weathersfield conferences was no less happily captured
by Clinton, and we have seen how clearly Washington had there expressed his reluctance to attempt striking the chief blow in the South.
A letter of Barras to La Luzerne, of May 27,
was also intercepted, and as luck would have it,
the sailor declared in it his intention to take the
fleet, of all places, to Boston (a real project, but
abandoned as soon as formed and replaced by
another which took him to the Chesapeake). A
most important letter of Rochambeau to La
Luzerne, explaining the real plan, was thereupon

intercepted; it was in cipher and the English managed to decipher it. But, as the stars shone propitious to the allies, it was only the English in London, and not those in New York, who could do it, and when the translation reached Clinton at last, he had no longer, for good causes, any doubt as to the real aims of Washington and Rochambeau.

The colonial secretary was, in the meantime, kept in a state of jubilation by so much treasure-trove and the news forwarded by Clinton, to whom he wrote: "The copies of the very important correspondence which so fortunately fell into your hands, inclosed in your despatch, show the rebel affairs to be almost desperate, and that nothing but the success of some extraordinary enterprise can give vigor and activity to their cause, and I confess I am well pleased that they have fixed upon New York as the object to be attempted."[1]   Clinton acknowledged a little later to Lord Germain the receipt of a "reinforcement of about 2,400 German troops and recruits," which he was careful to hold tight in New York till the end.

The combined armies had, in the meantime, done their best to confirm the English commander in such happy dispositions. They had built in the vicinity of New York brick ovens for baking

[1] July 14, 1781.

bread for an army, as in view of a long siege.
There had been reconnaissances, marches, and
countermarches, a sending of ships toward Long
Island without entering, however, "dans la baie
d'Oyster," skirmishes which looked like preliminaries to more important operations, and in one
of which, together with the two Berthiers and
Count de Vauban, Closen nearly lost his life in
order to save his hat. A camp proverb about
hats had been the cause of his taking the risk.
When he returned, "kind Washington," he writes
in his journal, "tapped me on the shoulder, saying: 'Dear Baron, this French proverb is not yet
known among our army, but your cold behavior
during danger will be it'" (in English in the original as being the very words of the great man to
the young one, though *cold* does probably duty
for *cool*, and the final *it* is certainly not Washington's).

Then on the sudden, on the 18th of August,
the two armies raised their camps, disappeared,
and, following unusual roads, moving northward
at first for three marches, reached in the midst
of great difficulties, under a torrid heat, greatly
encumbered with heavy baggage, the Hudson
River and crossed it at King's Ferry, without
being more interfered with than before. How
can such an inaction on the part of Clinton be explained? "It is for me," writes Count Guillaume

de Deux-Ponts in his journal, the manuscript of which was found on the quays in Paris,[1] and printed in America, "an undecipherable enigma, and I hope I shall never be reproached for having puzzled people with any similar ones."

The river once crossed, the double army moved southward by forced marches. Rochambeau, in order to hasten the move, prescribed the leaving behind of a quantity of effects, and this, says Closen, "caused considerable grumbling among the line," which grumbled but marched. The news, to be sure, of so important a movement came to Clinton, but, since the stars had ceased to smile on him, he chose to conclude, as he wrote to Lord Germain on the 7th of September, "this to be a feint." When he discovered that it was not "a feint," the Franco-American army was beyond reach. "What can be said as to this?" Closen writes merrily. "Try to see better another time," and he draws a pair of spectacles on the margin of his journal.

The march southward thus continued unhampered. They crossed first the Jerseys, "a land of Cockayne, for game, fish, vegetables, poultry." Closen had the happiness to "hear from the lips of General Washington, and on the ground itself, a

[1] In June, 1867, by S. A. Green, who printed it with an English translation: *My Campaigns in America, a journal kept by Count William de Deux-Ponts*, Boston, 1868.

description of the dispositions taken, the movements and all the incidents of the famous battles
of Trenton and Princeton." The young man, who
had made great progress in English, was now used
by the two generals as their interpreter; so nothing
escaped him. The reception at Philadelphia was
triumphal; Congress was most courteous; toasts
were innumerable. The city is an immense one,
"with seventy-two streets in a straight line. . . .
Shops abound in all kinds of merchandise, and
some of them do not yield to the *Petit Dunkerque*
in Paris." Where is now the *Petit Dunkerque?*
—"Mais où sont les Neiges d'antan?"[1] Women
are very pretty, "of charming manners, and very
well dressed, even in French fashion." Benezet,
the French Quaker, one of the celebrities of the
city, is found to be full of wisdom, and La Luzerne,
"who keeps a state worthy of his sovereign,"
gives a dinner to one hundred and eighty guests.

From Philadelphia to Chester, on the 5th of
September, Rochambeau and his aides took a
boat. As they were nearing the latter city, "we
saw in the distance," says Closen, "General Washington shaking his hat and a white handkerchief,

---

[1] The house at the entrance of the Pont-Neuf, where the *Petit
Dunkerque* was established, being then the most famous "magasin
de frivolités" in existence, survived until July, 1914. The sign of the
shop, a little ship with the inscription, "Au Petit Dunkerque," was
still there. It has been preserved and is now in the Carnavalet
Museum.

and showing signs of great joy." Rochambeau
had scarcely landed when Washington, usually
so cool and composed, fell into his arms; the
great news had arrived; de Grasse had come, and
while Cornwallis was on the defensive at Yorktown the French fleet was barring the Chesapeake.[1]

On the receipt of letters from Washington, Rochambeau, and La Luzerne telling him to what
extent the fate of the United States was in his
hands, the sailor, having "learned, with much
sorrow," he wrote to the latter, "what was the
distress of the continent, and the need there was
of immediate help," had decided that he would
leave nothing undone to usefully take part in the
supreme effort which, without his help, might be
attempted in vain.   Having left, on the 5th of
August, Cap Français (to-day Cap Haïtien), he
had added to his fleet all the available ships he
could find in our isles, including some which, having been years away, had received orders to go
back to France for repairs.   He had had great diffi-

---

[1] Washington's joy was in proportion to the acuteness of his
anxieties; only three days before he was writing to Lafayette:
"But, my dear marquis, I am distressed beyond expression to know
what has become of Count de Grasse, and for fear that the English
fleet, by occupying the Chesapeake, toward which, my last accounts
say, they were steering, may frustrate all our prospects in that quarter. . . .   Adieu, my dear marquis; if you get anything new from
any quarter, send it, I pray you, *on the spur of speed*, for I am almost
all impatience and anxiety."   Philadelphia, September 2, 1781.

culty in obtaining the money asked for, although
he had offered to mortgage for it his castle of
Tilly, and the Chevalier de Charitte, in command
of the *Bourgogne*, had made a like offer. But at
last, thanks to the Spanish governor at Havana,
he had secured the desired amount of twelve hundred thousand francs. He was bringing, moreover, the Marquis de Saint-Simon, with the 3,000
regular troops under his command. De Grasse's
only request was that operations be pushed on
with the utmost rapidity, as he was bound to be
back at the Isles at a fixed date. It can truly be
said that no single man risked nor did more for
the United States than de Grasse, the single one
of the leaders to whom no memorial has been
dedicated.

The news spread like wild-fire; the camp was
merry with songs and shouts; in Philadelphia the
joy was indescribable; crowds pressed before the
house of La Luzerne, cheering him and his country, while in the streets impromptu orators, standing on chairs, delivered mock funeral orations on
the Earl of Cornwallis. "You have," Rochambeau wrote to the admiral, "spread universal joy
throughout America, with which she is wild." [1]

Anxiety was renewed, however, when it was
learned shortly after that the French men-of-war
had left the Chesapeake, the entrance to which

[1] September 7, 1781.

now remained free. The English fleet, of twenty
ships and seven frigates, under Hood and Graves,
the same Graves who had failed to intercept Rochambeau's convoy, had been signalled on the
5th of September, and de Grasse, leaving behind
him, in order to go faster, some of his ships and a
number of sailors who were busy on land, had
weighed anchor, three-quarters of an hour after
sighting the signals, to risk the fight upon which
the issue of the campaign and, as it turned out,
of the war, was to depend. "This behavior of
Count de Grasse," wrote the famous Tarleton,
is "worthy of admiration." Six days later the
French admiral was back; he had had 21 officers
and 200 sailors killed or wounded, but he had
lost no ship, and the enemy's fleet, very much
damaged, with 336 men killed or disabled, and
having lost the *Terrible*, of 74 guns, and the
frigates *Iris* and *Richmond* of 40,[1] had been
compelled to retreat to New York. Admiral
Robert Digby thereupon arrived with naval re-

---

[1] Graves had rightly supposed that, to have been able to start so
quickly, de Grasse must have caused some of his ships to cut their
anchors' cables, marking the spot with buoys. The two frigates
had been sent to gather those buoys, and were bringing several as a
prize to the English admiral, when they were captured. (*Journal Particulier*, by Count de Revel, sublieutenant in the regiment of "Mon-
sieur-Infanterie," p. 131.) On the 15th of September Washington
wrote to de Grasse: "I am at a loss to express the pleasure which
I have in congratulating your Excellency . . . on the glory of having driven the British fleet from the coast and taking two of their
frigates."

inforcements; "yet I do not think," La Luzerne wrote to Rochambeau, "that battle will be offered again. If it is, I am not anxious about the result." Nothing was attempted. This "superiority at sea," Tarleton wrote in his *History of the Campaigns*, "proved the strength of the enemies of Great Britain, deranged the plans of her generals, disheartened the courage of her friends, and finally confirmed the independency of America."[1] "Nothing," Rochambeau had written in his notebook at starting, "without naval supremacy."

On re-entering the bay de Grasse had the pleasure to find there another French fleet, that of his friend Barras. As a lieutenant-general de Grasse outranked him, but as a "chef d'escadre" Barras was his senior officer, which might have caused difficulties; the latter could be tempted, and he was, to conduct a campaign apart, so as to personally reap the glory of possible successes. "I leave it to thee, my dear Barras," de Grasse had written him on the 28th of July, "to come and join me or to act on thy own account for the good of the common cause. Do only let me know, so that we do not hamper each other unawares." Barras preferred the service of the cause to his own interest; leaving Newport, going far out on

[1] *History of the Campaigns of 1780 and 1787*, by Lieutenant-Colonel Tarleton, commandant of the late British Legion, Dublin, 1787, pp. 403 ff.

the high seas, then dashing south at a great distance from the coast, he escaped the English and reached the Chesapeake, bringing the heavy siege artillery now indispensable for the last operations. The stars had continued incredibly propitious.

The well-known double siege now began, that of Yorktown[1] by Washington and Rochambeau, and that of Gloucester, on the opposite side of the river, which might have afforded a place of retreat to Cornwallis. De Grasse had consented to land, in view of the latter, 800 men under Choisy, whom Lauzun joined with his legion, and both acted in conjunction with the American militia under Weedon.[2] The two chiefs on the Yorktown side were careful to conduct the operations according to rules, "on account," says Closen, "of the reputation of Cornwallis, and the strength of the garrison." Such rules were certainly familiar to Rochambeau, whose fifteenth siege this one was.

From day to day Cornwallis was more narrowly pressed. As late as the 29th of September he was still full of hope. "I have ventured these

[1] A minute "Journal of the Siege" was kept by Mr. de Ménonville, aide major-general, a translation of which is in the *Magazine of American History*, 1881, VII, 283.

[2] The city of Gloucester consisted of "four houses on a promontory facing York," but very well defended by trenches, ditches, redoubts, manned by a garrison of 1,200 men. (Count de Revel, *Journal Particulier*, p. 171.) A detailed account of the Gloucester siege is in this journal. Choisy "had previously won a kind of fame by his defense of the citadel of Cracow, in Poland." (*Ibid.*, p. 139.)

two days," he wrote to Clinton, "to look General Washington's whole force in the face in the position on the outside of my works; and I have the pleasure to assure your Excellency that there was but one wish throughout the whole army, which was that the enemy would advance." A dozen days later the tone was very different. "I have only to repeat that nothing but a direct move to York River, which includes a successful naval action, can save me . . . many of our works are considerably damaged."

Lord Germain was, in the meantime, writing to Clinton in his happiest mood, on the 12th of October: "It is a great satisfaction to me to find . . . that the plan you had concerted for conducting the military operations in that quarter (the Chesapeake) corresponds with what I had suggested." The court, which had no more misgivings than Lord Germain himself, had caused to sail with Digby no less a personage than Prince William, one of the fifteen children of George III, and eventually one of his successors as William IV; but his presence could only prove one more encumbrance.

After the familiar incidents of the siege in which the American and French armies displayed similar valor and met with about the same losses, the decisive move of the night attack on the enemy's advanced redoubts had to be made, one of the redoubts to be stormed by the Americans with Lafayette, and the other by the French under Viomesnil. Rochambeau addressed himself especially to the grenadiers of the regiment of Gatinais, which had been formed with a portion of his old regiment of Auvergne, and said: "My boys, if I need you to-night, I hope you will not have forgotten that we have served together in that brave regiment of Auvergne sans tache (spotless Auvergne), an honorable surname deserved by it since its formation." They answered that if he would promise to have their former name restored to them he would find they were ready to die to the last. They kept their word, losing many of their number, and one of the first requests of Rochambeau when he reached Paris was that their old name be given back to them, which was done. Gatinais thus became Royal Auvergne, and is now the 18th Infantry.

On the 19th of October, after a loss of less than 300 men in each of the besieging armies, an act was signed as great in its consequences as any that ever followed the bloodiest battles, the capitulation of Yorktown. It was in a way the ratification of that other act which had been proposed for signature five years before at Philadelphia by men whose fate had more than once, in the interval, seemed desperate, the Declaration of Independence.

On the same day Closen writes: "The York garrison marched past at two o'clock, before the combined army, which was formed in two lines, the French facing the Americans and in full dress uniform. . . . Passing between the two armies, the English showed much disdain for the Americans, who so far as dress and appearances went represented the seamy side, many of those poor boys being garbed in linen *habits-vestes*, torn, soiled, a number among them almost shoeless. The English had given them the nickname of *Yanckey-Dudle*. What does it matter? the man of sense will think; they are the more to be praised and show the greater valor, fighting, as they do, so badly equipped." As a "man of sense," Rochambeau writes in his memoirs: "This justice must be rendered to the Americans that they behaved with a zeal, a courage, an emulation which left them in no case behind, in all that part of the siege intrusted to them, in spite of their being unaccustomed to sieges."

The city offered a pitiful sight. "I shall never forget," says Closen, "how horrible and painful to behold was the aspect of the town of York. . . . One could not walk three steps without finding big holes made by bombs, cannon-balls, splinters, barely covered graves, arms and legs of blacks and whites scattered here and there, most of the houses riddled with shot and devoid

of window panes. . . . We found Lord Cornwallis in his house. His attitude evinced the nobility of his soul, his magnanimity and firmness of
character. He seemed to say: I have nothing to
reproach myself with, I have done my duty and
defended myself to the utmost." This impression
of Lord Cornwallis was general.

As to Closen's description of the town, now so
quiet and almost asleep, by the blue water, amid
her sand-dunes, once more torn and blood-stained
during the Civil War, resting at the foot of the
great marble memorial raised a hundred years
later by Congress,[1] it is confirmed by Abbé Robin,
who notices, too, "the quantity of human limbs
which infected the air," but also, being an abbé,
the number of books scattered among the ruins,
many being works of piety and theological con-
troversy, and with them "the works of the famous
Pope, and translations of Montaigne's *Essays*, of

[1] As early as 1796, when La Rochefoucauld-Liancourt visited it,
the city, formerly a prosperous one, had become a borough of 800
inhabitants, two-thirds of which were colored. "The inhabitants,"
says the traveller, "are without occupation. Some retail spirits or
cloth; some are called lawyers, some justices of the peace. Most
of them have, at a short distance from the town, a small farm, which
they go and visit every morning, but that scarcely fills the mind or
time; and the inhabitants of York, who live on very good terms
with each other, occupy both better in dining together, drinking
punch, playing billiards; to introduce more variety in this mo-
notonous kind of life, they often change the place where they meet.
. . . The name of Marshal de Rochambeau is still held there in
great veneration." *Voyage dans les Etats-Unis*, Paris, "An VII,"
vol. VI, p. 283.

Gil Blas, and of the *Essay on Women* by Monsieur Thomas," that stern essay, so popular then in America, in which society ladies were invited to fill their soul with those "sentiments of nature which are born in retreat and grow in silence."

Nothing better puts in its true light the dominant characteristic of the French sentiment throughout the war than what happened on this solemn occasion, and more shows how, with their new-born enthusiasm for philanthropy and liberty, the French were pro-Americans much more than anti-English. No trace of a triumphant attitude toward a vanquished enemy appeared in anything they did or said. Even in the surrendering, the fact remained apparent that this was not a war of hatred. "The English," writes Abbé Robin, "laid down their arms at the place selected. Care was taken not to admit sightseers, so as to diminish their humiliation." Henry Lee (Light-horse Harry), who was present, describes in the same spirit the march past: "Universal silence was observed amidst the vast concourse, and the utmost decency prevailed, exhibiting in demeanor an awful sense of the vicissitudes of human life, mingled with commiseration for the unhappy."[1]

[1] *Memoirs of the War in the Southern Department of the United States*, Philadelphia, 1812, II, 343. In the same spirit Pontgibaud notes that the British army laid down its arms "to the noble confusion of its brave and unfortunate soldiers." *Mémoires du Comte de Moré* (Pontgibaud), 1898, p. 104.

The victors pitied Cornwallis and showed him every consideration; Rochambeau, learning that he was without money, lent him all he wanted. He invited him to dine with him and his officers on the 2d of November. "Lord Cornwallis," writes Closen, "especially distinguished himself by his reflective turn of mind, his noble and gentle manners. He spoke freely of his campaigns in the Carolinas, and, though he had won several victories, he acknowledged, nevertheless, that they were the cause of the present misfortunes. All, with the exception of Tarleton, spoke French, O'Hara in particular to perfection, but he seemed to us something of a brag."[1] A friendly correspondence began between the English general and some of the French officers, Viscount de Noailles, the one who had walked all the way, lending him, the week after the capitulation, his copy of the beforementioned famous work of Count de Guibert on *Tactics*, which was at that time the talk of Europe, and of which Napoleon

[1] Same good feeling on the Gloucester side. After the surrender, "les officiers anglais vinrent voir nos officiers qui étaient de service, leur firent toutes les honnêtetés possible, et burent à leur santé." (Revel, *Journal Particulier*, p. 168.) The British fleet appeared only on the 27th of October, at the entrance of the capes; thirty-one sails were counted on that day and forty-four on the next; after the 29th they were no longer seen. "Nous avons su depuis," Revel writes, "que l'Amiral Graves avait dans son armée le général Clinton, avec des troupes venues de New York pour secourir lord Cornwallis. Mais il était trop tard; la poule était mangée, et l'un et l'autre prirent le parti de s'en retourner." (*Ibid.*, p. 178.)

said later that "it was such as to form great men,"
the same Guibert who expected lasting repute
from that work and from his military services,
and who—irony of fate—general and Academician
though he was, is chiefly remembered as the hero
of the letters of Mademoiselle de Lespinasse.

Cornwallis realized quite well that the French
had fought for a cause dear to their hearts more
than from any desire to humble him or his nation.
He publicly rendered full justice to the enemy,
acknowledging that the fairest treatment had
been awarded him by them.   In the final report
in which he gives his own account of the catastrophe, and which he caused to be printed when
he reached England, he said: "The kindness and
attention that has been shown us by the French
officers . . . their delicate sensibility of our situation, their generous and pressing offers of money,
both public and private, to any amount, has really
gone beyond what I can possibly describe and
will, I hope, make an impression on the breast of
every British officer whenever the fortunes of war
should put any of them in our power."

The French attitude in the New World was in
perfect accord with the French sentiments in the
Old.   On receiving from Lauzun and Count de
Deux-Ponts, who for fear of capture had sailed
in two different frigates, the news of the taking
of Cornwallis, of his 8,000 men (of whom 2,000

were in hospitals), 800 sailors, 214 guns, and 22 flags, the King wrote to Rochambeau: "Monsieur le Comte de Rochambeau, the success of my arms flatters me only as being conducive to peace." And, thanking the "Author of all prosperity," he announced the sending of letters to the archbishops and bishops of his kingdom for a *Te Deum* to be sung in all the churches of their dioceses.

It was a long time since the old cocks of the French churches had quivered at the points of the steeples to the chant of a *Te Deum* for a victory leading to a glorious peace. The victory was over those enemies who, not so very long before, had bereft us of Canada. Nothing more significant than the pastoral letter of "Louis Apollinaire de la Tour du Pin Montauban, by the grace of God first Bishop of Nancy, Primate of Lorraine," appointing the date for the thanksgiving ceremonies, and adding: "This so important advantage has been the result of the wisest measures. Reason and humanity have gauged it and have placed it far above those memorable but bloody victories whose lustre has been tarnished by almost universal mourning. Here the blood of our allies and of our generous compatriots has been spared, and why should we not note with satisfaction that the forces of our enemies have been considerably weakened, their efforts baffled, the fruits of their immense expense lost, without our having caused rivers of their blood to be spilt, without our having filled their country with unfortunate widows and mothers?" For this, too, as well as for the victory, thanks must be offered; and for this, too, for such a rare and such a humane feeling, the name of Bishop de la Tour du Pin Montauban deserves to be remembered.

The nation at large felt like the bishop. One of the most typical of the publications inspired in France by the war and its outcome was the *Fragment of Xenophon, newly found in the ruins of Palmyra* . . . *translated from the Greek*, anonymously printed, in 1783,[1] in which under the names of Greeks and Carthaginians, the story of the campaign is told; the chief actors being easily recognized, most of them, under anagrams: Tusingonas is Washington; Cherambos, Rochambeau; the illustrious Filaatete, Lafayette; Tangides, d'Estaing, and the wise Thales of Milet, Franklin.

Critical minds, the author observes, will perhaps think they discover anachronisms, but such mean nothing; he will soon give an edition of the Greek original, splendidly printed, "so the wealthy amateurs will buy it, without being able to read it; the learned, who could read it, will be unable to buy it, and everybody will be pleased."

---

[1] The work of Gabriel Brizard, a popular writer in his day: *Fragment de Xenophon, nouvellement trouvé dans les ruines de Palmyre par un Anglois et déposé au Museum Britannicum—Traduit du Grec par un François*, Paris, 1783.

The author gives a detailed description of the Greeks and of the Carthaginians, that is, the French and their former enemies, the English: "Greece, owing to her intellectual and artistic predominance, seemed to lead the rest of the world, and Athens led Greece. The Athenians were, truth to say, accused of inconstancy; they were reproached for the mobility of their character, their fondness for new things, their leaning toward raillery; but there was something pleasing in their defects. Justice was, moreover, rendered to their rare qualities: gentle as they were and softened by their fondness for enjoyment, they nonetheless were attracted by danger and prodigal of their blood. They felt as much passion for glory as for pleasure; arbiters in matters of taste, they played the same rôle in questions of honor, an idol with them; somewhat light-minded, they were withal frank and generous. . . . This brilliant and famous nation was such that those among her enemies that cast most reproaches at her envied the fate of the citizens living within her borders."

Whether succeeding events have cured or not some of that light-mindedness, any one can see to-day and form his judgment.

As to Carthaginians (the English), no animosity, no hatred, but, on the contrary, greater praise than was accorded to his own compatriots by many an English writer: "It must

be acknowledged that they never made a finer
defense. . . . They faced everywhere all their
enemies, and, disastrous as the result may have
proved for them, this part of their annals will
remain one of the most glorious. Why should
we hesitate to render them justice? Yes, if the
intrepid defender of the columns of Hercules[1] were
present in person at our celebration, he would
receive the tribute of praise and applause that
Greeks know how to pay to any brave and generous enemy."

This way of thinking had nothing exceptional.
One of the most authoritative publicists of the
day, Lacretelle, in 1785, considering, in the *Mercure de France*, the future of the new-born United
States, praised the favorable influence exercised
on them by the so much admired British Constitution—"the most wonderful government in Europe.
For it will be England's glory to have created
peoples worthy of throwing off her yoke, even
though she must endure the reproach of having
forced them to independence by forgetfulness of
her own maxims."

As to the members of the French army who
had started for the new crusade two years before,
they had at once the conviction that, in accor-

[1] General Eliott, later Lord Heathfield, defender of Gibraltar, well
known in France not only as an enemy, but as a former pupil of the
military school at La Fère.

dance with their anticipation, they had witnessed something great which would leave a profound trace in the history of the world. They brought home the seed of liberty and equality, the "virus," as it was called by Pontgibaud, who, friend as he was of Lafayette, resisted the current to the last and remained a royalist. "The young French nobility," says Talleyrand in his memoirs, "having enlisted for the cause of independence, clung ever after to the principle which it had gone to defend."[1] Youthful Saint-Simon, the future Saint-Simonian, thus summed up his impressions of the campaign: "I felt that the American Revolution marked the beginning of a

---

[1] Mathieu-Dumas availed himself of his stay in Boston before sailing to go and visit, with some of his brother officers, several of the heroes of independence—Hancock, John Adams, Doctor Cooper: "We listened with avidity to the latter, who, while applauding our enthusiasm for liberty, said to us: 'Take care, take care, young men, that the triumph of the cause on this virgin soil does not influence overmuch your hopes; you will carry away with you the germ of these generous sentiments, but if you attempt to fecund them on your native soil, after so many centuries of corruption, you will have to surmount many more obstacles; it cost us much blood to conquer liberty; but you will shed torrents before you establish it in your old Europe.' How often since, during our political turmoils, in the course of our *bad days*, did I not recall to mind the prophetic leave-taking of Doctor Cooper. But the inestimable prize which the Americans secured in exchange for their sacrifices was never absent from my thought." (*Souvenirs du Lieutenant-Général Comte Mathieu-Dumas, publiés par son fils*, I, 108.) The writer notices the early formation of a "national character, in spite of the similitude of language, customs, manners, religion, principles of government with the English." (*Ibid.*, 113.)

new political era; that this revolution would
necessarily set moving an important progress in
general civilization, and that it would, béfore
long, occasion great changes in the social order
then existing in Europe."[1] Many experienced
the feeling described in the last lines of his journal by Count Guillaume de Deux-Ponts, wounded
at the storming of the redoubts: "With troops as
good and brave and well-disciplined as those
which I have had the honor to lead against the
enemy, one can undertake anything. . . . I owe
them the greatest day in my life, the souvenir of
which will never die out. . . . Man's life is
mixed with trials, but one can no longer complain when having enjoyed the delightful moments
which are their counterpart; a single instant
effaces such troubles, and that instant, well re-
sented, causes one to desire new trials so as to
once more enjoy their recompense."

[1] *Œuvres*, 1865, I, 12.

VIII

For one year more Rochambeau remained in America. Peace was a possibility, not a certainty. In London, where so late as November 20, the most encouraging news continued to be received, but where that of the catastrophe, brought by the *Rattlesnake*, arrived on the 25th, George III and his ministers refused to yield to evidence, Lord Germain especially, for whom the shock had been great, and who was beseeching Parliament "to proceed with vigor in the prosecution of the war and not leave it in the power of the French to tell the Americans that they had procured their independence, and were consequently entitled to a preference, if not an exclusive right, in their trade." This was not to know us well; our treaty of commerce had been signed three years before, at a time when anything would have been granted to propitiate France, but there was not in it, as we saw, one single advantage that was not equally accessible to any one who chose, the English included.

As for King George, he decided that the 8th of February, 1782, would be a day of national fasting, to ask pardon for past sins, and implore

Heaven's assistance in the prosecution of the
war. Franklin was still beseeching his compatriots to be on their guard: "It seems the [Eng-
lish] nation is sick of [the war] . . . but the King
is obstinate. . . . The ministry, you will see,
declare that the war in America is for the future
to be only *defensive*. I hope we shall be too prudent to have the least dependence on this declaration. It is only thrown out to lull us; for, depend upon it, the King hates us cordially, and will
be content with nothing short of our extirpation."[1]

With his French *admiratrices* the sage exchanged merry, picturesque letters. Madame
Brillon writes, in French, from Nice on the 11th
of December, 1781: "My dear Papa, I am sulky
with you . . . yes, Mr. Papa, I am sulky. What!
You capture whole armies in America, you burgoy-
nize Cornwallis, you capture guns, ships, ammunition, men, horses, etc., etc., you capture everything and of everything, and only the gazette
informs your friends, who go off their heads
drinking your health, that of Washington, of independence, of the King of France, of the Marquis de Lafayette, of Mr. de Rochambeau, Mr.
de Chastellux, etc., and you give them no sign of
life! . . ."

With his valiant pen, which feared nothing, not
even French grammar, Franklin answered: "Passy,

[1] To Robert Livingston, Passy, March 4, 1782.

25 Décembre 1781.—Vous me boudés, ma chère amie, que je n'avois pas vous envoyé tout de suite l'histoire de notre grande victoire. Je suis bien sensible de la magnitude de notre avantage et de ses possibles bonnes conséquences, mais je ne triomphe pas. Sçachant que la guerre est pleine de variétés et d'incertitudes, dans la mauvaise fortune j'espère la bonne, et dans la bonne je crains la mauvaise."

The future continued doubtful. In June Washington was still writing: "In vain is it to expect that our aim is to be accomplished by fond wishes for peace, and equally ungenerous and fruitless will it be for one State to depend upon another to bring this to pass."[1] French and American regiments remained, therefore, under arms and waited, but scarcely did anything on the continent but wait. For if George III was still for war, the mass of his people were not. Rochambeau availed himself of his leisure to visit the accessible parts of the country, give calls and dinners to his neighbors, study the manners and resources of the inhabitants, go fox-hunting "through the woods, accompanied by some twenty sportsmen. We have forced more than thirty foxes; the packs of hounds of the local gentlemen are perfect," states Closen. The different usages of the French and the Americans are for each other a cause of merri-

[1] To Archibald Cary, June 15, 1782.

ment. "On New Year's Day the custom of the
French to embrace, even in the street, caused much
American laughter," but, the young aide observes
with some spite, "their *shake hands*, on the other
side, those more or less prolonged and sometimes
very hard-pressed twitchings of the hands are certainly on a par with European embracings."

Rochambeau had established himself at Williamsburg, the quiet and dignified capital of the
then immense State of Virginia, noted for its
"Bruton church," its old College of William and
Mary, designed by Sir Christopher Wren, and the
birthplace of the far-famed Phi Beta Kappa fra-
ternity, its statue of the former English governor,
Lord Botetourt,[1] in conspicuous marble wig and
court mantle. "America, behold your friend,"
the inscription on the pedestal reads.

That other friend of America, Rochambeau,
took up his quarters in the college, one of the
buildings of which, used as a hospital for our
troops, accidentally took fire, but was at once paid
for by the French commander. Seeing more of
the population, Rochambeau was noting a number of traits which were to be taken up again by
Tocqueville, the diffusion of the ideas of religious
tolerance, the absence of privileges, equality put
into practise. "The husbandman in his habita-
tion is neither a castellated lord nor a tenant,

[1] White marble; signed and dated, Richard Hayward, London,
1773.

but a landowner." It takes him thirty to forty
years to rise from "the house made of logs and
posts," with the house "of well-joined boards"
as an intermediary stage, to the "house in bricks,
which is the acme of their architecture." Labor
is expensive and is paid a dollar a day. The country has three million inhabitants, but will easily
support a little more than thirty, which was
not such a bad guess since the thirteen States
of Rochambeau's day have now thirty-seven.
Men are fond of English furniture, and women
"have a great liking for French fashions." In
every part where the ravages of the war have not
been felt people live at their ease, "and the little
negro is ever busy clearing and laying the table."

Faithful Closen, who had been proposed for promotion on account of his gallant conduct at the
siege, accompanied the general everywhere, and
also explored separately, on his own account, led
sometimes by his fondness for animals, of which
he was making "a small collection, some living
and some stuffed ones, only too glad if they can
please the persons for whom I destine them."
He takes notes on raccoons, investigates opossums,
and visits a marsh "full of subterranean habitations of beavers," and he sees them at work. He is
also present at one of those cock-fights so popular
then in the region, "but the sight is a little too
cruel to allow one to derive enjoyment from it."

Sent to Portsmouth with letters for Mr. de

Vaudreuil, in command of our fleet, Closen becomes acquainted "with a very curious animal
which the people of the region call a musk-cat, but
which I believe to be the *puant*" (the stinking
one), and a careful description shows that, in any
case, the name well fitted the animal. He also
studies groundhogs on the same occasion. The
charm and picturesqueness of wild life in American
forests is a trait which French officers noted with
amused curiosity in their journals. Describing
his long journey on foot from the Chesapeake,
where he had been shipwrecked, to Valley Forge,
where he was to become aide to his Auvergnat
compatriot, Lafayette, youthful Pontgibaud, with
no luggage nor money left, sleeping in the open,
writes of the beauty of birds, and the delightful
liveliness of innumerable little squirrels, "who
jumped from branch to branch, from tree to tree,
around me. They seemed to accompany the triumphal march of a young warrior toward glory.
. . . It is a fact that, with their jumps, their
gambols, that quantity of little dancers, so nim-
ble, so clever, retarded my walk. . . . Such is
the way with people of eighteen; the present moment makes them forget all the rest."[1]

Rochambeau, his son, and two aides, one of

----

[1] *Mémoires du Comte de Moré* (formerly Chevalier de Pontgibaud),
1898, p. 56; first ed., Paris, 1827, one of Balzac's ventures as a
printer.

whom was Closen, journey to visit at Monticello
the already famous Jefferson; they take with
them fourteen horses, sleep in the houses where
they chance to be at nightfall, a surprise party
which may, at times, have caused embarrassment,
but this accorded with the customs of the day.
The hospitality is, according to occasions, brilliant
or wretched, "with a bed for the general, as ornamented as the canopy for a procession," and elsewhere "with rats which come and tickle our ears."
They reach the handsome house of the "philosopher," adorned with a colonnade, "the platform
of which is very prettily fitted with all sorts of
mythological scenes."

The lord of the place dazzles his visitors by his
encyclopædic knowledge. Closen describes him
as "very learned in belles-lettres, in history, in
geography, etc., etc., being better versed than any
in the statistics of America in general, and the
interests of each particular province, trade, agriculture, soil, products, in a word, all that is of
greatest use to know. The least detail of the wars
here since the beginning of the troubles is familiar to him. He speaks all the chief languages
to perfection, and his library is well chosen, and
even rather large in spite of a visit paid to the
place by a detachment of Tarleton's legion, which
has proved costly and has greatly frightened his
family."

Numerous addresses expressing fervent gratitude were received by Rochambeau, from Congress, from the legislatures of the various States,
from the universities, from the mayor and inhabitants of Williamsburg, the latter offering their
thanks not only for the services rendered by the
general in his "military capacity," but, they said,
"for your conduct in the more private walks of
life, and the happiness we have derived from the
social, polite, and very friendly intercourse we
have been honored with by yourself and the officers
of the French army in general, during the whole
time of your residence among us." The favorable impression left by an army permeated with
the growing humanitarian spirit, is especially
mentioned in several of those addresses: "May
Heaven," wrote "the Governor, council and representatives of the State of Rhode Island and
Providence Plantations in General Assembly convened," "reward your exertions in the cause of
humanity and the particular regard you have paid
to the rights of the citizens."

Writing at the moment when departure was im-
minent, the Maryland Assembly recalled in its
address the extraordinary prejudices prevailing
shortly before in America against all that was
French: "To preserve in troops far removed from
their own country the strictest discipline and *to
convert into esteem and affection deep and ancient*

prejudices was reserved for you. . . . We view with regret the departure of troops which have so conducted, so endeared, and so distinguished themselves, and we pray that the laurels they have gathered before Yorktown may never fade, and that victory, to whatever quarter of the globe they direct their arms, may follow their standard."

The important result of a change in American sentiment toward the French, apart from the military service rendered by them, was confirmed to Rochambeau by La Luzerne, who wrote him: "Your well-behaved and brave army has not only contributed to put an end to the success of the English in this country, but has destroyed in three years prejudices deep-rooted for three centuries."[1]

The "President and professors of the University of William and Mary," using a style which was to become habitual in France but a few years later, desired to address Rochambeau, "not in the prostituted language of fashionable flattery, but with the voice of truth and republican sincerity," and, after thanks for the services rendered and the payment made for the building destroyed "by an accident that often eludes all possible precaution," they adverted to the future intellectual intercourse between the two nations, saying:

[1] October 8, 1782. This letter, as well as the addresses, in the Rochambeau papers.

"Among the many substantial advantages which this country hath already derived, and which must ever continue to flow from its connection with France, we are persuaded that the improvement of useful knowledge will not be the least. A number of distinguished characters in your army afford us the happiest presage that science as well as liberty will acquire vigor from the fostering hand of your nation."

They concluded: "You have reaped the noblest laurels that victory can bestow, and it is, perhaps, not an inferior triumph to have obtained the sincere affection of a grateful people."

In order to "foster," as the authors of the address said, such sentiments as to a possible intellectual intercourse, the French King sent to this university, as the college was then called, "two hundred volumes of the greatest and best French works," but, La Rochefoucauld adds after having seen them in 1796, they arrived greatly damaged, "because the Richmond merchant who had undertaken to convey them to the college forgot them for a pretty long time in his cellar in the midst of his oil and sugar barrels." Fire has since completed the havoc, so that of the two hundred only two are now left, exhibited under glass in the library-museum of the college. They are parts of the works of Bailly, then of European fame as an astronomer and scientist, who was, however, to count in history for something else than his *Traité sur l'Atlantide de Platon*, for he was the same Bailly who a few years later presided over the National Assembly, sending to the royal purchaser of his works the famous reply: "The nation assembled can receive no orders," and who, two days after the fall of the Bastille, was acclaimed by the crowd mayor of Paris, while Lafayette was acclaimed commander-in-chief of the National Guard.

Another gift of books was sent, with the same intent, by the King of France to the University of Pennsylvania, and, though many have disappeared, the fate of this collection has been happier. A number of those volumes are still in use at Philadelphia, works which had been selected as being likely to prove of greatest advantage, on science, surgery, history, voyages, and bearing the honored names of Buffon, of Darwin's forerunner, Lamarck, of Joinville, Bougainville, the Bénédictins (*Art de vérifier les Dates*), and the same Bailly.

Rochambeau, who had begun learning English, set himself the task of translating the addresses received by him, and several such versions in his handwriting figure among his papers.

Closen, intrusted with the care of taking to Congress the general's answer to its congratulations, rode at the rate of over one hundred miles

a day, slept "a few hours in a bed not meant to
let any one oversleep himself, thanks either to
its comfort or to the biting and abundant company
in it," met by chance at Alexandria "the young,
charming, and lovely daughter-in-law of General
Washington," Mrs. Custis, and the praise of her
is, from now on, ceaseless: "I had already heard
pompous praise of her, but I confess people had
not exaggerated. This lady is of such a gay disposition, so prepossessing, with such perfect education, that she cannot fail to please everybody."
He hands his despatches to Congress, some to
Washington, returns at the same rate of speed,
having as guide a weaver, so anxious to be through
with his job (two couriers had just been killed),
that he rode at the maddest pace. He reached
Williamsburg on the 11th of May, having covered,
deduction made of the indispensable stoppings,
"nine hundred and eighty miles in less than nine
times twenty-four hours."

As the summer of 1782 was drawing near, the
French army, which had wintered in Virginia,
moved northward in view of possible operations.
This was for Closen an occasion to visit Mount
Vernon, where Rochambeau had stopped with
Washington the year before when on their way
to Yorktown. "The house," says the aide, "is
quite vast and perfectly distributed, with handsome furniture, and is admirably kept, without

luxury. There are two pavilions connected with it, and a number of farm buildings. . . . Behind the pavilion on the right is an immense garden, with the most exquisite fruit in the country."

Mrs. Washington gracefully entertains the visitor, as well as Colonel de Custine, the same who was to win and lose battles and die beheaded in the French Revolution. Some ten officers of the Saintonge regiment, which was in the neighborhood, are also received. "Mr. de Bellegarde came ahead of Mr. de Custine, and brought, on his behalf, a porcelain service, from his own manufacture, at Niderviller, near Phalsbourg, of great beauty and in the newest taste, with the arms of General Washington, and his monogram surmounted by a wreath of laurel.[1] Mrs. Washington was delighted with Mr. de Custine's attention, and most gracefully expressed her gratitude."

All leave that same evening except Closen, who had again found there the incomparable Mrs. Custis (whose silhouette he took and inserted in his journal), and who remained "one day more, being treated with the utmost affability by these ladies, whose society," he notes, "was most sweet and pleasant to me." He leaves at last, "rather sad."

---

[1] A large bowl from the original set is preserved in the National Museum (Smithsonian Institution) at Washington. It bears only the monogram and not the family arms. The wreath is of roses with a foliage which may be laurel.

Moving northward by night marches, the troops again start not later than two o'clock in the morning, as in the previous summer; the French officers notice the extraordinary progress realized since their first visit. At Wilmington, says Closen, "some fifty brick houses have been built, very fine and large, since we first passed, which gives a charming appearance to the main street." At Philadelphia La Luzerne is ready with another magnificent entertainment; a Dauphin has been born to France, and a beautiful hall has been built on purpose for the intended banquet by "a French officer serving in the American corps of Engineers," Major L'Enfant, the future designer of the future "federal city."

On the 14th of August Washington and Rochambeau were again together, in the vicinity of the North River, and the American troops were again reviewed by the French general. They are no longer in tatters, but well dressed, and have a fine appearance; their bearing, their manœuvres are perfect; the commander-in-chief, "who causes his drums," Rochambeau relates, "to beat the French March," is delighted to show his soldiers to advantage; everybody compliments him.

During his stay at Providence, in the course of his journey north, Rochambeau gave numerous fêtes, a charming picture of which, as well as of the American society attending them, is furnished us by Ségur: "Mr. de Rochambeau, desirous to the very last of proving by the details of his conduct, as well as by the great services he had rendered, how much he wished to keep the affection of the Americans and to carry away their regrets, gave in the city of Providence frequent assemblies and numerous balls, to which people flocked from ten leagues around.

"I do not remember to have seen gathered together in any other spot more gayety and less confusion, more pretty women and more happily married couples, more grace and less coquetry, a more complete mingling of persons of all classes, between whom an equal decency allowed no untoward difference to be seen. That decency, that order, that wise liberty, that felicity of the new Republic, so ripe from its very cradle, were the continual subject of my surprise and the object of my frequent talks with the Chevalier de Chastellux." [1]

[1] *Mémoires, souvenirs et anecdotes*, I, 402.

IX

In the autumn of 1782 a general parting took place, Rochambeau returning to France[1] and the army being sent to the Isles, believed now to be threatened by the English; for if the war was practically at an end for the Americans on the continent, it was not yet the same elsewhere for us, and Suffren especially was prosecuting in the Indies his famous naval campaign, which, owing to the lack of means of communication, was to be continued long after peace had been signed.

So many friendships had been formed that there was much emotion when the last days arrived.[2] On the 19th of October, being the anniversary of

---

[1] On which occasion the Marquis de Vaudreuil, in command of the fleet, wrote him from Boston, November 18, 1782: "Je suis vraiment touché, Monsieur, de ne pouvoir pas avoir l'honneur de vous voir ici; je m'estimais heureux de renouveler la connaissance que j'avais faite avec vous à Brest chez M. d'Orvilliers. Mais je ne puis qu'applaudir au parti que vous prenez d'éviter la tristesse des adieux et les témoignages de la sensibilité de tous vos officiers en se voyant séparés de leur chef qu'ils respectent et chérissent sincèrement." (Rochambeau papers.)

[2] An anecdote in the *Autobiography* of John Trumbull, the painter, well shows how lasting were the feelings for the land and the people taken home with them by the French. The artist tells of his reaching Mulhouse in 1795, finding it "full of troops," with no accommodation of any sort. He is taken to the old general in command:

"The veteran looked at me keenly and asked bluntly: 'Who are you, an Englishman?'"

Yorktown, Washington offered a dinner to the French officers, who on the same day took leave of him, never to see him again. "On that evening," says Closen, "we took leave of General Washington and of the other officers of our acquaintance, our troops being to sail on the 22d. There is no sort of kindness and tokens of good will we have not received from General Washington; the idea of parting from the French army, probably forever, seemed to cause him real sorrow, having, as he had, received the most convincing proofs of the respect, the veneration, the esteem, and even the attachment which every individual in the army felt for him."

"'No, general, I am an American of the United States.'
"'Ah! do you know Connecticut?'
"'Yes, sir, it is my native State.'
"'You know, then, the good Governor Trumbull?'
"'Yes, general, he is my father.'
"'Oh! mon Dieu, que je suis charmé. . . . Entrez, entrez!'"
And all that is best is placed at the disposal of the newcomer by the soldier, who turns out to be a former member of the Lauzun legion. The artist adds: "The old general kept me up almost all night, inquiring of everybody and of everything in America." Some papers are brought for him to sign, which he does with his left hand, and, Trumbull noticing it, "'Yes,' said he, 'last year, in Belgium, the Austrians cut me to pieces and left me for dead, but I recovered, and, finding my right hand ruined, I have learned to use my left, and I can write and fence with it tolerably.'

"'But, sir,' said I, 'why did you not retire from service?'
"'Retire!' exclaimed he. 'Ha! I was born in a camp, have passed all my life in the service, and will die in a camp, or on the field.'

"This is," Trumbull concludes, "a faithful picture of the military enthusiasm of the time—1795."

After having taken leave, "in tenderest fashion," of the American commander, who promised "an enduring fraternal friendship," Rochambeau, carrying with him two bronze field-pieces taken at Yorktown, presented by Congress, and adorned with inscriptions, the engraving of which had been supervised by Washington,[1] sailed for France on the *Emeraude*, early in January, 1783. An English warship which had been cruising at the entrance of the Chesapeake nearly captured him, and it was only by throwing overboard her spare masts and part of her artillery that the *Emeraude*, thus become lighter and faster, could escape. The general learned, on landing, of the peace which Vergennes had considered, from the first, as a certain, though not immediate, consequence of the taking of Yorktown. "The homages of all Frenchmen go to you," he had written to Rochambeau, adding: "You have restored to our arms all their lustre, and you have laid the cornerstone for the raising, which we expect, of an honorable peace." The hour for it had now struck, and while Suffren had yet to win the naval battle of Goudelour, the preliminaries had been signed at Versailles on the 20th of January, 1783.

---

[1] ". . . An inscription engraved on them, expressive of the occasion. I find a difficulty in getting the engraving properly executed. When it will be finished, I shall with peculiar pleasure put the cannon into your possession." Washington to Rochambeau, February 2, 1782.

The King, the ministers, the whole country gave Rochambeau the welcome he deserved. At his first audience on his return he had asked Louis XVI, as being his chief request, permission to divide the praise bestowed on him with the unfortunate de Grasse, now a prisoner of the English after the battle of the Saintes, where, fighting 30 against 37, he had lost seven ships, including the *Ville de Paris* (which had 400 dead and 500 wounded), all so damaged by the most furious resistance that, owing to grounding, to sinking, or to fire, not one reached the English waters.[1] Rochambeau received the blue ribbon of the Holy Ghost, was appointed governor of Picardy, and a few years later became a marshal of France. Owing to the proximity of his new post, he was able twice to visit England, where he met again his dear La Luzerne, now French ambassador• in London, and his former foe, Admiral Hood, who received him with open arms. But the tokens of friendship which touched him most came from officers of Cornwallis's army: "They manifested," he writes, "in the most public manner their gratitude for the humanity with which they had been treated by the French army after their surrender."

[1] De Grasse died in January, 1788. "The Cincinnati in some of the States have gone into mourning for him." Washington to Rochambeau, April 28, 1788.

Rochambeau was keeping up with Washington a most affectionate correspondence, still partly unpublished, the great American often reminding him of his "friendship and love" for his "companions in war," discussing a possible visit to France, and describing his life now spent "in rural employments and in contemplation of those friendships which the Revolution enabled me to form with so many worthy characters of your nation, through whose assistance I can now sit down in my calm retreat." Dreaming of a humanity less agitated than that he had known, dreaming dreams which were not to be soon realized, he was writing to Rochambeau, from Mount Vernon, on September 7, 1785: "Although it is against the profession of arms, I wish to see all the world at peace."

"Much as he may wish to conceal himself and lead the life of a plain man, he will ever be the first citizen of the United States," La Luzerne had written to Vergennes, and the truth of the statement was shown when a unanimous election made of the former commander-in-chief the first President of the new republic, in the year when the States General met in France and our own Revolution began.

Knowing the friendly dispositions preserved by Rochambeau toward Americans,[1] Washington

---

[1] Jefferson seems to have feared that the souvenir of Rochambeau might soon fade. He wrote to Madison, February 8, 1786: "Count

often gave those going abroad letters of introduction to him; one day the man was Gouverneur Morris, so well known afterward; another day it was a poet of great fame then, of not so great now. Less sure of his ground when the question was of Parnassus than when it was of battlefields, Washington had described this traveller to Lafayette as being "considered by those who are good judges to be a genius of the first magnitude." To Rochambeau he introduced him as "the author of an admirable poem in which he has worthily celebrated the glory of your nation in general, and of yourself in particular."[1] The poet was that Joel Barlow, of Hartford, who, having become later minister of the United States to France, died in a Polish village in the course of a journey undertaken to present his credentials to the chief of the state, who, for important reasons, had been unable to grant him an audience elsewhere than in Russia, the year being 1812, and the sovereign Emperor Napoleon.[2]

The poem alluded to by Washington was an

Rochambeau, too, has deserved more attention than he has received. Why not set up his bust, that of Gates, Greene, Franklin in your new Capitol?" No bust was placed in the Capitol, but the raising of the statue in Lafayette Square, Washington, in 1902, has proved that, after so many years, Rochambeau was not forgotten in America.

[1] May 28, 1788.

[2] In a letter of July 31, 1789, Rochambeau informs Washington of Barlow's arrival, "and I made him all the good reception that he deserves by himself and by the honorable commendation that you give to him." In Rochambeau's English; Washington papers.

epic one, called the *Vision of Columbus*, in which an angel appears to the navigator in his legendary prison and reveals to him, in Virgilian fashion, the future of America. Washington, Wayne, Greene are thus shown him, as well as

> Brave Rochambeau in gleamy steel array'd,

a description which, if brave Rochambeau ever saw it, must have made him smile.

Rochambeau's letters are in such English as we have seen he had been able, with commendable zeal, to learn late in life. The French general keeps the American leader informed of what goes on in France, in England, and Europe, bestows the highest praise on Pitt, "a wise man who sets finances (of the English) in good order," and gives an account of a visit paid him by Cornwallis at Calais: "I have seen Cornwallis last summer at Calais. . . . I gave him a supper in little committee;[1] he was very polite, but, as you may believe, I could not drink with him your health in toast."[2]

He tells Washington of Franklin's departure from France, very old, very ill, greatly admired, "having the courage to undertake so long a voyage to go and die in the bosom of his native country. It will be impossible for him, at his

---

[1] Fr., "en petit comité"—a small party of friends.
[2] January 7, 1786. Washington papers.

coming back [to] America, to go and visit you, but I told him that you would certainly go and see him, and that I had always heard you speaking of him in the best terms and having a great consideration for his respectable character. He will have a great joy to see you again, and I should be very happy if I could enjoy the same pleasure."[1]

An affectionate interest for one another and one another's families appears in all these letters, as well as a cherishing of common souvenirs. Rochambeau asks to be remembered to his former American comrades: "A thousand kindness[es] and compliments to Mr. Jefferson, to Mr. Knox, and to all my *anciens camarades* and friends which are near you."[2]

The Countess de Rochambeau sometimes takes up the pen, and in one of her letters appeals to Washington in favor of dear Closen who, though he had every right to be included in it, had been forgotten when the list of the original Cincinnati had been drawn up.[3] The request was at once granted.

---

[1] Paris, June, 1785 (*ibid*).
[2] "Rochambeau near Vendôme, April 11, 1790."
[3] Here is this letter in full:

Paris the 18th November, 1790.

SIR:

I hope that your Excellency will give me the leave to beg a favor of your justice. I think it just to intercede for the Baron de Closen who was an aide-de-camp to Mr. Rochambeau during the American war. He longs with the desire to be a member of the associa-

Two *gouaches* had been painted by the famous miniaturist Van Blarenberghe, one representing the storming of the redoubts at Yorktown, the other the surrender of the garrison. They were for the King, and are well known nowadays to every one familiar with the Versailles Museum. Their topographical accuracy is so remarkable that it had always been believed the painter had had the help of some French officer present at the siege. Rochambeau writes to Washington about those pictures and gives us the name of the officer who had actually helped the miniaturist, a well-known name, that of Berthier: "[There have] been presented yesterday to the King, my dear general, two pictures to put in his closet (study), which have been done by an excellent painter, one representing the siege of York, and the other the defile of the British army between the American and the French armies.

"Mr. le Marshal de Ségur promised me copies of them which I will place in my closet on the right and left sides of your picture. Besides that they are excellent paintings, they have been

tion of the Cincinnati. The officers who were employed in the French army and younger than him in the military service have been decorated with this emblem of liberty, and such a reward given by your Excellency's hand shall increase its value.

I flatter myself that you will receive the assurances of the respect and veneration I have for your talents and your virtue, well known in the whole world.

I have (etc.),   La Comtesse de Rochambeau.

drawn both by the truth and by an excellent design by the young Berthier, who was deputed
quartermaster at the said siege."[1]

Washington having alluded, as he was fond of
doing, to the rest he had at last secured for the
remnant of his life, as he thought, under the
shadow of his own vine and fig-tree, Rochambeau
in his answer courteously and sincerely compliments him on the "philosophical" but not definitive quiet he now enjoys under the shadow—"of
his *laurel*-tree."[2]

The War of the Austrian Succession had found
Rochambeau already an officer in the French army;
the Revolution found him still an officer in the
French army, defending the frontier as a marshal
of France and commander-in-chief of the northern
troops. In 1792 he definitively withdrew to Rochambeau, barely escaping with his life during
the Terror. A striking and touching thing it is
to note that, when a prisoner in that "horrible
sepulchre," the Conciergerie, he appealed to the

---

[1] June, 1785. Two of the Berthier brothers had taken part, as we
saw, in the expedition. The one alluded to here is the younger,
César-Gabriel, not the older, Louis-Alexandre, who became Prince
de Wagram. Both are described in their "états de service," preserved among the Rochambeau papers, as expert draftsmen. The
notice concerning the younger, who was a captain of dragoons, reads:
"Il s'est fait remarquer ainsi que son frère par son talent à dessiner
et lever des plans."

[2] Concerning this correspondence, as continued during the French
Revolution, see below, pp. 245 ff.

"Citizen President of the Revolutionary Tri-
bunal," and invoked as a safeguard the great
name of Washington, "my colleague and my friend
in the war we made together for the liberty of
America."

Luckier than many of his companions in arms
of the American war, than Lauzun, Custine,
d'Estaing, Broglie, Dillon, and others, Rochambeau escaped the scaffold. He lived long enough
to see rise to glory that young man who was teaching the world better military tactics than even the
book of Count de Guibert, Bonaparte, now First
Consul of the French Republic. Bonaparte had
great respect for the old marshal, who was presented to him by the minister of war in 1803; he
received him surrounded by his generals, and as
the soldier of Klostercamp and Yorktown entered
he said, "Monsieur le Maréchal, here are your
pupils"; and the old man answered: "They have
surpassed their master."

After having been very near death from his
wounds in 1747, Rochambeau died only in 1807,
being then in his castle of Rochambeau, in Vendomois, and aged eighty-two. He was buried in
the neighboring village of Thoré, in a tomb of
black and white marble, in the classical style
then in vogue. An inscription devised by his
wife at the evening of a very long life, draws a
touching picture of those qualities which had won

her heart more than half a century before: "A
model as admirable in his family as in his armies,
an enlightened mind, indulgent, ever thinking of
the interests of others . . . a happy and honored
old age has been for him the crowning of a spotless life. Those who had been his vassals had
become his children. . . . His tomb awaits me;
before descending to it I have desired to engrave
upon it the memory of so many merits and virtues, as a token of gratitude for fifty years of
happiness." On a parallel slab one reads: "Here
lies Jeanne Thérèse Telles d'Acosta, who died at
Rochambeau, aged ninety-four, May 19, 1824."

In the castle are still to be seen the exquisite portrait, by Latour, of her who in her old age had
written the inscription, several portraits of the
marshal, and of his ancestors from the first Vimeur, who had become, in the sixteenth century,
lord of Rochambeau, the portrait in the white
uniform of Auvergne of the old soldier's son, who
died at Leipzig, the sword worn at Yorktown, the
eagle of the Cincinnati side by side with the star
of the Holy Ghost, the before-mentioned *gouaches*
by Van Blarenberghe, a portrait of Washington, given by him to his French friend and also
mentioned in their correspondence, and many
other historical relics. But the two bronze field-
pieces offered by Congress are no longer there,
having been commandeered during the Revolu-

tion. In front of the simple and noble façade
of the slate-roofed castle, at the foot of the ter-
race, the Loir flows, brimful, between woods and
meadows, the same river that fills such a great
place in French literature, because of a distant
relative of the Rochambeaus of old, Pierre de
Ronsard.

Visiting some years ago the place and the tomb,
and standing beside the grave of the marshal, it
occurred to me that it would be appropriate if
some day trees from Mount Vernon could spread
their shade over the remains of that friend of
Washington and the American cause. With the
assent of the family and of the mayor of Thoré,
and thanks to the good will of the ladies of the
Mount Vernon Association, this idea was realized,
and half a dozen seedlings from trees planted by
Washington were sent to be placed around Rochambeau's monument: two elms, two maples,
two redbuds, and six plants of ivy from Washington's tomb. The last news received about
them showed that they had taken root and were
growing.

X

Some will, perhaps, desire to know what became of Closen. Sent to the Islands (the West Indies) with the rest of the army, he felt, like all his comrades, greatly disappointed, more even than the others, on account of his bride, whom American beauties had not caused him to forget. He had inserted in his journal a page of silhouettes representing a dozen of the latter, with the name inscribed on each; but he had taken care to write underneath: "Honni soit qui mal y pense." When about to go on board he writes: "I scarcely dare say what I experienced and which was the dominating sentiment, whether my attachment to all that I love or ambition added to sensitiveness on the principles of honor. Reason, however, soon took the lead and decided in favor of the latter. . . . Let me be patient and do my duty."

To leave Rochambeau was for him one more cause of pain: "I shall never insist enough, nor sufficiently describe the sorrow I felt when separated from my worthy and respectable general; I lose more than any one else in the army. . . . Attentive as I was to all he had to say about battles, marches, the selection of positions, sieges, in a word, to all that pertains to the profession, I have always tried to profit by his so instructive talks. . . . I must be resigned."

Once again, therefore, life begins on those detested "sabots," a large-sized *sabot*, this time, namely the *Brave*, of seventy-four guns, "quite recently lined with copper," a sad place of abode, however, in bad weather, or even in any weather: "One can scarcely imagine the bigness of the sea, the noise, the height of the waves, such pitching and rolling that it was impossible to stand; the ships disappearing at times as if they had been swallowed by the sea, to touch it the instant after only with a tiny bit of the keel. What a nasty element, and how sincerely we hate it, all of us of the land troops! The lugubrious noise of the masts, the *crics-cracs* of the vessel, the terrible movements which on the sudden raise you, and to which we were not at all accustomed, the perpetual encumbrance that forty-five officers are for each other, forty having no other place of refuge than a single room for them all, the sad faces of those who are sick . . . the dirt, the boredom, the feeling that one is shut up in a *sabot* as in a state prison . . . all this is only part of what goes to make life unpleasant for a land officer on a vessel, even a naval one. . . . Let us take courage."[1]

[1] December 29, 1782.

Few diversions. They meet a slave-ship under the Austrian flag, an "abominable and cruel sight," with "that iron chain running from one end of the ship to the other, the negroes being tied there, two and two," stark naked and harshly beaten if they make any movement which displeases the captain. The latter, who is from Bordeaux, salutes his country's war flag with three "Vive le Roi!" They signal to him an answer which cannot be transcribed. No one knows where they go. "Sail on," philosophically writes Closen.

They touch at Porto Rico, at Curaçao, where the fleet is saddened by the loss of the *Bourgogne*, at Porto Cabello (Venezuela), where they make some stay, and where Closen loses no time in resuming his observations on natives, men and beasts, tatous, monkeys, caimans, "enormous lizards quite different from ours," houses which consist in one ground floor divided into three rooms. The "company of the Caracque" (Caracas) keeps the people in a state of restraint and slavery. Taxation is enormous." Religious intolerance is very troublesome: "Though the Inquisition is not as rigorous in its searches as in Europe, for there is but one commissioner at Caracque, there is, however, too much fanaticism, too many absurd superstitions, in a word, too much ignorance among the inhabitants, who can

never say a word or walk a step without saying an
Ave, crossing themselves twenty times, or kissing
a chaplet which they ever have dangling from
their neck with a somewhat considerable accom-
paniment of relics and crosses. One gentleman,
in order to play a trick on me, in the private
houses where I had gained access so as to satisfy
my curiosity and desire of instruction, told a few
people that I was a Protestant. What signs of
the cross at the news! And they would ceaselessly repeat: *Malacco Christiano*—a bad Christian!"

On the 24th of March (1783) great news reached
them: the French vessel *Andromaque* arrived,
"with the grand white flag on her foremast, as a
signal of peace. The minute after all our men-
of-war were decked with flags." There were a
few more incidents, like the capture of some
French officers, who were quietly rowing in open
boats, by "the *Albemarle*, of twenty-four guns,
commanded by Captain Nelson, of whom these
gentlemen speak in the highest terms." As soon
as the news of the peace was given him they were
released by the future enemy of Napoleon.

The hour for the return home had struck at
last. It was delayed by brief stays in some parts
of the French West Indies, notably Cap Français, Santo Domingo (now Cap Haïtien). "A few
days before our arrival at the Cape Prince William,

Duke of Lancaster, third son of the King of England, had come and spent there two days, while
the English squadron was cruising in the roads.
Great festivities had been arranged in his honor,"
—for there was really no hatred against the enemy
of the day before.

Some calms and some storms also delayed the
return, with the usual "criiiiicks craaaaaks" of
the masts, the journey being occupied in transcribing the "notes and journals on the two
Americas," and enlivened by the saving of the
parrakeet of a Spanish lady who had been admitted with her family on board the *Brave*.
"Frightened by something, the little parrakeet
flies off and falls into the sea. The lady's negro,
luckily happening to be on the same side, jumps
just as he is, with no time to think, dives, reap-
pears, cries, 'Cato! Cato!' joins the parrakeet,
puts her on his woolly head, and returns to the
ship." Delighted, the lady "allows this black
saviour to kiss her hand, a unique distinction for
a slave, and bestows on him a life pension of one
hundred francs. Many sailors would have liked
to do the same, had they known."

Land is now descried; they see again the sights
noted when sailing for America: these "coasts
thick-decked with live people, fruit-trees and other
delightful objects." All is delightful; the joy is
universal; they make arrangements to reach

Paris, which Closen did in magnificent style. "And I," we read in his journal, "after having bought a fine coach where I could place, before, behind, on the top, my servants, consisting of a white man and of my faithful and superb black Peter, and with them three monkeys, four parrots, and six parrakeets, posted to Paris in this company, a noisy one and difficult to maintain clean and in good order. . . . The next day (June 22) I was at Saint-Pol-de-Léon, my last quarters before sailing for America, and saw again with hearty rejoicings the respectable Kersabiec family which had so well tended me throughout my convalescence after a deadly disease." He thought he could do no less than present them with one of his parrakeets as a token of "gratitude and friendship."

At Guingamp he finds the Du Dresnays, other friends of his, and reaches Paris, he writes, on the 30th of June, with "all my live beings of all colors, myself looking an Indian so tanned and sunburnt was my face, exception made for my forehead, which my hat had preserved quite white."

The Rochambeau family made him leave his inn and stay with them in their beautiful house of the Rue du Cherche-Midi. The general ("my kind and respectable military father," says Closen) presented him to the minister of war, Marshal de Ségur, who granted the young officer a flattering welcome, and the journal closes as novels used to end in olden days, and as the first part of well-ordered, happy lives will ever continue to end. Leaving Paris with the promise of a colonelcy *en second*—"a very eventual ministerial bouquet"— he went home to Deux-Ponts: "There I found my beautiful fiancée, my dear, my divine Doris, who had had the constancy to keep for me her heart and her hand during the four years of my absence in America, in spite of several proposals received by her, even from men much better endowed with worldly goods, my share consisting only in the before mentioned ministerial promise and in the reputation of an honest man and a good soldier."

I shall only add that the ministerial promise was kept, and that it was as a colonel and a knight of Saint Louis that Closen found himself aide-de-camp again to his old chief, Rochambeau, charged with the defense of the northern frontier at the beginning of the Revolution.[1]

Faded inks, hushed voices. The remembrance of the work remains, however, and cannot fade;

[1] A lithographed portrait mentions the later-day titles and dignities of: "I. C. Louis, Baron de Closen, Maréchal de Camp, chambellan et chevalier des ordres français pour le Mérite et de la Légion d'honneur, ainsi que de celui de Cincinnatus des Etats Unis de l'Amérique Septentrionale." Reproduced by C. W. Bowen, who first drew attention to this journal, *Century Magazine*, February, 1907. Closen died in 1830, aged seventy-five.

for its grandeur becomes, from year to year, more apparent. In less than a century and a half New York has passed from the ten thousand inhabitants it possessed under Clinton to the five million and more of to-day. Philadelphia, once the chief city, "an immense town," Closen had called it, has now ten times more houses than it had citizens. Partly owing again to France, ceding, unasked, the whole territory of Louisiana in 1803, the frontier of this country, which the upper Hudson formerly divided in its centre, has been pushed back to the Pacific; the three million Americans of Washington and Rochambeau have become the one hundred million of to-day. From the time when the flags of the two countries floated on the ruins of Yorktown the equilibrium of the world has been altered.

There is, perhaps, no case in which, with the unavoidable mixture of human interests, a war has been more undoubtedly waged for an idea. The fact was made obvious at the peace, when victorious France, being offered Canada for a separate settlement, refused,[1] and kept her word not to accept any material advantage, the whole

---

[1] Which was done in a letter giving as a reason "that, whenever the two crowns should come to treat, his Most Christian Majesty would show how much the engagements he might enter into were to be relied on, by his exact observance of those he had already had with his present allies." Quoted, as "a sentence which I much liked," by Franklin, writing to John Adams, April 13, 1782.

nation being in accord, and the people illuminating for joy.

The cause was a just one; even the adversary, many among whom had been from the first of that opinion, was not long to acknowledge it. Little by little, and in spite of some fitful re-awakening of former animosities, as was seen in the second War of Independence, hostile disposi-tions vanished. The three nations who had met in arms in Yorktown, the three whose ancestors had known a Hundred Years' War, have now known a hundred years' peace. "I wish to see all the world at peace," Washington had written to Rochambeau. For over a century now the three nations which fought at Yorktown have become friends, and in this measure at least the wish of the great American has been fulfilled.

II

MAJOR L'ENFANT AND THE FEDERAL CITY

MAJOR L'ENFANT AND THE
FEDERAL CITY

I

LITTLE more than a century ago the hill
on which rises the Capitol of the federal
city and the ground around it were covered with woods and underbrush; a few scattered
farms had been built here and there, with one or
two exceptions mere wooden structures whose
low roofs scarcely emerged from their leafy surroundings. Not very long before, Indians had
used to gather on that eminence and hold their
council-fires.

As far now as the eye can reach the picturesque
outline of one of the finest cities that exist is discovered; steeples and pinnacles rise above the
verdure of the trees lining the avenues within
the unaltered frame supplied by the blue hills of
Maryland and Virginia.

The will of Congress, the choice made by the
great man whose name the city was to bear, the
talents of a French officer, caused this change.

Debates and competitions had been very keen;
more than one city of the North and of the South
had put forth pleas to be the one selected and

become the capital: Boston, where the first shot
had been fired; Philadelphia, where independence
had been proclaimed; Yorktown, where it had
been won—Yorktown, modest as a city, but glorious by the events its name recalled, now an out-
of-the-way borough, rarely visited, and where
fifty white inhabitants are all that people the
would-be capital of the new-born Union. New
York also had been in the ranks, as well as King-
ston, Newport, Wilmington, Trenton, Reading,
Lancaster, Annapolis, Williamsburg, and several
others. Passions were stirred to such an extent
that the worst was feared, and that, incredible as
it may now seem, Jefferson could speak of the
"necessity of a compromise to save the Union."

A compromise was, in fact, resorted to, which
consisted in choosing no city already in existence,
but building a new one on purpose. This solution had been early thought of, for Washington
had written on October 12, 1783, to Chevalier de
Chastellux: "They (Congress) have lately determined to make choice of some convenient spot
near the Falls of the Delaware for the permanent
residence of the sovereign power of these United
States." But would-be capitals still persisted in
hoping they might be selected.

Congress made up its mind for good on the 16th
of July, 1790, and decided that the President
should be intrusted with the care of choosing "on

the river Potomac" a territory, ten miles square,
which should become the "Federal territory" and
the permanent seat of the Government of the
United States.

Washington thereupon quickly reached a decision; a great rider all his life, the hills and vales
of the region were familiar to him; it soon became certain that the federal city would rise one
day where it now stands. The spot seemed to
him a particularly appropriate one for a reason
which has long ceased to be so very telling, and
which he constantly mentions in his letters as
the place's "centrality."

But what sort of a city should it be? A resi-
dential one for statesmen, legislators, and judges,
or a commercial one with the possibilities, considered then of the first order, afforded by the
river, or a mixture of both? Should it be planned
in view of the present or of the future, and of
what sort of future?

With the mind of an artist and in some sense of
a prophet, perceiving future time as clearly as if
it were the present, a man foresaw, over a century ago, what we now see with our eyes. He
was a French officer who had fought for the cause
of independence, and had remained in America
after the war, Major Pierre Charles L'Enfant.

Some researches in French and American
archives have allowed me to trace his ancestry,

and to add a few particulars to what was already known of him.

Born at Paris, on August 2, 1754, he was the son of Pierre L'Enfant, "Painter in ordinary to the King in his Manufacture of the Gobelins." The painter, whose wife was Marie Charlotte Leullier, had for his specialty landscapes and battle-scenes. Born at Anet, in 1704, on a farm which he bequeathed to his children, he was a pupil of Parrocel and had been elected an Academician in 1745. Some of his pictures are at Tours; six are at Versailles, representing as many French victories: the taking of Menin, 1744; of Fribourg, 1744; of Tournay, 1745; the battle of Fontenoy, 1745 (a favorite subject, several times painted by him); the battle of Laufeldt, 1747, where that young officer, destined to be Washington's partner in the Yorktown campaign, Count Rochambeau, received, as we have seen before, his first wounds. The painter died a very old man, in the Royal Manufacture, 1787.

Young L'Enfant grew up among artistic surroundings, and, as subsequent events showed, received instruction as an architect and engineer. The cause of the United States had in him one of its earliest enthusiasts. In 1777, being then twenty-three, possessed of a commission of lieutenant in the French colonial troops, he sailed for America on one of those ships belonging to

Beaumarchais's mythical firm of "Hortalez and Co.," a firm whose cargoes consisted in soldiers and ammunition for the insurgents, and which was as much a product of the dramatist's brain as Figaro himself. Figaro, it is averred, has had a great influence in this world; Hortalez and Co. had not a small one, either. The ship had been named after the secretary of state, who was to sign, the following year, the United States' only alliance, *Le Comte de Vergennes*, a name, wrote Beaumarchais, "fit to bring luck to the cargo, which is superb." The superb cargo consisted, as usual, in guns and war supplies, also in men who might be of no less use for the particular sort of trade Hortalez and Co. were conducting. "Some good engineers and some cavalry officers will soon arrive," Silas Deane was then writing to Congress. One of the engineers was Pierre Charles L'Enfant. His coming had preceded by one month the sailing of another ship with another appropriate name, the ship *La Victoire*, which brought Lafayette.

L'Enfant served first as a volunteer and at his own expense. "In February, 1778," we read in an unpublished letter of his to Washington, "I was honored with a commission of captain of engineers, and by leave of Congress attached to the Inspector-general. . . . Seeing [after the winter of 1778–9] no appearance of an active campaign to the northward, my whole ambition was to attend the Southern army, where it was likely the seat of war would be transferred." He was, accordingly, sent to Charleston, and obtained "leave to join the light infantry, under Lieutenant-Colonel Laurens; his friendship furnished me," he relates, "with many opportunities of seeing the enemy to advantage."[1]

Not "to advantage," however, did he fight at Savannah, when the French and Americans, under d'Estaing and Lincoln, were repulsed with terrible loss. The young captain was leading one of the vanguard columns in the American contingent and, like d'Estaing himself, was grievously wounded. He managed to escape to Charleston. I was, he said, "in my bed till January, 1780. My weak state of health did not permit me to work at the fortifications of Charleston, and when the enemy debarked, I was still obliged to use a crutch."[2] He took part, however, in the fight, replacing a wounded major, and was made a prisoner at the capitulation. Rochambeau negotiated his exchange in January, 1782, for Captain von Heyden, a Hessian officer.

"Your zeal and active services," Washington wrote back to L'Enfant, "are such as reflect the

[1] Philadelphia, February 18, 1782. Washington papers, Library of Congress.
[2] Same letter.

highest honor on yourself and are extremely
pleasing to me, and I have no doubt they will
have their due weight with Congress in any
future promotion in your corps." [1] They had,
in fact, in the following year, when, by a vote of
the assembly, L'Enfant was promoted a major
of engineers, 1783.

His knowledge of the art of fortification, his
merit as a disciplinarian, the part he had taken, as
he recalls in a letter to Count de La Luzerne,[2] in
devising the earliest "system of discipline and
exercises which was finally adopted in the American army" (all that was done in that line was not
by Steuben alone), rendered his services quite
useful. His gifts as an artist, his cleverness at
catching likenesses made him welcome among
his brother officers. He would in the dreary days
of Valley Forge draw pencil portraits of them,
one, we know, of Washington, at the request of
Lafayette, who wanted also to have a painted
portrait. "I misunderstood you," the general
wrote him from Fredericksburg, on September 25,
1778; "else I would have had the picture made
by Peale when he was at Valley Forge. When
you requested me to sit to Monsieur Lanfang"—
thus spelled, showing how pronounced by Wash-

[1] March 1, 1782. Washington papers.
[2] Brother of the minister to the United States, New York, December 10, 1787; unpublished. Archives of the French Ministry of
Colonies.

ington—"I thought it was only to obtain the outlines and a few shades of my features, to have some prints struck from."

Some such pencil portraits by L'Enfant subsist, for example in the Glover family at Washington, and are creditable and obviously true-to-nature sketches.

Whenever, during the war or after, something in any way connected with art was wanted, L'Enfant was, as a matter of course, appealed to, whether the question was of a portrait, of a banqueting hall, of a marble palace, a jewel, a solemn procession, a fortress to be raised, or a city to be planned. A man of many accomplishments, with an overflow of ideas and few competitors, he was the factotum of the new nation. When the French minister, La Luzerne, desired to arrange a grand banquet in honor of the birth of the Dauphin (the first one, who lived only eight years), he had a hall built on purpose, in Philadelphia, and L'Enfant was the designer. Baron de Closen, Rochambeau's aide, writes as to this in his journal: "M. de La Luzerne offered a dinner that day to the legion of Lauzun, which had arrived the same morning (August 2, 1782). The hall which he caused to be built on purpose for the fête he gave on the occasion of the birth of the Dauphin, is very large and as beautiful as it can be. One cannot imagine a building in

better taste; simplicity is there united with an
air of dignity. It has been erected under the
direction of Mr. de L'Enfant, a French officer, in
the service of the American corps of engineers."
Closen adds that "Mr. Barbé de Marbois,[1] coun-
selor of embassy of our court, is too modest to
admit that his advice had something to do with
the result."

When peace came, those officers who had fought
shoulder to shoulder with the Americans returned home, bringing to the old continent new
and fruitful ideas, those especially pertaining to
equality and to the unreasonableness of class distinctions. Liberty had been learned from England; equality was from America.

L'Enfant was one of those who went back to
France, but he did not stay. He had been away
five years and wanted to see his old father, the
painter, whose end now was near. A royal brevet
of June 13, 1783, had conferred on the officer a
small French pension of three hundred livres, "in
consideration of the usefulness of his services, and
of the wounds received by him during the American war."[2] He sailed for France late in the same
year, reaching Havre on the 8th of December.

The Society of the Cincinnati had been founded
in May. For the insignia appeal had been made

[1] Mentioned before, p. 21.
[2] Brevet 14,302. Archives of the Ministry of War, Paris.

as usual to the artist of the army,[1] L'Enfant, who was, moreover, commissioned by Washington, first president of the association, to avail himself of his journey to order from some good Paris jeweller the eagles to be worn by the members, L'Enfant himself being one. He was also to help in organizing the French branch of the society. Difficulties had first been encountered, for the reason that no foreign order was then allowed in France, but it was recognized that this could scarcely be considered a foreign one. In an unpublished letter to Rochambeau, Marshal de Ségur, minister of war, said: "His Majesty the King asks me to inform you that he allows you to accept this honorable invitation (to be a member). He even wants you to assure General Washington, in his behalf, that he will always see with extreme satisfaction all that may lead to a maintenance and strengthening of the ties formed between France and the United States. The successes and the glory which have been the result and fruit of this union have shown how

---

[1] Steuben writes him from West Point on July 1, 1783, sending him "a resolution of the convention of the Cincinnati of June 19, 1783, by which I am requested," he says, "to transmit their thanks to you for your care and ingenuity in preparing the designs which were laid before them by the president on that day." Original in the L'Enfant papers, in the possession of Doctor James Dudley Morgan, of Washington, a descendant of the Digges family, the last friends of L'Enfant. To him my thanks are due for having allowed me to use those valuable documents.

advantageous it is, and that it should be perpetuated." Concerning the institution itself the minister wrote: "It is equally honorable because of the spirit which has inspired its creation and of the virtues and talents of the celebrated general whom it has chosen as its president."[1]

L'Enfant sent to Washington glowing accounts of the way the idea had been welcomed in France, and told him of the first meetings held, one at the house of Rochambeau, Rue du Cherche-Midi, for officers in the French service, and another at the house of Lafayette, Rue de Bourbon, for French officers who held their commissions from Congress, both groups deciding thereupon to unite, under Admiral d'Estaing as president-general.[2]

What proved for L'Enfant, according to circumstances, one of his chief qualities, as well as one of his chief defects, was that, whatever the occasion, he ever saw "en grand." It had been understood that he would pay the expenses of his journey, and that the Society of the Cincinnati would only take charge of those resulting from the making of the eagles. His own modest resources had been, as Duportail testified, freely spent by him during the war for the good of the cause, and little enough was left him. Never-

[1] December 18, 1783. Rochambeau papers.
[2] Asa Bird Gardner, *The Order of the Cincinnati in France*, 1905, pp. 9 ff.

theless, did he write to Alexander Hamilton, "being arrived in France, everything there concurred to strengthen the sentiment which had made me undertake that voyage, and the reception which the Cincinnati met with soon induced me to appear in that country in a manner consistent with the dignity of the society of which I was regarded as the representative." He spent without counting: "My abode at the court produced expenses far beyond the sums I had at first thought of." He ordered the eagles from the best "artists, who rivalled each other for the honor of working for the society,"[1] but wanted, however, to be paid; and a letter to Rochambeau, written later, shows him grappling with the problem of satisfying Duval and Francastel of Paris, who had supplied the eagles on credit, and to whom the large sum of twenty-two thousand three hundred and three livres were still due. These money troubles caused L'Enfant to shorten his stay in France; he was back in New York on the 29th of April, 1784, and after some discussion and delay, the society "Resolved, that, in consideration of services rendered by Major L'Enfant, the general meeting make arrangements for advancing him the sum of one thousand five hundred and forty-eight dollars, being the amount of the loss

[1] An undated memoir (May, 1787?), in the Hamilton papers, Library of Congress.

incurred by him in the negotiation for a number
of eagles, or orders, of the Cincinnati." [1]

[1] Text annexed to L'Enfant's letter to Rochambeau, June 15, 1786.
(Rochambeau papers.) On August 1, 1787, however, Francastel was
still unpaid, for at that date one of L'Enfant's friends, Duplessis,
i. e., the Chevalier de Mauduit du Plessis, who, like himself, had
served as a volunteer in the American army, writes him: "J'ai vu
ici M. Francastel le bijoutier qui vous a fait une fourniture con-
sidérable de médailles de Cincinnatus et qui m'a dit que vous lui
deviez 20,000 livres, je crois, plus ou moins. Je l'ai fort rassuré
sur votre probité." (L'Enfant papers.)

II

The country was free; war was over now, people felt; for ever, many fondly hoped. Settled in New York, where appeals to his talents as an architect and engineer made him prosperous for a time, L'Enfant believed such hopes to be vain, and that the country should at once make preparations so exhaustive that its wealth and defenselessness should not tempt any greedy enemy. He placed the problem before Congress, in a memoir still unprinted, which offers particular interest in our days, when the same problem is being again discussed.

"Sensible," wrote L'Enfant, in the creditable if not faultless English he then spoke,[1] "of the situation of affairs, and well impregnated with the spirit of republican government, I am far from intimating the idea of following other nations in their way of securing themselves against insult or invasions, surrounded as they are with powerful neighbors, who, being the objects of reciprocal jealousy, are forced to secure not only their fron-

---

[1] Only his orthography is corrected in the quotations. Orthography was not L'Enfant's strong point in any language. His mistakes are even worse in French than in English, the reason being, probably, that he took even less pains.

tier, but even their inland towns with fortifications, the much happier situation of the United
States rendering those measures of little or no
necessity."

The States must act differently; but not to
act at all would be folly. "How and upon what
foundations could it be supposed that America
will have nothing to fear from a rupture between
any of the European Powers? . . . A neutral
Power, it will be said, receives the benefit of a
universal trade, has his possessions respected, as
well as his colors, by all the Powers at war. This
may be said of a powerful nation, but this America
is not to expect; a neutral Power must be ready
for war, and his trade depends on the means of
protecting and making his colors respected.
America, neutral without [a] navy, without troops
or fortified harbors could have nothing but ca-
lamity to expect." She cannot live free and develop in safety without "power to resent, ability
to protect."

A noteworthy statement, to be sure, and which
deserves to be remembered. L'Enfant draws,
thereupon, a plan of defense, especially insisting,
of course, on the importance of his own particular
branch, namely engineering.[1]

[1] Unpublished, n. d., but probably of 1784. (Papers of the Continental Congress—Letters, vol. LXXVIII, p. 583, Library of Congress.) His ambition would have been to be asked to realize his
own plan, "as Brigadier-General Kosciusko, at leaving this conti-

Houdon's brief visit, shortly after, in order to make Washington's statue for the State of Virginia,[1] must have been particularly pleasant to the major, to whom the great sculptor could bring news of his co-Academician, the old painter of the Gobelins Manufacture, father of the officer.

An unprinted letter of L'Enfant to the secretary of Congress, sitting then in New York, gives a number of details on Houdon's stay in America. The Federal Congress had thought of ordering, in its turn, a statue of Washington, which would have been an equestrian one; but what would the cost be? A most important question in those days. On behalf of Houdon, who knew no English, L'Enfant wrote to Charles Thomson that Mr. Houdon could not "properly hazard to give him any answer relating [to] the cost of the general's equestrian statue"; there are a great many ways of making such work, and Congress must say which it prefers. A book belonging to Mr. Houdon will shortly reach these shores, where particulars as to the "performance of the several statues which have been created in Europe are mentioned, together with their cost." The book is on a vessel, soon expected, and which brings back Doctor Franklin's "bagage."

nent, gave me the flattering expectation of being at the head of [such] a department."

[1] On this visit, see below, p. 225.

Congress had thought also of a marble bust for the hall where it sat. Houdon was taking home with him a finished model of the head of the great man, and had exhibited it, for every one to say his say, in the "room of Congress."

Such busts, L'Enfant wrote, are "generally paid in Europe five thousand French livres"; but as many duplicates will probably be ordered from him, Houdon will lower the price to one hundred guineas. "He begs leave, however, to observe that a bust of the size of nature only may be fit for a private and small room, but not for such a large one as that devoted for the assembly of a Congress, where it should be necessary to have a bust of a larger size to have it appear to advantage."

The price had been asked, too, of duplicates in plaster of Paris, for private citizens. The answer was: four guineas, also in the thought that a goodly number would be wanted, "provided that there be a subscription for a large number, and that the gentlemen who will have any of these busts in their possession consider themselves as engaged to prevent any copy from being taken; this last condition he humbly insists upon."

As for the original, Houdon is anxious to know what the compatriots of the general think of it; any criticism would be welcome: "Mr. Houdon hopes that Congress is satisfied with the bust he has had the honor to submit to their examination, begs the gentlemen who may have some objections to communicate them to him, and he flatters himself that Congress will favor him with their opinion in writing, which he will consider as a proof of their satisfaction and keep as a testimony of their goodness."

He is just about to sail, and the bust has to be removed at once: "Mr. Houdon, being to embark to-morrow morning, begs leave to take out the general's bust from the room of Congress this afternoon."[1]

L'Enfant's chief work in New York consisted in the remodelling of the old, or rather older (but not oldest), City Hall, the one which preceded that now known, in its turn, as the old one. The undertaking was of importance, the question being of better accommodating Congress, which had left Philadelphia with a grudge toward that city, and was now sitting in New York. A large sum, for those days, had been advanced by patriotic citizens, which sum, however, L'Enfant's habit to see things "en grand" caused to be insufficient by more than half. The city hoped that the devising of such a structure would be for it one more title to be selected as the federal capital, and it therefore did not protest, but on the contrary

[1] New York, 3d November, 1785. Papers of the Continental Congress—Letters, l. 78, vol. XIV, p. 677.

caused a "testimonial" to be officially presented
to L'Enfant, highly praising his work: "While
the hall exists it will exhibit a most respectable
monument of your eminent talents, as well as of
the munificence of the citizens."[1] L'Enfant received "the freedom of the city" by "special
honorifick patent," as he wrote later, and he was,
moreover, offered ten acres of land near Provost
Lane, "which latter he politely declined."[2]

The building won general admiration for its
noble appearance, the tasteful brilliancy of its
ornamentation, and its commodious internal arrangements. The only objections came from the
Anti-Federalists, who called it the "Fools' Trap,"
in which appellation politics had, obviously, more
to do than architecture.

L'Enfant, a man of ideas, had tried to make of
the renovated hall something characteristically
American, if not in the general style, which was
classical, at least in many details. National resources had been turned into use; in the Senate
chamber the chimneys were of American marble,
which, "for beauties of shade and polish, is equal to
any of its kind in Europe."[3] The capitals of the
pilasters were "of a fanciful kind, the invention of
Major L'Enfant, the architect. . . . Amidst their

[1] October 13, 1789.
[2] Taggart, *Records of the Columbia Historical Society*, XI, 215.
[3] Thomas E. V. Smith, *The City of New York in 1789*, p. 46, quoting
contemporary magazines.

foliage appears a star and rays, and a piece of
drapery below suspends a small medallion with
U. S. in a cipher.   The idea is new and the effect
pleasing; and although they cannot be said to be of
any ancient order, we must allow that they have
an appearance of magnificence."[1]   The frieze outside was so divided as to give room for thirteen
stars in so many metopes.   A much-talked-of
eagle, with thirteen arrows in its talons, which,
unluckily, could not be ready for March 4, 1789,
when Congress met in the hall for the first time
under the newly voted Constitution, was the chief
ornament on the pediment.   On the 22d of April
the news could be sent to the *Salem Mercury*:
"The eagle in front of the Federal State-House
is displayed.   The general appearance of this
front is truly august."[2]   The emblem was thus
at its proper place when the chief event that
Federal Hall, as it was then called, was to witness
occurred, on the 30th of the same month, the day
of the first inauguration of the first President of
the United States.

Crowds came to visit what was then the most
beautiful building in the country; but better than
crowds came, and one visit was for the major
more touching and flattering than all the others

[1] *Ibid.*
[2] C. M. Bowen, *The Centennial Celebration of the Inauguration of
George Washington*, 1892, pp. 15, 16.

put together—the wife of his general, now the President, Mrs. Washington, caused Colonel Humphreys and Mr. Lear to make arrangements with L'Enfant for her to inspect the hall, in June of the inauguration year.[1]

The expensive and greatly admired monument was to experience the strange fate of being survived by its author. Becoming again City Hall when Congress, soon after, left New York to go back, reconciled, to Philadelphia, it was pulled down in 1812, the building itself being sold at auction for four hundred and twenty-five dollars: and thus disappeared, to the regret of all lovers of ancient souvenirs, the beautiful chimneys in American marble, the "truly august" eagle with its thirteen arrows, and the first really American capitals ever devised, and which, though in a new style, were yet "magnificent."

One solitary souvenir of the building remains, however, that is, the middle part of the railing on which Washington must have leaned when taking the oath; a piece of wrought iron of a fine ornamental style, now preserved with so many other interesting relics of old New York on the ground floor of the New York Historical Society's Museum. In the same room can be seen several

[1] "Mr. Lear does himself the honor to inform Major L'Enfant that Mrs. Washington intends to visit the federal building at six o'clock this evening.—Saturday morning, 13th June, 1789." (L'Enfant papers.)

contemporary views of Federal Hall, one in water-color, by Robertson, 1798; another, an engraving, showing every detail of the façade, represents, as the inscription runs, "Federal Hall, the Seat of Congress.—Printed and sold by A. Doolittle, New Haven, 1790.—A. Doolittle Sc.   Pet. Lacour del."

Shortly before the inauguration of the first President, L'Enfant had had to lend his help for the devising of a grand, artistic, historical, and especially political procession, a Federalist one, arranged in the hope of influencing public opinion and securing the vote of the Constitution by the State of New York. This now revered text was then the subject of ardent criticism; famous patriots like Patrick Henry had detected in it something royalistic, which has long ceased to be apparent, and were violent in their denunciation of this instrument of tyranny. New York was in doubt; its convention had met at Poughkeepsie in June, 1788, and it seemed as if an adverse vote were possible. The procession was then thought of.

It took place on Monday, the 23d of July, and was a grand affair, with artillery salute, trumpeters, foresters, Christopher Columbus on horseback, farmers, gardeners, the Society of the Cincinnati "in full military uniform," brewers showing in their ranks, "mounted on a tun of ale, a beautiful boy of eight years, in close-fitting, flesh-colored silk, representing Bacchus, with a silver goblet in his hand," butchers, tanners, cordwainers "surrounding the car of the Sons of Saint Crispin," furriers exhibiting "an Indian in native costume, loaded with furs, notwithstanding it was one of the hottest days in July." [1]

The chief object of wonder was the good ship *Hamilton*, presented by the ship-carpenters, mounted on wheels, a perfect frigate of thirty-two guns, with its crew, complete, firing salutes on its way. The confectioners surrounded an immense "Federal cake." The judges and lawyers were followed by "John Lawrence, John Cozine, and Robert Troup, bearing the new Constitution elegantly engrossed on vellum, and ten students of law followed, bearing in order the ratification of the ten States." [2] The tin-plate workers exhibited "the Federal tin warehouse, raised on ten pillars, with the motto:

> When three more pillars rise,
> Our Union will the world surprise."

—tin-plate poetry, for the tin warehouse. Then came learned men, physicians, clergymen, the re-

[1] Martha J. Lamb, *History of the City of New York*, 1881, vol. II, pp. 321 ff.

[2] Ten had already voted the Constitution, which made its enactment certain, for Congress had decided that an adoption by nine States would be enough for that. As is well known, there remained in the end only two dissenting States, North Carolina and Rhode Island.

gent and students of Columbia University, scholars, and among them Noah Webster, famous since as a lexicographer, and then as a professor and journalist, now admired by everybody, but, in those days of strife, only by Federalists—"a mere pedagogue," disdainfully wrote Jefferson later, "of very limited understanding and very strong prejudices," in saying which he himself, maybe, showed some prejudice, too.[1]

A grand banquet, at which, according to the *New York Journal and Weekly Register*,[2] bullocks were roasted whole for the "regale" of the guests, was held at the extreme point reached by the procession, called by the same paper the "parade des fêtes champêtres." The President and members of Congress sat under a dome devised by L'Enfant. It was "surmounted by a figure of Fame, with a trumpet proclaiming a new era, and holding a scroll emblematic of the three great epochs of the war: *Independence—Alliance with France—Peace.*"[3]

This was greatly admired. "The committee," we read in a note printed by their order in the *Imperial Gazetteer*, "would be insensible of the zeal and merit of Major L'Enfant were they to omit expressing the obligation which they are under to him for the elegance of the design and

[1] To James Madison, August 12, 1801.
[2] Number of July 24, 1788.   [3] Martha J. Lamb, *ibid.*

the excellence of the execution of the pavilion and tables." [1]

The whole was a considerable success. "As it redounds much to the credit of the citizens, . . ." another paper observes, "it ought to be remarked that there was not the least outrage, or even indecency, notwithstanding 6,000 or 7,000 people (as supposed, spectators included) had collected, and that the whole company was dismissed at half after five o'clock." [2]

Three days after the procession the vote was taken at Poughkeepsie, and if *any* influence at all could be attributed to the effect on public opinion of the quasi-mediæval pageant, its organizers must have felt proud, for in an assembly of fifty-seven the Constitution was actually voted by a majority of two.

[1] July 26, 1788.   [2] *New York Journal*, July 24.

III

The same year in which the New York Federal Hall had seen the inauguration of the first President, the chance of his life came to L'Enfant. He deserved it, because he not only availed himself of it, but went forth to meet it, giving up his abode in New York, "where I stood at the time," he wrote later, "able of commanding whatever business I liked." This was the founding of the federal city.

The impression was a general one among the French that those insurgents whom they had helped to become a free nation were to be a great one, too. Leaving England, where he was a refugee during our Revolution, Talleyrand decided to come to the United States, "desirous of seeing," he says in his memoirs, "that great country whose history begins." General Moreau, also a refugee, a few years later spoke with the same confidence of the future of the country: "I had pictured to myself the advantages of living under a free government; but I had conceived only in part what such happiness is: here it is enjoyed to the full. . . . It is impossible for men who have lived under such a government to allow themselves ever to be subjugated; they would be

very great cowards if they did not perish to the
last in order to defend it."[1]

L'Enfant, with his tendency to see things "en
grand," could not fail to act accordingly, and the
moment he heard that the federal city would be
neither New York nor Philadelphia, nor any other
already in existence, but one to be built expressly,
he wrote to Washington a letter remarkable by
his clear understanding of the opportunity offered
to the country, and by his determined purpose to
work not for the three million inhabitants of his
day, but for the one hundred of ours, and for all
the unborn millions that will come after us.

The letter is dated from New York, 11th of
September, 1789. "Sir," he said, "the late deter-
mination of Congress to lay the foundation of a
city which is to become the capital of this vast
empire offers so great an occasion of acquiring
reputation to whoever may be appointed to conduct the execution of the business that your
Excellency will not be surprised that my ambition and the desire I have of becoming a useful
citizen should lead me to wish a share in the
undertaking.

"No nation, perhaps, had ever before the opportunity offered them of deliberately deciding
on the spot where their capital city should be

[1] To his brother, Philadelphia, November 17, 1806. *Revue des
Deux Mondes*, November 15, 1908, p. 421.

fixed. . . . And, although the means now within
the power of the country are not such as to pursue the design to any great extent it will be obvious that the plan should be drawn on such a
scale as to leave room for that aggrandizement and
embellishment which the increase of the wealth
of the nation will permit it to pursue at any period,
however remote.   Viewing the matter in this light,
I am fully sensible of the extent of the undertaking."[1]

Washington knew that L'Enfant was afflicted,
to be sure, with an "untoward" temper, being
haughty, proud, intractable, but that he was
honest withal, sincere, loyal, full of ideas, and remarkably gifted.   He decided to intrust him with
the great task, thus justifying, a little later, his
selection: "Since my first knowledge of the gentleman's abilities in the line of his profession, I have
received him not only as a scientific man, but one
who has added considerable taste to professional
knowledge; and that, for such employment as he
is now engaged in, for prosecuting public works
and carrying them into effect, he was better quali-
fied than any one who had come within my knowledge in this country."[2]   The President informed
L'Enfant that he was to set to work at once, and

[1] Original (several times printed in part) in the Library of Congress, *Miscellaneous—Personal*.   The rest of the letter treats of the
necessity of fortifying the coasts.
[2] To David Stuart, November 20, 1791.

so bestir himself as to have at least a general
plan to show a few months later, when he himself
would return from a trip South. On March 2,
1791, Washington announced to Colonel Dickens,
of Georgetown, the coming of the major: "An
eminent French military engineer starts for Georgetown to examine and survey the site of the federal
city." A few days later the arrival of "Major
Longfont" was duly recorded by the *Georgetown
Weekly Ledger*.[1]

L'Enfant's enthusiasm and his desire to do
well and quickly had been raised to a high pitch.
He reached the place a few days later and found it
wrapped in mist, soaked in rain, but he would
not wait. "I see no other way," he wrote to Jefferson on the 11th, "if by Monday next the weather
does not change, but of making a rough draft as
accurate as may be obtained by viewing the
ground in riding over it on horseback, as I have
already done yesterday through the rain, to obtain a knowledge of the whole. . . . As far as
I was able to judge through a thick fog, I passed
on many spots which appeared to me really beautiful, and which seem to dispute with each other
[which] commands."[2]

When he could see the place to better advantage, his admiration knew no bounds. In an un-

[1] W. B. Bryan's *History of the National Capital*, 1914, p. 127.
[2] *Records of the Columbia Historical Society*, II, 151.

published letter to Hamilton he says: "Now, when you may probably have heard that I am finally charged with delineating a plan for the city, I feel a sort of embarrassment how to speak to you as advantageously as I really think of the situation determined upon; for, as there is no doubt, I must feel highly interested in the success of the undertaking, I become apprehensive of being charged with partiality when I assure you that no position in America can be more susceptible of grand improvement than that between the eastern branch of the Potomac and Georgetown." [1]

A few weeks later L'Enfant was doing the honors of the spot to a brother artist, the painter Trumbull, just back from Yorktown, where he had been sketching in view of his big picture of the surrendering of Cornwallis, and who wrote in his autobiography: "Then to Georgetown, where I found Major L'Enfant drawing his plan of the city of Washington; rode with him over the ground on which the city has since been built. Where the Capitol now stands was then a thick wood." (May, 1791.)

Another visitor of note came in the same year, namely the French minister, a former companion in arms of Lafayette and of L'Enfant himself, Ternant, back from a three days' stay at Mount

[1] April 8, 1791. Hamilton Papers, vol. XI, Library of Congress.

Vernon, and who gave his government an account of what he had observed: "I would not leave Georgetown without having seen the ground destined for the federal city. The position seemed to me a most interesting one from every point of view. The French engineer who has already traced the streets, is busy preparing a detailed plan. . . . The President shows the greatest interest in this new Salente, which is to bear his name." [1]

The city, L'Enfant thought, must be great, beautiful, and soon peopled, drawn "on that grand scale on which it ought to be planned";[2] meant to absorb "Georgetown itself, whose name will before long be suppressed, and its whole district become a part of the cession." [3] It must be quickly filled with inhabitants, because this will strengthen the Union: "I earnestly wish all that the Eastern States can spare may come this way, and believe it would answer as good a purpose as that of their emigration to the West. It would deface that line of markation which will ever

[1] September 30, October 24, 1791. *Correspondence of the French Ministers*, ed. F. J. Turner, 1904, p. 62. "Salente," the ideal city, in Fénelon's *Télémaque*. During the War of Independence Chevalier Jean de Ternant had served as a volunteer officer in the American army. He was at Valley Forge, at Charleston, took part under Greene in the Southern campaign and was promoted a colonel by a vote of Congress.

[2] To Jefferson, March 11, 1791.

[3] To Hamilton, April 8, 1791.

oppose the South against the East, for when objects are seen at a distance the idea we form of
them is apt to mislead us . . . and we fancy
monstrous that object which, from a nearer view,
would charm us. . . . Hence arises a natural
though unwarrantable prejudice of nations against
nations, of States against States, and so down to
individuals, who often mistrust one another for
want of being sufficiently acquainted with each
other." [1]

The city must be beautiful, due advantage
being taken of the hilly nature of the spot for
grand or lovely prospects, and of its water resources for handsome fountains and cascades:
"five grand fountains intended, with a constant
spout of water—a grand cascade" at the foot of
Capitol Hill,[2] etc., a part of the plan which was,
unluckily, left in abeyance. Some had spoken of
a plain rectangular plan, "a regular assemblage
of houses laid out in squares, and forming streets
all parallel and uniform." This might be good
enough, L'Enfant declared, "on a well-level plain,
where, no surrounding object being interesting,
it becomes indifferent which way the opening
street may be directed." But the case is quite
different with the future federal city: "Such

[1] Same letter to Hamilton.
[2] L'Enfant's *Observations Explanatory of the Plan*, inscribed on the
plan itself.

regular plans, however answerable they may appear on paper . . . become at last tiresome and insipid, and it could never be, in its origin, but a mean continence of some cool imagination wanting a sense of the really grand and truly beautiful, only to be met with where nature contributes with art and diversifies the objects."[1] We may imagine what his feelings would be if he saw, in our days, the steam-shovel busy around the city, dumping as many hills as possible into as many vales, and securing a maximum platitude.

But the city must be more than that; besides being beautiful, healthy, commodious, it should be full of sentiment, of associations, of ideas; everything in it must be evocative and have a meaning and a "raison d'être." Rarely was a brain more busy than that of L'Enfant during the first half of the year 1791. Surveying the ground, mapping out the district, sketching the chief buildings of the model city that was to be,[2] he presented three reports to Washington, the first, giving only his general ideas, before the end of

[1] First report to the President, March 26, 1791.
[2] For he was depended upon for that, too: "M. L'Enfant," Ternant wrote, "aura aussi la direction des bâtimens que le Congrès se propose d'y faire élever." September 30, 1791. See also the documents quoted by W. B. Bryan, *History of the National Capital*, 1914, p. 165, note. L'Enfant actually made drawings for the Capitol, the President's house, the bridges, the market, etc., which he complained later the commissioners to have unjustly appropriated. *Records of the Columbia Historical Society*, II, 140.

March, the second in June, the last in August,
the two latter accompanied with plans, the last
of which being the one which was followed in
the building of the city.

By the amplitude of its scope, the logic of the
arrangements, the breadth of the streets and
avenues, the beauty of the prospects cleverly
taken into account, the quantity of ground set
apart for gardens and parks, the display of waters,
the plan was a unique monument. The selection
of the place for what we call the Capitol and the
White House, which were then called the Federal
House and the Palace for the President, near
which the ministerial departments were to be
built, had been the result of a good deal of thinking and comparing. "After much menutial [sic]
search for an eligible situation, prompted, as I
may say, from a fear of being prejudiced in favor
of a first opinion, I could discover no one so advantageously to greet the congressional building
as is that on the west end of Jenkins heights,
which stand as a pedestal waiting for a monument. . . . Some might, perhaps, require less
labor to be made agreeable, but, after all assistance
of arts, none ever would be made so grand." On
that very pedestal now rises the Capitol of the
United States.

As for the "Presidential Palace," L'Enfant made
his choice with the object, he says, of "adding to

the sumptuousness of a palace the convenience
of a house and the agreeableness of a country
seat," which are the three main qualities actually
combined in the present White House. He selected a spot which Washington had himself
noticed as a convenient one, at some distance
from Congress, it is true, but that would not matter
much, L'Enfant thought, with his old-world notions of etiquette, for "no message to nor from
the President is to be made without a sort of
decorum which will doubtless point out the propriety of committee waiting on him in carriage,
should his palace be even contiguous to Congress."
Since it was a question of driving, it little mat-
tered whether the drive was to be a little more
or less long.

For different reasons President Washington approved of that distance; *major e longinquo amicitia*,
he apparently thought. "Where and how," he
once wrote to Alexander White, "the houses for
the President and other public officers may be
fixed is to me as an individual a matter of moon-
shine, but . . . the daily intercourse which the
secretaries of the departments must have with
the President would render a distant situation
extremely inconvenient to them; and not much
less so would one be close to the Capitol, for it was
the universal complaint of them all, that while
the legislature was in session they could do little

or no business, so much were they interrupted by
the individual visits of members (in office hours)
and by calls for papers. Many of them have declared to me that they have often been obliged
to go home and deny themselves in order to
transact the current business."[1]   In that respect,
carriage or no carriage, distance would have its
merits.

L'Enfant's letters and the notes accompanying
his plans show that everything in the future city
had been devised, indeed, with an intention:
ever-flowing fountains and a cascade for health
and beauty; an avenue of noble buildings, leading from the Capitol to the Presidential House,
and increasing the dignified appearance of both:
"The grand avenue," he wrote, "connecting both
the Palace and the Federal House will be most
magnificent and most. convenient," with a number of handsome monuments, a very characteristic one being a temple for national semireligious
celebrations, "such as public prayer, thanks-
givings, funeral orations, etc., and assigned to
the special use of no particular sect or denomination, but equally opened to all."   It would also
be a pantheon for the illustrious dead, "as may
hereafter be decreed by the voice of a grateful
nation."   A column, as yet never built, was "to
be erected to celebrate the first rise of a navy,

[1] March 25, 1798.

and to stand a ready monument to consecrate
its progress and achievements." The squares
were to be allotted, one to each of the States
forming the Union: "The centre of each square
will admit of statues, columns, obelisks, or any
other ornaments . . . to perpetuate not only the
memory of such individuals whose counsels or
military achievements were conspicuous in giving
liberty and independence to this country, but also
those whose usefulness hath rendered them worthy
of general imitation, to invite the youth of succeeding generations to tread in the paths of those
sages or heroes whom their country has thought
proper to celebrate."   This was a way, L'Enfant
considered, of fortifying the Union and of giving
to the very city that educational value to which
he attached so much importance.

Chief among those patriotic objects was to be,
at some distance north of the place where the
Washington monument now rises, "the equestrian
figure of George Washington, a monument voted
in 1783 by the late Continental Congress."   And
L'Enfant must certainly have hoped that the
author would be his illustrious compatriot, the
sculptor Houdon, on whose behalf we have seen
him writing to Congress, in 1785, as to the probable cost.

Distant views and prospects were, of course,
to be used to the best advantage: "Attention has

been paid to the passing of those leading avenues
over the most favorable ground for prospect and
convenience." But, above all, L'Enfant was per-
sistent in his request that, on no account, the
grandeur of his conception be in any way cur-
tailed: it was to remain commensurate with the
greatness of the United States of future times.
The plan "must leave to posterity a grand idea
of the patriotic interest which promoted it." [1]
He foresaw much opposition to some of his ideas,
but besought the President to stand by him, and
especially to prevent any dwarfing of his views:
"I remain assured you will conceive it essential
to pursue with dignity the operation of an undertaking of a magnitude so worthy of the concern
of a grand empire . . . over whose progress the
eyes of every other nation, envying the opportunity denied them, will stand judge." [2]

To make a man of that temper and enthusiasm,
having a reason for each of his propositions, accept hints and change his mind was almost an
impossibility. In vain did Jefferson object "to
the obligation to build the houses at a given distance from the street. . . . It produces a dis-
gusting monotony; all persons make this complaint against Philadelphia." In the same record
of his views, however, and much more to his credit,

[1] L'Enfant's *Observations Explanatory of the Plan*, inscribed on it.
[2] Conclusion of his third report.

Washington's secretary of state is seen foreseeing
the sky-scraper and its dangers: "In Paris it is
forbidden to build a house beyond a given height,
and it is admitted to be a good restriction. It
keeps down the price of grounds, keeps the houses
low and convenient, and the streets light and airy.
Fires are much more manageable when houses
are low,"[1] as was only too well evidenced since
in the fires at Chicago, Baltimore, and San Francisco.

As for the President himself, he had well-deter-
mined, practical ideas on some points, such as the
befitting distance between the places of abode
of Congress and of the chief of the state, and,
what was of more import, the necessarily large
extent of the ground to be reserved for the building of the future capital.[2] On the rest, with his
habit of trusting those who knew, he seems to

[1] "Opinion on Capital," November 29, 1790. *Writings*, ed. Ford,
V, 253.
[2] Which agreed perfectly with L'Enfant's constant desire to ever
do things "en grand." Washington writes to him that, "although
it may not be *immediately* wanting," a large tract of ground must be
reserved. The lands to be set apart, "in my opinion are those between Rock Creek, the Potowmac River, and the Eastern Branch,
and as far up the latter as the turn of the channel above Evens's
point; thence including the flat back of Jenkins's height; thence
to the road leading from Georgetown to Bladensburg as far easterly
along the same as to include the Branch which runs across it, some-
where near the exterior of the Georgetown Session. Thence in a
proper direction to Rock Creek at or above the ford, according to
the situation of ground." Mount Vernon, April 4, 1791, Washington's manuscript *Letter Book*, vol. XI, Library of Congress.

have left free rein to L'Enfant. Submitting to
him certain suggestions, some from Jefferson, he
allows him to use them or not, as he pleases,
and he personally seems to incline toward not:
"Sir, although I do not conceive that you will
derive any material advantage from an examination of the inclosed papers, yet, as they have been
drawn under different circumstances and by different persons, they may be compared with your own
ideas of a proper plan for the federal city. . . .
The rough sketch by Mr. Jefferson was done
under an idea that no offer worthy of consideration would come from the landholders in the
vicinity of Carrollsburgh, from the backwardness
which appeared in them, and therefore was ac-
commodated to the grounds about Georgetown."[1]

Criticism of L'Enfant's plan turned out to be
insignificant, and the approbation general. "The
work of Major L'Enfant, which is greatly admired,
will show," Washington said, "that he had many
objects to attend to and to combine, not on paper
merely, but to make them correspond with the
actual circumstances of the ground."[2]   Jefferson,
who had the good taste not to stick to his own
former suggestions, was sending, a little later,
copies of the plan to Gouverneur Morris, then
minister to France, for him to exhibit in various

[1] Same letter.
[2] To the Commissioners, December 18, 1791.

cities as a thing for the United States to be proud
of: "I sent you by the way of London a dozen
plans of the city of Washington in the Federal
territory, hoping you would have them displayed
to public view where they would be most seen by
those descriptions of men worthy and likely to be
attracted to it. Paris, Lyons, Rouen, and the
seaport towns of Havre, Nantes, Bordeaux, and
Marseille would be proper places to send them
to."[1]

Three assistants had been given to L'Enfant,
two of the Ellicot brothers (Andrew and Benjamin) and Isaac Roberdeau, the major's trustiest
second. Three Commissioners of the District had
been appointed, Thomas Johnson and Daniel
Carroll, both of Maryland, and David Stuart, of
Virginia. They notified L'Enfant, on the 9th of
September, 1791, that a name had been selected
for the district and the city: "We have agreed
that the federal district shall be called 'the
Territory of Columbia,' and the federal city
'the City of Washington.' The title of the map
will therefore be 'A map of the City of Washington in the District of Columbia.'"

For the expropriation of the ground with a
minimum actual outlay, an ingenious system, also
applied elsewhere, had been adopted: "The terms
entered into by me," Washington wrote to Jeffer-

[1] Philadelphia, March 12, 1793.

son, "on the part of the United States with the
landowners of Georgetown and Carrollsburgh, are
that all the land from Rock Creek along the river
to the Eastern Branch . . . is ceded to the public, on condition that, when the whole shall be
surveyed and laid off as a city, which Major L'Enfant is now directed to do, the present proprietors
shall retain every other lot, and for such parts
of the land as may be taken for public use they
shall be allowed at the rate of twenty-five pounds
per acre, the public having the right to reserve
such parts of the wood on the land as may be
thought necessary to be preserved for ornament;
the landholders to have the use and profit of all
the grounds until the city is laid off into lots,
which by this agreement became public property.
Nothing is to be allowed for the ground which
may be occupied as streets or alleys." The President was confident that everybody would acquiesce
and show good-will, "even the obstinate Mr.
Burns."[1]

But it turned out that there were other obstinate people besides Mr. Burns, L'Enfant himself
chief among them. He had evinced from the
first a great fear of speculators, and was at once
at war with them. "How far," he boldly wrote
to Hamilton, "I have contributed to overset that
plotting business, it would not do for me to tell;

[1] March 31, 1791.

besides, I am not wholly satisfied whether I would
be thanked for by the people among whom you
live."[1]   The three Commissioners had notions of
their own, but could never bring L'Enfant to
take into account either their persons or their
ideas; he would acknowledge no chief except
Washington, who, gently at first, firmly afterward, sternly later, and vainly throughout, tried
to make the major understand that he was one
of the Commissioners' subordinates.   A great reciprocal irritation, which even the President's
painstaking diplomacy could not assuage, began
between them from the first.   Out of fear of speculators, L'Enfant wanted the sale of the lots to be
delayed, while the Commissioners desired to make
a beginning as soon as possible.   The officer kept,
accordingly, his plan to himself, and refused to
have it shown to would-be purchasers.   How, then,
Washington exclaimed, could they be "induced
to buy, to borrow an old adage, a *pig in a poke*"?[2]

The major would not be persuaded, and, giving
an early example of an unconquerable fear of
what would now be called a "trust," he persisted
in refusing to show his plan to any individual or
association.   He had declared beforehand, in one
of his reports to the President, what were his views
and how things should be delayed until the plan

[1] April 8, 1791. Hamilton papers, vol. XI.
[2] To David Stuart, November 20, 1791.

could be engraved, distributed all over the country, and made known to all people at the same time: "A sale made previous the general plan of the distribution of the city is made public, and before the circumstance of that sale taking place has had time to be known through the whole continent, will not call a sufficient concurrence, and must be confined to a few individuals speculating . . . and the consequence of a low sale in this first instance may prove injurious to the subsequent ones by serving as precedents." He was afraid of the "plotting of a number of certain designing men," of the forming of a "society" organized "to engross the most of the sale and master the whole business."[1]

When one of the chief landowners of the district, Daniel Carroll, of Duddington, a relative of one of the Commissioners, decided, in spite of all warnings, to go on with the building of a house across what was to be New Jersey Avenue, matters came to a crisis. Washington tried to pacify L'Enfant, whose indignation knew no bounds. "As a similar case," he wrote to him, "cannot happen again (Mr. Carroll's house having been begun before the federal district was fixed upon), no precedent will be established by yielding a little in the present instance; and it will always be found sound policy to conciliate the good-will

[1] Report to the President, August 19, 1791.

rather than provoke the enmity of any man,
where it can be accomplished without much difficulty, inconvenience, or loss."

But even at the request of a leader whom he
worshipped, L'Enfant would not be persuaded.
With no authority from the Commissioners, he
sent his faithful Roberdeau to raze the house to
the ground, which was but partly done when the
Commissioners had Roberdeau arrested. L'Enfant thereupon came in person with some labor-
ers, and saw the work of destruction perfected
(November 22). He barely escaped arrest himself. Washington, who, as he wrote to Jefferson,
was loath to lose "his services, which in my opinion would be a serious misfortune," severely re-
monstrated now with the major. "In future I
must strictly enjoin you to touch no man's property without his consent, or the previous order
of the Commissioners," adding in kindlier tones:
"Having the beauty and regularity of your plan
only in view, you pursue it as if every person or
thing were obliged to yield to it."[1]

But so they are, thought L'Enfant. For him
the city was his city, his child, and a father has a
right to rear his child as he pleases. Remon-
strating went on some time. Jefferson came to
the rescue of the President, used the fairest means,
asked the major to dine with him "tête à tête,"

[1] December 2, 1791.

so as to quietly discuss the federal city, the hour for the meal differing rather widely from ours: "Mr. Jefferson presents his compliments to Major L'Enfant, and is sorry to have been absent when he was so kind as to call on him, as he wishes to have some conversation with him on the subject of the federal city. He asks the favor of him to come and take a private dinner with him to-morrow at half after three, which may afford time and opportunity for the purpose.—Saturday January 7, 1792."[1] Nothing resulted. Another landowner, Notley Young, had been found in December building a house which had, "contrary to expectation, fallen into a principal street. But I hope," Washington wrote the Commissioners, "the major does not mean to proceed to the demolition of this also."

On no point would L'Enfant yield, so that on March 6, 1792, Jefferson wrote to the Commissioners: "It having been found impracticable to employ Major L'Enfant in that degree of subordination which was lawful and proper, he has been notified that his services were at an end."

A consolation and a comfort to him was the immediate signing by all the landowners of the district, except two, of a testimonial "lamenting" his departure, wishing for his return, praising his work, "for we well know that your time and the

[1] L'Enfant papers.

whole powers of your mind have been for months entirely devoted to the arrangements in the city which reflect so much honor on your taste and judgment."[1]

[1] March 9, 1792. *Records of the Columbia Historical Society*, II, 137.

IV

The bright part of L'Enfant's life was over. His fame was great, and appeals continued for some time to be made to him when important works were contemplated. But his same tendency to ever see things "en grand," his unyielding disposition, his increasing and almost morbid fear of speculators wrecked more than one of his undertakings.

Almost on his leaving his work at Washington he was asked to draw the plans of the first manufacturing city, devised as such, in the United States, and which is to-day one of the most important in existence, Paterson, N. J. "Major L'Enfant, it is said," wrote Washington, who still retained a friendly feeling for him, "is performing wonders at the new town of Paterson."[1] The moving spirit was Hamilton, under whose influence had been founded the "Society for the Establishing Useful Manufactures." The chief point was to transform into a city a spot where only ten houses were in existence, and to make of it an industrial one by turning into use the Falls of the Passaic. Several letters of the major to Hamilton, giving an account of the work, in

[1] To the Commissioners, November 30, 1792.

which faithful Roberdeau was helping, and of the increasing difficulties with all sorts of peop'e, are preserved in the Library of Congress. After one year's toil, L'Enfant was once more notified that his services were no longer wanted.

He is found in the same year and the following one working as an engineer at Fort Mifflin, on the Delaware, and as an architect at a mansion in Philadelphia which was to surpass in magnificence any other in the States. It had been ordered of him by Robert Morris, the financier of the Revolution, and the richest man in America.[1] Here was, if ever, an occasion to do things "en grand." L'Enfant, however, did them "en plus grand" than even the financier had dreamed; improvements and afterthoughts, the use of marble for columns and façades increased the delay and the expense. His being busy at Paterson had also been at first another cause of complaint. "Dear Sir," Morris beseechingly wrote him from Philadelphia, "I had like to have stopped my house for fear of wanting money; that difficulty being removed, it will now be stopped for want of Major L'Enfant."[2] The roof had at last been put on, and one could judge of the beauty of the ensemble, quite remarkable, as we can see from

[1] Morris had bought for it a whole block, limited on its four sides by Chestnut, Walnut, Seventh, and Eighth Streets.
[2] May 9, 1793. (L'Enfant papers.)

a sketch by Birch the Elder preserved in the Philadelphia Library, when Morris's catastrophe occurred, putting an end to the work, and swallowing part, if not all, of L'Enfant's savings.[1]

In his delight at being intrusted with the plan of the federal city he had never said a word about any remuneration, and he had not copyrighted his plan. At the time of his dismissal Washington had written to the Commissioners: "The plan of the city having met universal applause (as far as my information goes), and Major L'Enfant having become a very discontented man, it was thought that less than from two thousand five hundred to three thousand dollars, would not be proper to offer him for his services; instead of this, suppose five hundred guineas and a lot in a good part of the city were substituted?"

The offer was made; L'Enfant refused, without giving reasons. More and more gloomy times were in store for him; mishaps and disappointments multiplied. He had laid great store on the selling of copies of his plan, but since he had not copyrighted it, no royalty on the sale was re-

[1] He seems to have tried to help the financier rather than to be helped by him. Ill-satisfied as he was with the house, for which he, apparently, never paid l'Enfant anything, Morris wrote: "But he lent me thirteen shares of bank stock disinterestedly, and on this point I feel the greatest anxiety that he should get the same number of shares with the dividends, for the want of which he has suffered great distress." Written about 1800. W. B. Bryan, *History of the National Capital*, 1914, p. 181.

served for him. He protested against this,
against the way in which the engraving had been
made, with grievous "errors of execution," and
against the suppression of his name on it, "de-
priving me of the repute of the projector." Contrary, however, to the fear expressed at first by
Washington, that out of spite he might, in his
discontent, side with the many who disapproved
of the vast and difficult undertaking, he remained
loyal to it, and "there is no record of any act or
word that tarnishes his life history with the
blemish of disloyalty to the creation of his genius.
He bore his honors and disappointments in hu-
mility and poverty." [1]

Poverty was, indeed, at his door, and soon in
his house. Haunted by the notion of his wrongs,
some only too real, some more or less imaginary,
he sent to Congress memoir after memoir, recalling what he had done, and what was his destitu-
tion, the "absolute destruction of his family's
fortune in Europe," owing to the French Revolution, his being reduced "from a state of ease and
content to one the most distressed and helpless,"
living as he did, upon "borrowed bread"; but he
would not doubt of "the magnanimity and justice
of Congress." [2]

[1] S. C. Busey, *Pictures of the City of Washington in the Past*, 1898,
p. 108.
[2] Memoirs of 1801, 1802, 1813, in the Jefferson papers, Library of
Congress.

The family's fortune had been reduced, indeed, to a low ebb, his own lack of attention to his financial affairs making matters worse. His inability to properly attend to them is only too well evidenced by some letters from French relatives, showing that, while he was himself in absolute want, he neglected to receive the pension bestowed on him by the French Government, and which, in spite of the Revolution, had been maintained. He had also inherited from the old painter, his father, a small farm in Normandy, but had taken no steps about it, so that the farmer never ceased to pocket the revenues.[1]

One of these letters, which tells him of the death of his mother, who "died with the piety of an angel," shows what reports reached France as to the major's standing among his American friends: "All the persons whom I have seen and who know you, assured me that you enjoyed public esteem. This is everything in a country of which people praise the morals, the virtues, and the probity as worthy of our first ancestors."[2]

On two occasions, after many years, Congress

[1] Letter from his cousin, Destouches, Paris, September 15, 1805, greatly exaggerating, as shown by the letter mentioned below, his mother's state of poverty. (L'Enfant papers.)

[2] From his cousin, Mrs. Roland, née Mallet, whose husband had a modest position at the Ministry of the Navy; Paris, May 5, 1806. The mother's furniture and silver plate was valued at 1,500 livres. Allusion is made to L'Enfant's deceased sister and to her "mariage projeté avec Mr. Leclerc." (L'Enfant papers.)

voted modest sums for L'Enfant, but they were at once appropriated by his creditors. He was, moreover, appointed, in 1812, "professor of the art of military engineering in the Military Academy of the United States," a nomination which, in spite of the entreaties of James Monroe, then secretary of state, he declined. He is found in September, 1814, working at Fort Washington, when fifty men with spades and axes are sent him.

He survived eleven years, haunting the lobbies of the Capitol, pacing the newly marked avenues of "his" city, watching its growth, deploring the slightest deviation from his original design, for, as Washington had early noticed, he was "so tenacious of his plans as to conceive that they would be marred if they underwent any change or alteration,"[1] visiting the friends he had among the early settlers. "Mr. W. W. Corcoran, who lately departed this life in the city of Washington, full of years and honor . . . had a very distinct recollection of the personal appearance of L'Enfant, the latter having been a frequent visitor at his father's house. He described him to me as a tall, erect man, fully six feet in height, finely proportioned, nose prominent, of military bearing, courtly air, and polite manners, his figure usually enveloped in a long overcoat and surmounted by

[1] To David Stuart, November 20, 1791.

a bell-crowned hat—a man who would attract attention in any assembly."[1]

He ended his days, the permanent guest of the Digges family, in their house near Washington. His death occurred there in 1825, and he was buried in their property at the foot of a tree. An inventory of his "personal goods and chattels" showed that they consisted in three watches, three compasses, some books, maps, and surveying instruments, the whole being valued at forty-six dollars.

The federal city, Washington had written in 1798 to Mrs. Sarah Fairfax, then in England, will be a great and beautiful one "a century hence, if this country keeps united, and it is surely its policy and interest to do it." It took, indeed, a great many years, and for a long time doubters could enjoy their doubts, and jokers their jokes. The Duke de La Rochefoucauld-Liancourt visited the incipient town in 1797; he found that it possessed one hundred and fifty houses, scattered here and there; the house for the President was ready to be covered the same year, and the only wing of the Capitol yet begun was to receive its roof the year following, both being "handsome buildings, in white stones very well wrought."

[1] Hugh T. Taggart, in *Records of the Columbia Historical Society*, XI, 216.

But the unredeemable fault, in his eyes, was the very magnitude and beauty of the plan. "The plan," he wrote, "is fine, cleverly and grandly designed, but it is its very grandeur, its magnificence, which causes it to be nothing but a dream." The distance, so heartily approved of by Washington, between the President's house and the Capitol, seemed to the traveller a serious objection; the raising of five hundred houses would be necessary to connect the two buildings; not one is in existence. "If this gap is not filled, communication will be impracticable in winter, for one can scarcely suppose that the United States would undergo the expense for pavement, footpaths, and lamps for such a long stretch of uninhabited ground."[1]   This   wonder   has,   however,   been seen.

For a long time, for more than half the present duration of the city's life, deriders could deride to their heart's content. Few cities have ever been so abundantly nicknamed as Washington, the "wilderness city," the city "of magnificent distances," the "village monumental," the city, as reported by Jean-Jacques Ampère, the son of the great scientist, who visited it in 1851, of "streets without houses, and of houses without streets."   He saw in its fate "a striking proof of this truth that one cannot create a great city at

[1] *Voyage en Amérique*, VI, 122 ff.

will." But this truth, as some others, has proved an untruth.

The growth was slow, indeed, but constant, and when the century was over, Washington's prophecy and L'Enfant's foresight were justified by the event. A city had risen, ample and beautiful, a proper capital for a wealthy and powerful nation, one quite apart, copied on no other, "not one of those cities," as was remarked, in our days, by one of Washington's successors, Mr. Roosevelt, "of which you can cut out a piece and transplant it into another, without any one perceiving that something has happened."

Then at last came L'Enfant's day. What he had always expected for "his" city took place; what he had never expected for himself took place also. In January, 1902, both the "Park Commission," composed of Daniel H. Burnham, Charles F. McKim, Augustus Saint-Gaudens, and F. L. Olmsted, and the Senate committee presented their reports on the improvement and development of Washington; the conclusions were: "The original plan of the city of Washington, having stood the test of a century, has met universal approval. The departures from that plan are to be regretted, and wherever possible, remedied." It was thus resolved to revert, as much as circumstances allowed, and in spite of a heavy outlay, to several of L'Enfant's ideas, especially to one which he considered of greatest importance, and which had been kept so long in abeyance, the giving of its proper character to that "grand avenue" between the Capitol and the White House, meant to be "most magnificent and most convenient." It is now going to be both.

As for L'Enfant himself, one more appropriation, this time not to go to his creditors, was voted by Congress on account of the major, and it was resolved that his ashes, the place of which continued to be marked only by a tree, should be removed to Arlington National Cemetery, to lie in that ever-growing army of the dead, former members of the regiments of that Republic for which he had fought and bled. His remains were brought to what had been "Jenkins's Hill," and placed under the great dome of the Capitol. In the presence of the chief of the state, President Taft, of representatives of Congress, the Supreme Court, the Society of the Cincinnati, and other patriotic and artistic societies, and of a vast crowd, on the 28th of April, 1909, orations were delivered by the Vice-President of the United States, James Sherman, and by the Chief Commissioner of the District, Henry B. McFarland, the latter amply making up, by his friendly and eloquent address, for the long-forgotten troubles of his predecessors with L'Enfant. The Vice-President courteously concluded thus: "And turn-

ing to you, Mr. Ambassador . . . I express the
hope that the friendship between our nations,
which has existed for more than a century, will
be but intensified as time passes, and that we will
in the future join hands in advancing every good
cause which an all-wise Providence intrusts to our
care." The hearse, wrapped in the three colors
of France and America, was accompanied to Arlington by the French naval and military attachés,
and an escort from one of those regiments of engineers to which the major himself had belonged.

A handsome monument was unveiled two years
later by Miss E. C. Morgan, the great-grand-
daughter of William Digges, who had befriended
L'Enfant in his last days, the chief speeches being
delivered by President Taft, and by the secretary
of state, Elihu Root.[1] "Few men," Mr. Root said,
"can afford to wait a hundred years to be remembered. It is not a change in L'Enfant that brings
us here. It is we who have changed, who have
just become able to appreciate his work. And
our tribute to him should be to continue his work."
The monument, by W. W. Bosworth, who, like
L'Enfant had received in Paris his artistic education, is in the shape of a table, on which has been
engraved a facsimile of the original plan of the
city by the French soldier-artist. From the slope
where it has been raised can be seen, on the other

[1] May 22, 1911.

side of the river, the ceaselessly growing federal
capital, called Washington, "a revered name,"
another French officer, the Chevalier de Chastellux, had written, when visiting, in 1782, another
and earlier town of the same name in Connecticut,
"a revered name, whose memory will undoubtedly
last longer than the very city called upon to perpetuate it."

III

WASHINGTON AND THE FRENCH

WASHINGTON AND THE FRENCH

I

WASHINGTON'S acquaintance with things French began early and was of a mixed nature. As a pupil of the French Huguenot Maryes, who kept a school at Fredericksburg, and did *not* teach him French,[1] we find him carefully transcribing, in his elegant youthful hand, those famous "Rules of Civility and Decent Behavior in Company and Conversation," which have recently been proved to be French. Whether this French teaching given him by a Frenchman engraved itself in his mind or happened to match his natural disposition, or both, certain it is that he lived up to the best among those maxims, those, for example, and they are remarkably numerous, that deprecate

---

[1] He kept all his life a feeling that his early educa ion had been incomplete. Strongly advised by David Humphreys to write an account of the great events in which he had taken part, he answered that he would not, on account of a lack of leisure, and a "consciousness of a defective education." July 25, 1785. When Lafayette was beseeching him to visit France some day, he answered: "Remember, my good friend, that I am unacquainted with your language, that I am too far advanced in years to acquire a knowledge of it." September 30, 1779. Franklin added later his entreaties to those of Lafayette; see Washington's answer, October 11, 1780.

jokes and railing at the expense of others, or those of a noble import advising the young man to be "no flatterer," to "show no sign of choler in reproving, but to do it with sweetness and mildness," those prescribing that his "recreations be manful, not sinful," and giving him this advice of supreme importance, which Washington observed throughout life: "Labor to keep alive in your breast that little spark of celestial fire called conscience."

Another chance that Washington had to become acquainted with things French was through his reading, and was less favorable to them. An early note in his hand informs us that, about the year 1748, he, being then sixteen, had, "in the *Spectator*, read to No. 143." All those numbers had been written by Steele and Addison at a period of French wars, at the moment when we were fighting "Monsieur Malbrouk." Not a portrait of the French in those numbers that is not a caricature; they are a "ludicrous nation"; their women are "fantastical," their men "vain and lively," their fashions ridiculous; not even their wines find grace in the eyes of Steele, who could plead, it is true, that he was not without experience on the subject, and who declares that this "plaguy French claret" is greatly inferior to "a bottle or two of good, solid, edifying port."

Washington was soon to learn more of French

people, and was to find that they were something else than mere ludicrous and lively puppets.

A soldier born, with all that is necessary to prove a good one and to become an apt leader, having, as he himself wrote, "resolution to face what any man durst."[1]   Washington rose rapidly in the ranks, becoming a colonel in 1754, at the age of twenty-two.   He was three times sent, in his younger days, to observe, and check if he could, the progress of his future allies, in the Ohio and Monongahela Valleys.   His journal and letters show him animated toward them with the spirit befitting a loyal subject of George II, none of his judgments on them being spoiled by any undue leniency.

On the first occasion he was simply ordered to hand to the commander of a French fort a letter from the governor of Virginia, and to ask him to withdraw as having "invaded the King of Great Britain's territory."   To which the Frenchman, an old officer and Knight of Saint Louis, Mr. de Saint-Pierre, who shortly before had been leading an exploration in the extreme West, toward the Rockies,[2] politely but firmly declined to assent,

[1] "For my own part I can answer I have a constitution hardy enough to encounter and undergo the most severe trials and, I flatter myself, resolution to face what any man durst."   To Governor Dinwiddie, May 29, 1754.

[2] In continuation of the La Verendrie's (father and sons) bold attempt to reach the great Western sea, a token of which, a leaden

writing back to the governor: "I am here by the orders of my general, and I entreat you, sir, not to doubt but that I shall try to conform myself to them with all the exactness and resolution which must be expected from a good officer." He has "much the air of a soldier," Washington wrote of him.

Mr. de Saint-Pierre added, on his part, a word on the bearer of Governor Dinwiddie's message, who was to be the bearer also of his answer, and in this we have the first French comment on Washington's personality: "I made it my particular care to receive Mr. Washington with a distinction suitable to your dignity as well as to his own personal merit.—From the Fort on the Rivière-aux-Bœufs, December 15, 1753." Having received plentiful supplies as a gift from the French, but entertaining the worst misgivings as to their "artifices," the young officer began his return journey, during which, in spite of all trouble, he managed to pay a visit to Queen Aliquippa: "I made her a present," he wrote, "of a match-coat and a bottle of rum, which latter was thought much the best present of the two." On the 16th of January, 1754, he was back at Williamsburg, handed to the governor Mr. de Saint

tablet with a French and Latin inscription and the arms of France, was recently discovered near Fort Pierre, South Dakota. See *South Dakota Historical Collections*, 1914, pp. 89 ff.

Pierre's negative answer, and printed an account of his journey.[1]

The second expedition, a military one, was marked next year by the sad and famous Jumonville incident and by the surrendering, to the brother of dead Jumonville, of Fort Necessity, where the subjects of King George and their youthful colonel, after a fight lasting from eleven in the morning till eight in the evening, had to capitulate, being permitted, however, by the French to withdraw with "full military honors, drum-beating, and taking with them one small piece of ordnance." (July 3, 1754.) The fort and the rest of the artillery remained in the hands of the captors, as well as part of that diary which, although with interruptions, Washington was fond of keeping, whenever he could, his last entry being dated Friday, December 13, 1799, the day before his death. The part found at Fort Necessity—March 31 to June 27, 1754—was sent to Paris, translated into French, printed in 1756 by the royal government,[2] and the text given in Washington's writings is only a retranslation from

---

[1] *The Journal of Major George Washington, sent by the Hon. Robert Dinwiddie, Esq., his Majesty's Lieut.-Governor and Commander in chief of Virginia, to the commandant of the French forces in Ohio.* Williamsburg, 1754.

[2] *Mémoire contenant le précis des faits avec leurs pièces justificatives pour servir de response aux observations envoyées par les ministres d'Angleterre dans les cours d'Europe,* Paris, 1756.

the French, the original English not having been preserved.

The third occasion was the terrible campaign of 1755, which ended in Braddock's death and the defeat of the English regulars on the Monongahela, not far from the newly built Fort Duquesne, later Pittsburgh (July 9). Contrary to expectation[1] (there being "about three hundred French and Indians," wrote Washington; "our numbers consisted of about thirteen hundred well-armed men, chiefly regulars"[2]), the French won the day, nearly doing to death their future commander-in-chief. A rumor was even spread that he had actually succumbed after composing a "dying speech," and Washington had to write to his brother John to assure him that he had had as yet no occasion for such a composition, though very near having had it: "By the all-powerful dispensation of Providence, I have been protected beyond all human probability and expectation; for I had four bullets through my coat, and two horses shot under me, yet escaped unhurt, although death was levelling my companions on every side of me. We have been most scandalously beaten."[3]

[1] "As to any danger from the enemy, I look upon it as triflin
Washington to his brother, John, May 14, 1755.

[2] Washington to Dinwiddie, July 18, 1755.

[3] Same date. Washington revisited the region in October, 1770, but the entries in his journal contain no allusion to previous events:

By an irony of fate, in this expedition against the French, in which George Washington acted as aide-de-camp to the English general, the means of transportation had been supplied by Post-master Benjamin Franklin.

The French were indubitably different from the airy fops of Addison's *Spectator*, but they were as far as ever from commanding young Washington's sympathy. It was part of his loyalism to hate them and to interpret for the worst anything they could do or say. The master of an ampler vocabulary than he is some-times credited with, we find him writing to Rich-ard Washington, in 1757, that the means by which the French maintain themselves in the Ohio Valley are—"hellish."[1]

"We lodged [at Fort Pitt] in what is called the town, about three hundred yards from the fort. . . . These houses, which are built of logs, and ranged into streets, are on the Monongahela, and, I sup-pose, may be twenty in number, and inhabited by Indian traders, etc. The fort is built on the point between the rivers Allegheny and Monongahela, but not so near the pitch of it as Fort Duquesne."

[1] To Richard Washington, merchant, London; from Fort Loudoun, April 15, 1757. The same letter enlightens us as to Washington's tastes concerning things material. He orders "sundry things" to be sent him from London, adding: "Whatever goods you may send me where the prices are not absolutely limited, you will let them be fashionable, neat and good in their several kinds." Same tastes shown in his letter to Robert Cary and Co., ordering a chariot "in the new taste, handsome, genteel, and light," painted preferably green, but in that he would be "governed by fashion." (June 6, 1768.) The chariot was sent in September; it was green, "all the framed work of the body gilt, handsome scrawl, shields, ornamented with flowers all over the panels."

A few years later the tone is greatly altered, not yet toward the French, but toward the British Government and King. In sad, solemn words, full already of the spirit of the Washington of history, he warns his friend and neighbor George Mason, the one who was to draw the first Constitution of Virginia, of the great crisis now looming: "American freedom" is at stake; "it seems highly necessary that something should be done to avert the stroke and maintain the liberty which we have derived from our ancestors. But the manner of doing it, to answer the purpose effectually, is the point in question.

"That no man should scruple or hesitate a moment to use a-ms [*sic*] in defense of so valuable a blessing, on which all the good and evil of life depends, is clearly my opinion. Yet a-ms, I would beg leave to add, should be the last resource, the *dernier resort*." [1] Absolutely firm, absolutely moderate, such was Washington to continue to the end of the impending struggle, and, indeed, of his days. The life of the great Washington was now beginning.

[1] Mount Vernon, April 5, 1765.

II

Some more years elapse, and when the curtain rises again on scenes of war, momentous changes have occurred. To the last hour the former officer of the colonial wars, now a man of forty-two, was still expressing the wish "that the dispute had been left to posterity to determine: but the crisis has arrived when we must assert our rights or submit to every imposition that can be heaped upon us, till custom and use make us as tame and abject slaves as the blacks we rule over with such arbitrary sway." It was hard for him to reconcile himself to the fact that the English were really to be the enemy; he long tried to believe that the quarrel was not with England and her King, but only with the ministry and their troops, which he calls the "ministerials." Writing on the 31st of May, 1775, from Philadelphia, where he was attending the second Continental Congress, to G. W. Fairfax in England, he gave him an account of the clash between the "provincials" of Massachusetts and "the ministerial troops: for we do not, nor can we yet prevail upon ourselves to call them the King's troops." [1]

[1] This continued until the proclamation of independence. By letter of March 19, 1776, Washington notified the President of Con-

The war was to be, in his eyes, a fratricidal one: "Unhappy it is, though, to reflect that a brother's sword has been sheathed in a brother's breast, and that the once happy and peaceful plains of America are either to be drenched with blood or inhabited by slaves. Sad alternative! But can a virtuous man hesitate in his choice?"

Two weeks later the signer of this letter was appointed, on the proposition of John Adams, of Massachusetts, commander-in-chief of a new body of troops just entering history, and called the "Continental Army." [1] Braddock's former aide was to become the leader of a yet unborn nation, in an eight-year conflict with all-powerful Britain, mistress of the coasts, mistress of the seas.

What that conflict was, and what the results have been, all the world knows. There were sad days and bright days; there were Valley Forge and Saratoga. "No man, I believe," Washington

gress of the taking of Boston, and the retreat of the "ministerial army." The flag of the "insurgents" was then the British flag with thirteen white and red stripes, emblematic of the thirteen colonies.

[1] An appointment accepted in a characteristically modest spirit, as shown by his letter to his "dear Patsy," his wife, giving her the news, and that to Colonel Bassett, where he says: "I can answer but for three things, a firm belief in the justice of our cause, close attention in the prosecution of it, and the strictest integrity. If these cannot supply the place of ability and experience, the cause will suffer, and, more than probable, my character along with it, as reputation derives its principal support from success." June 9, 1775.

wrote concerning his own fate, "had a greater choice of difficulties."[1]

The French had ceased by then to inspire Washington with disdain or animosity; he was beginning to render them better justice, but his heart was far as yet from being won. French volunteers had early begun to flock to the American army, some of them as much an encumbrance as a help. "They seem to be genteel, sensible men," wrote Washington to Congress, in October, 1776, "and I have no doubt of their making good officers as soon as they can learn so much of our language as to make themselves well understood." One of them, the commander-in-chief learned, was a young enthusiast who had left wife and child to serve the American cause as a volunteer, and without pay, like George Washington himself. He had crossed the ocean, escaping the British cruisers, on a boat called *La Victoire*, he being called Lafayette. One more encumbrance, audibly muttered the general, who wrote to Benjamin Harrison: "What the designs of Congress respecting this gentleman were, and what line of conduct I am to pursue to comply with their design and his expectation, I know no more than the child unborn, and beg to be instructed."[2]

"Give me a chance," pleaded Lafayette, still

[1] To his brother, John, December 18, 1776.
[2] August 19, 1777.

in Philadelphia; "I do not want to be an honorary soldier." He came to camp, and it was a case of friendship at first, or at least second, sight, which would need the pen of a Plutarch to be told. In August, Washington had been wondering what to do with the newcomer. On the 1st of November he wrote to Congress: ". . . Besides, he is sensible, discreet in his manner, has made great proficiency in our language, and from the disposition he discovered in the battle of Brandywine possesses a large share of bravery and military ardor."

Then it was that Washington had a chance to learn what those men really were who had lodged so many bullets in his coat on the occasion of Braddock's defeat; not at once, but by degrees he came to consider that one peculiar trait in those former enemies made them worthy of his friendship: their aptitude for disinterested enthusiasm for a cherished idea.

Not at once; early prejudices and associations had left on him too deep an imprint to be easily removed. He resisted longer than old Franklin, and with a stiffer pen than that of the Philadelphia sage he would note down his persisting suspicions and his reluctance to admit the possibility of generous motives inspiring the French nation's policy. "I have from the first," he wrote, in 1777, to his brother, John, "been among those few who never built much upon a French war. I never did and still do think they never meant more than to give us a kind of underhand assistance; that is, to supply us with arms, etc., for our money and trade. This may, indeed, if Great Britain has spirit and strength to resent it, bring on a war; but the declaration of it on either side must, I am convinced, come from the last-mentioned Power." It was not, however, to be so.

Even after France alone had recognized the new nation, and she had actually begun war on England, Washington remained unbending, his heart would not melt. "Hatred of England," he wrote, "may carry some into an excess of confidence in France. . . . I am heartily disposed to entertain the most favorable sentiments of our new ally, and to cherish them in others to a reasonable degree. But it is a maxim founded on the universal experience of mankind that no nation is to be trusted farther than it is bound by its interest, and no prudent statesman or politician will venture to depart from it." [1]

After the Declaration of Independence, envoys had been sent to Europe intrusted with the mission of securing the alliance, not especially of France, but of all nations who might be touched by the fate of the struggling colonists and inclined to help them in their fight for liberty. Some of the

[1] November 14, 1778.

envoys were not even admitted to the capitals of the countries assigned to their efforts; others received only good words.

Sent to Prussia, Arthur Lee, who had been previously refused admittance to Madrid, could reach the capital (June 4, 1777), but not the King. "There is no name," Lee wrote appealingly to the monarch, "so highly respected among us as that of your Majesty. Hence there is no King the declaration of whose friendship would inspire our own people with so much courage." But the King would not be persuaded; he refused all help in "artillery, arms, and money," though, Lee wrote to the committee of foreign affairs, "I was well informed he had a considerable sum in his treasury." Frederick would not relent, giving as a reason that, if he agreed, the result would be much "inconvenience" for himself. He even refused to receive Lee, whom he, however, allowed to see his army: a mechanism without peer, the American envoy wrote to Washington, but only a mechanism:

"The Prussian army, which amounts to 220,000 horse and foot, are disciplined by force of hourly exercise and caning to move with a rapidity and order so as to certainly exceed any troops in Europe." They practise each day: "Every man is filed off singly, and passes in review before different officers, who beat his limbs into the posi-

tion they think proper, so that the man appears
to be purely a machine in the hand of a work-
man." [1]

The furthest Frederick consented to go was to
cause Lee to be assured, when he left Prussia the
following month (July, 1777), that he would always receive with pleasure the news of any English reverse.

To the American appeal France alone answered,
Adsum: for what motives, has been shown above,[2]
love of liberty rather than hatred of England
being the chief reason, and the rebellious colonies
being popular in France not so much because they
wanted to throw off an English yoke as because
they wanted to throw off a yoke.

Up to the time when Rochambeau arrived
Washington had seen during the war more or less
numerous specimens of the French race, but only
isolated specimens. He had heard of what they
were doing as soldiers and sailors, without himself seeing them in action. As gentlemen and

[1] To Washington, June 15, 1777. Same impression later (1785)
on Lafayette, who saw the Prussian grand manœuvres, and sent
an account of them to Washington: "The Prussian army is a perfectly regular piece of machinery. . . . All the situations which
may be imagined in war, all the movements which they may cause,
have been by constant habit so well inculcated in their heads that
all those operations are performed almost mechanically." February
8, 1786. *Mémoires, correspondance et manuscrits du Général Lafayette,* Bruxelles, 1838, I, 204.

[2] Pp. 10 ff.

soldiers he held them, at that date, to be fit representatives of a nation "old in war, very strict in military etiquette, and apt to take fire where others scarcely seem warmed." [1] He noticed, however, after Savannah, that with all that warmth they could, when put to the test, prove steady, level-headed, and careful of their words: "While," he said to General Lincoln, "I regret the misfortune, I feel a very sensible pleasure in contemplating the gallant behavior of the officers and men of the French and American army; and it adds not a little to my consolation to learn that, instead of the mutual reproaches which often follow the failure of enterprises depending upon the co-operation of troops of different nations, their confidence in and esteem of each other is increased." [2]

Concerning the French as sailors Washington did not conceal, however, to his intimate friends his misgivings. He early felt that the issue of the whole war and the independence of his country might depend on an at least momentary domination of the sea, but felt great doubt as to the possibility of this goal being reached. "In all probability," he thought, "the advantage will be on the side of the English. And then what would become of America? We ought not

[1] To General Sullivan, September, 1778.
[2] December 12, 1779.

to deceive ourselves. . . . It is an axiom that the nation which has the most extensive commerce will always have the most powerful marine. . . . It is true, France in a manner created a fleet in a very short space, and this may mislead us in the judgment we form of her naval abilities. . . . We should consider what was done by France as a violent and unnatural effort of the government, which for want of sufficient foundation cannot continue to operate proportionable effects." Moreover, though "the ability of her present financier (Necker) has done wonders," France is not a rich country.[1]

When Rochambeau came with his 5,000 troops, on Ternay's fleet, which carried numerous naval officers and sailors besides, Washington took, so to say, personal contact with France herself, and was no longer dependent upon his reading of hostile books, his souvenirs of the colonial wars, or his impression from acquaintanceship with separate individuals. The portraits in the *Spectator* could less and less be considered as portraits. Washington found himself among men of steady mind and courteous manners, noteworthy not only for their fighting qualities, but their sense of duty, their patience and endurance, their desire to do well. As for the troops, they observed, as is well known, so strict a discipline that the in-

[1] To President Reed, May 28, 1780.

habitants, who expected nothing of the sort, rather the reverse, were astonished and delighted.

Little by little Washington's heart was won. We did not, in that war, conquer any land for ourselves, but we conquered Washington. For some time more he remained only officially ours; the praise bestowed by him on his allies and their country found place in his letters to themselves, or in his reports to Congress, which were, in fact, public documents. At last the day came when, writing only for himself, in a journal not meant to be seen by anybody, he inscribed those three words: "our generous allies." That day, May 1, 1781, Washington's heart was really won.

From that moment what Washington wrote concerning the French, were it addressed to themselves or to Congress, can be taken at its face value, and very pleasant reading it is to this day for the compatriots of those officers and soldiers who had the great man for their commander-in-chief—such statements as this one, for example, sent to Congress seven days before the Yorktown capitulation: "I cannot but acknowledge the infinite obligations I am under to his Excellency, the Count de Rochambeau, the Marquis de Saint-Simon, commanding the troops from the West Indies, the other general officers, and indeed the officers of every denomination in the French army, for the assistance which they afford me. The experience of many of those gentlemen in the business before us is of the utmost advantage in the present operation. . . . The greatest harmony prevails between the two armies. They seem actuated by one spirit, that of supporting the honor of the allied armies." [1] When, in the course of the following year, the two armies which have never met since, were about to part, their leader thus summed up his impressions: "It may, I believe, with much truth be said that a greater harmony between two armies never subsisted than that which has prevailed between the French and Americans since the first junction of them last year." [2]

By the beginning of 1783 peace and American independence had been practically secured. Washington is found duly solemnizing the anniversary of the French alliance which had rendered those events possible. "I intended," he says to General Greene, "to have wrote you a long letter on sundry matters, but Major Burnet popped in unexpectedly at a time when I was preparing for the celebration of the day, and was just going to a review of the troops, previous to the *feu de joie*." The orders issued by him on the occasion read thus: "The commander-in-chief, who wishes on

---

[1] "Before York," October 12, 1781.
[2] To Lafayette, October 20, 1782.

the return of this auspicious day to diffuse the feelings of gratitude and pleasure as extensively as possible, is pleased to grant a full and free pardon to all military prisoners now in confinement." [1]

The orderly book used by Washington is still in existence, and from it we learn that the parole given for the day was "America and France," and the countersigns, "United," "Forever."

[1] February 6, 1783.

III

No less characteristic of Washington's sentiments thereafter is the correspondence continued
by him with a number of French people when the
war was a thing of the past and no further help
could be needed. With Rochambeau, with d'Estaing, Chastellux, La Luzerne, then ambassador
in London, whom he had seen with keen regret
leave the United States,[1] and, of course, with
Lafayette, he kept up a correspondence which
affords most pleasant reading: a friend writes to
his friends and tells them of his feelings and ex-
pectations. The attitude of France at the peace
is the subject of a noble letter to La Luzerne:
"The part your Excellency has acted in the cause
of America and the great and benevolent share
you have taken in the establishment of her independence are deeply impressed on my mind, and
will not be effaced from my remembrance, or that

[1] Sending him a farewell letter in which he said: "You may rest
assured that your abilities and dispositions to serve this country
were so well understood, and your service so properly appreciated
that the residence of no public minister will ever be longer remembered
or his absence more sincerely regretted. It will not be forgotten
that you were a witness to the dangers, the sufferings, the exertions
and the successes of the United States from the most perilous crises
to the hour of triumph." February 7, 1788.

of the citizens of America. . . . The articles of
the general treaty do not appear so favorable to
France, in point of territorial acquisitions, as
they do to the other Powers.[1] But the magnani-
mous and disinterested scale of action which that
great nation has exhibited to the world during
this war, and at the conclusion of peace, will
insure to the King and nation that reputation
which will be of more consequence to them than
every other consideration." [2]

Washington keeps his French friends aware of
the progress of the country and of his hopes for
its greatness; he wants to visit the United States
to the limit of what was then the extreme West.
"Prompted by these actual observations," he
writes to Chastellux, "I could not help taking a
more contemplative and extensive view of the
vast inland navigation of these United States
from maps and the information of others, and
could not but be struck with the immense diffusion
and importance of it, and with the goodness of
that Providence which has dealt her favors to us
with so profuse a hand. . Would to God we may
have wisdom enough to improve them. I shall
not rest contented till I have explored the Western

[1] They merely sanctioned some territorial exchanges and restitu-
tions on both sides in the colonies, and stipulated that the British
agent in Dunkirk, who had been expelled at the beginning of the war,
would not return.
[2] March 29, 1783.

country and traversed those lines, or great part
of them, which have given new bounds to a new
empire."[1]   To La Luzerne he wrote some years
later: "The United States are making great progress toward national happiness, and if it is not
attained here in as high a degree as human nature
will admit of, I think we may then conclude that
political happiness is unattainable."[2]

That rest for which Washington had been longing ("I pant for retirement," he had written to
Cary in June, 1782) had been granted him by
the end of 1783, when, the definitive treaty having
been concluded, he had resigned his commission
in the hands of Congress, at Annapolis on the
23d of December, "bidding an affectionate farewell," he said, "to this august body under whose
orders I have so long acted."   It was at first
difficult for him to enjoy, in his dear Mount Vernon, that so-much-desired quiet life, and "to get
the better," he wrote to General Knox, "of my
custom of ruminating as soon as I waked in the
morning on the business of the ensuing day, and
of my surprise at finding, after revolving many
things in my mind, that I was no longer a public
man, nor had anything to do with public transactions."   But he soon came to the thorough en-

[1] Princeton, October 12, 1783. He started for that journey the
following autumn.
[2] September 10, 1791.

joyment of his peaceful surroundings and happy family life, writing about his new existence to Rochambeau and Lafayette, not without a tinge of melancholy, as from one whose life's work is a thing of the past. To the man of all men for whom his manly heart felt most tenderness, to Lafayette, it is that he wrote the beautiful letter of February 1, 1784, unaware that his rest was only temporary, and that he was to become the first President of the country he had given life to:

"At length, my dear marquis, I am become a private citizen on the banks of the Potomac, and under the shadow of my own vine and my own fig-tree, free from the bustle of a camp and the busy scenes of public life, I am solacing myself with those tranquil enjoyments of which the soldier who is ever in pursuit of fame, the statesman whose watchful days and sleepless nights are spent in devising schemes to promote the welfare of his own, perhaps the ruin of other countries, as if the globe was insufficient for us all . . . can have very little conception. I have not only retired from all public employments, but I am retiring within myself, and shall be able to view the solitary walk of private life with heartfelt satisfaction. Envious of none, I am determined to be pleased with all; and this, my dear friend, being the order for my march, I will move gently down the stream of life until I sleep with my fathers."

With Lafayette the great man unbends, he becomes affectionate, poetical as in the passage just quoted, sometimes even jocose, which was so rare with him. He wants Madame de Lafayette to come to America and visit Mount Vernon, saying to her: "Your own doors do not open to you with more readiness than mine would." [1] She never came, but her husband returned for a few months, the same year, and this was the first of his two triumphant journeys to the freed United States; it was then that he parted at Annapolis from his chief, never to see him again; a very sad parting for both, Washington sending him from Mount Vernon, in time for it to reach him before he sailed, the most touching, perhaps, of all his letters:

"In the moment of our separation, upon the road as I travelled, and every hour since, I have felt all that love, respect, and attachment for you which length of years, close connection, and your merits have inspired me. I often asked myself, when our carriages separated, whether that was the last sight I should ever have of you. And though I wished to say, no, my fears answered, yes. I called to mind the days of my youth and found they had long since fled, to return no more;

[1] Mount Vernon, April 4, 1784.

that I was now descending the hill I had been fifty-two years climbing, and that, though I was blessed with a good constitution, I was of a short-lived family and might soon expect to be entombed in the mansion of my fathers. These thoughts darkened the shades and gave a gloom to the picture, and consequently to my prospect of seeing you again. But I will not repine; I have had my day."[1]

A portrait of Lafayette, his wife, and children was received the following year by Washington, and caused him great pleasure; this, he said to the sender, "I consider as an invaluable present and shall give it the best place in my house."[2]

He continued to the end to be Lafayette's confidant and adviser. In one of his most notable letters, passing judgment on the great warrior Frederick II and on his brother, Prince Henry, whom Lafayette had recently visited, he clearly outlined what should be his correspondent's ideal as to the government of men. "To be received," he says, "by the King of Prussia and Prince Henry, his brother (who as soldiers and politicians yield the palm to none), with such marks of attention and distinction, was as indicative of their discernment as it is of your merit. . . . It is to be lamented, however, that great characters

[1] December 8, 1784. Bayard Tuckerman, *Lafayette*, 1889, I, 165.
[2] July 25, 1785.

are seldom without a blot. That one man should
tyrannize over millions will always be a shade in
that of the former, while it is pleasing to hear
that due regards to the rights of mankind is characteristic of the latter."

. During those years of comparative rest—only
comparative, for he had to receive innumerable
visitors, to answer an unbelievable quantity of
letters, because everybody wanted his counsels,
to take part in the framing of the Constitution
as a delegate of Virginia in 1787—his fame went
on increasing in France from whence tokens of
admiration came for him of every kind, some noble,
some simple, some high-flown, like that letter
from the Chevalier de Lormerie, who made bold
to "present a *Plan of Perpetual Peace* to a general
who is even more of a philosopher than a warrior."[1]

Besides letters, French visitors would now and
then appear at the door of Mount Vernon. One
did so by appointment, and even in virtue of a
law, namely Jean Antoine Houdon, the famous
sculptor, whose coming was the result of an act
passed by the Assembly of Virginia, prescribing
"that the executive be requested to take measures
for procuring a statue of General Washington, to

[1] "Excellence, Vos vertus civiles et vos talents militaires ont donné
à votre patrie la liberté et le bonheur; mais leur influence sur celui
du globe entier est encore préférable à mes yeux. C'est à ce grand
but que tend tout homme qui se sent digne d'arriver à l'immortalité,"
etc. May 28, 1789. Papers of the Continental Congress, LXXVIII,
759, Library of Congress.

be of the finest marble and the best workman-
ship."

The sculptor might be of any nationality, provided he were the best alive. "The intention of
the Assembly," the Governor informed Jefferson,
then in Paris, "is that the statue should be the
work of the most masterly hand. I shall therefore
leave it to you to find out the best in any of the
European states."[1]   Once more it was France's
good fortune to be able to answer, *Adsum.*

The "executive," Governor Harrison, not over-
well versed in matters artistic, had thought that
all a sculptor could need to perform his task was
a painted portrait of the model, so he ordered one
from Peale, which would, he thought, enable the
artist "to finish his work in the most perfect
manner."[2] Houdon decided that he would rather
undertake the journey, insisting only that, as he
was the support of his father, mother, and sisters,
his life be insured, a condition which, owing to
the risks, was not fulfilled without difficulty. It
finally was, however, so that we know, to a cent,
what the life of the great sculptor was worth: it
was worth two thousand dollars.

Houdon came on the same ship which brought

[1] June 22, 1784. *Jean Antoine Houdon*, by C. H. Hart and Ed.
Biddle, Philadelphia, 1911, p. 182.

[2] *Ibid.*, p. 189. Peale's full-length portrait, with "a perspective
view of York and Gloucester, and the surrender of the British army,"
price thirty guineas, reached Paris in April, 1785, and has since
disappeared.

back Franklin after his long mission to France,
and he reached Mount Vernon on October 2,
1785, having been preceded by a letter, in which
Jefferson had thus described him to Washington:
"I have spoken of him as an artist only, but I
can assure you also that, as a man, he is disinterested, generous, candid, and panting for glory;
in every circumstance meriting your good opinion."[1]   He remained at Mount Vernon a fortnight,
an interpreter having been provided from Alexandria for the occasion. The antique costume
with which the artist and the model had been
threatened at one time was discarded; Washington was represented, not as a Greek, which he
was not, but as an American general, which he
was, the size being "precisely that of life." Any
one who wants to see with his eyes George Washington, to live in his atmosphere, to receive the
moral benefit of a great man's presence, has only
to go to Richmond. To those who know how to
listen the statue will know how to speak. No
work of art in the whole United States is of
greater worth and interest than this one, and no
copy gives an adequate idea of the original, copies
being further from the statue than the statue was
from the model. One must go to Richmond.

Unfortunately, no notes on his journey, and on
his stay at Mount Vernon, were left by Houdon.

[1] July 10, 1785. *Ibid.*, p. 191.

As was usual with him, what he had to say he said in marble.

Other French visitors of more or less note called at Mount Vernon. Popular in France, even at the time of their worst troubles, when failure seemed threatening, the United States were much more so now, and men wanted to go and see with their own eyes what was the power of liberty, and whether it could, as reported, transform a country into an Eden, and cities into modern "Salentes." The year of the alliance, 1778, Sébastien Mercier, in his *De la Littérature*, had drawn up a picture of the French people's expectation: "Perhaps it is in America that the human race will transform itself, adopt a new and sublime religion, improve sciences and arts, and become the representative of the nations of antiquity. A haven of liberty, Grecian souls, all strong and generous souls will develop or meet there, and this great example given to the universe will show what men can do when they are of one mind and combine their lights and their courage." Turgot, as mentioned before, had written in the same strain, the same year.[1]

The results of the war had increased those hopes; the success of the unprecedented crusade for liberty caused an enthusiasm which found its expression in verse and prose. The very year of

[1] Above, p. 12.

the treaty securing independence an epic poem was published, written in French Alexandrine verse, divided into cantos, adorned with all the machinery of the Greek models, Jupiter and the gods playing their part:

Ainsi parla des Dieux le monarque suprême

—with invocations to abstract virtues:

Fille aimable des Dieux, divine Tolérance.

Preceding by several years Joel Barlow's own, this epic, due to the pen of L. de Chavannes de La Grandière, appeared with ample annotations by the author himself, and dedicated to John Adams, under the title of *L'Amérique Délivrée*.[1]

The new Tasso, who justly foresaw the immense influence that the change in America would have on Europe, addressed, in tones of the most ardent admiration, Washington and Congress:

Illustre Washington, héros dont la mémoire
Des deux mondes vengés embellira l'histoire;
Toi que la main des Dieux, en nos siècles pervers,
Envoya consoler, étonner l'univers
Par le rare assemblage et l'union constante
D'un cœur pur et sans fard, d'une âme bienfaisante,
Aux talents de Turenne, aux vertus des Catons,
Et qui te vois plus grand que les deux Scipions,
Jouis de ton triomphe, admire ton ouvrage.

[1] Amsterdam, 1783. The author is strongly anti-English and is indignant at the "guilty Anglomania" still existing in France.

Congress is a Greek Areopagus, whose members have Themis and Minerva for their advisers:

> Auguste Aréopage, où Minerve elle-même
> Prononce avec Thémis par l'organe suprême
> De tant de Sénateurs, ornements des Etats,
> Une foule d'arrêts où tous les potentats
> Du droit des nations devraient venir apprendre
> Les principes sacrés, et jusqu'où peut s'étendre
> Le sceptre qu'en leurs mains les peuples ont commis,

—you have cast on us "a torrent of light and shown us how to break the detestable bonds of tyrants." A prophetical foot-note, commenting on this passage, announces that "this will per- haps, be seen sooner than one thinks. Happy the sovereigns who will know how to be nothing but just, pacific, and benevolent." Six years later the French Revolution began.

Using humble prose, but reaching a much wider public, Lacretelle, of the same group of thinkers as d'Alembert, Condorcet, and Turgot, himself later a member of the French Academy, was also writing in a strain of exultant admiration: "Since Columbus's discovery, nothing more important has happened among mankind than American in- dependence"; and addressing the new-born United States, he told them of the world's expectation and of their own responsibilities, so much depend- ing on their success or failure: "New-born Re-

publics of America, I salute you as the hope of
mankind, to which you open a refuge, and promise
great and happy examples. Grow in force and
numbers, amid our benedictions. . . .

"In adopting a democratic régime, you pledge
yourself to steadfast and pure morality. . . .
But you do not give up those comforts in life,
that splendor of society brought with them by
riches, sciences, and arts. . . . The vicinity of
corruption will not alter your morals; you will
allow the vicinity, not the invasion. While per-
mitting wealth to have its free play, you will see
that exorbitant fortunes be dispersed, and you
will correct the great inequality in enjoyments
by the strictest equality in rights. . . .

"Lawmaking peoples, never lose sight of the
majesty of your function and of the importance
of your task. Be nobly proud and holily enthusiastic at the prospect of your destinies' vast influence. By you the universe is held in expectation;
fifty years from now it will have learned from you
whether modern peoples can preserve republican
constitutions, whether morals are compatible with
the great progress of civilization, and whether
America is meant to improve or to aggravate the
fate of humanity." [1]

---

[1] In the *Mercure de France*, 1785, prefacing a review of Crèvecœur's
Letters from an American Farmer, and reproduced at the beginning of
the French edition of the *Letters*, 1787.

This sense of the responsibility of the new republic toward mankind of the future, and of the importance for all nations of its success or failure caused French thinkers to concern themselves with the problem, to express faith and admiration, but to submit also such recommendations as their studies of humanity's past made them consider of use. The *Observations on the Government and the Laws of the United States*, of modest, liberal, and noble-minded Abbé de Mably, are, for example, the outcome of such reflections.[1]

The visitor most representative of the views thus prevalent in the French nation, knocked at the gate of Mount Vernon, provided with that infallible *open sesame*,[2] a letter of introduction from Lafayette. "This gentleman," the letter read, "intends to write a history of America, and you would, therefore, make him very happy if

[1] *Observations sur le gouvernement et les loix des Etats Unis d'Amérique*, Amsterdam, 1784, 12mo; in the form of letters to John Adams. The Constitutions under discussion are those of the original States. "Tandis," says Mably, "que presque toutes les nations de l'Europe ignorent les principes constitutifs de la société et ne regardent les citoyens que comme les bestiaux d'une ferme qu'on gouverne pour l'avantage particulier du propriétaire, on est étonné, on est édifié que vos treize Républiques ayent connu à la fois la dignité de l'homme et soient allé puiser dans les sources de la plus sage philosophie les principes humains par lesquels elles veulent se gouverner." (P. 2.)

[2] Wanting, on his return to America, to make Washington's acquaintance, Franklin's own grandson called similarly provided. Lafayette to Washington, warmly praising the young man, July 14, 1785. *Mémoires, correspondance et manuscrits du Général Lafayette, publiés par sa Famille*, Brussels, 1837, I, 201.

you allowed him to glance at your papers.   He
seems to deserve this favor, since he loves America
very much, writes well, and will represent things
under their true light." [1]

The bearer, a sincere admirer and friend of
the new republic, and who had the advantage of
speaking English fluently, was Brissot, so famous
shortly after for the part he played in the French
Revolution, then already penetrated with its principles, and having written, young as he was, on
the reform of criminal laws, declared in favor
of the emancipation of the Jews, founded a
"Society of the Friends of the Blacks " and, what
is more to the point, a *Société Gallo-Américaine*,
first of its kind, for the members thereof to "exchange views on the common interests of France
and the United States."   To become a member
one had to prove "able and willing to bring to the
notice of the others universal ideas on the happiness of man and societies, because, though its
special and titular object be the interest of France
and the United States, nevertheless, it fully embraces in its considerations the happiness of mankind." [2]   In which appears the vastness of humanitarian plans so fondly cherished among us—
six years before the Reign of Terror.

[1] May 25, 1788.   J. P. Brissot, *Correspondance et Papiers*, ed.
Perroud, Paris, 1912, p. 192.
[2] 1787.   Text of the reports of the sittings.   *Ibid.*, pp. 105 ff.

The "particular object" of the association was, however, to "help the two countries to better know each other, which can only be realized by bringing nearer together the French individual and the American individual." Books were to be published by the society, the first one to be dedicated "to the Congress of the United States and the friends of America in the two worlds." Newspapers, books, the texts of laws, the journals of Congress were to be imported from "free America." The society would "welcome Americans whom their business should call to France, and whose knowledge would enable them to impart useful information there"; nothing more natural, since the aim of the society was "the welfare of the two nations." Lafayette and Jefferson had been asked to join. One of the founders was Saint-Jean de Crèvecœur, already known by his *Letters from an American Farmer*, who when he left France to return to the United States was intrusted with the care of "making the society known to the Americans, availing himself of newspapers, or of other means; his expenses, if any, to be repaid."[1] But the farmer-consul, very active in other matters, proved in this one very remiss.

Brissot reached Boston in July, 1788, and found that America was exactly what he had ex-

[1] *Ibid.*, pp. 114, 116, 126, 127, 136.

pected it to be: "Sanctuary of liberty," he wrote
on landing, "I salute thee ! . . .   Would to heaven
thou wert nearer Europe; fewer friends of liberty
would vainly bewail its absence there."   The inhabitants, he wrote, "have an air of simplicity
and kindness, but they are full of human dignity,
conscious of their liberty, and seeing in all men
their brothers and equals. . . .   I thought I was
in that Salente, so attractively depicted by
Fénelon."

Equality is what strikes him most, as it does the
mass of his compatriots; this was the particularly
American trait which, as mentioned before, was
imported from the United States into France on
the eve of our Revolution.

Luxury, the visitor admits, is, of course, a
danger; but they know it and arm against it:
"The most respectable inhabitants of the State
of Massachusetts have formed a society to prevent the increase of luxury"—an attempt which,
however, never succeeded, but at Salente.

After having seen the chief cities and paid a
visit to Franklin, found very ill but with his
great mind unimpaired, Brissot reached Mount
Vernon in November, and remained there three
days.   Different from Houdon, he luckily took
notes on the place and on the inhabitants thereof:
"The general arrived only in the evening; he returned very tired from a tour over part of his

domains where he was having a road traced.
You have often heard him compared to Cincinnatus; the comparison is a just one. This
celebrated general is now but a good farmer, ever
busy with his farm, as he calls it, improving cul-
tivation and building barns. He showed me one
of enormous dimensions, just being erected from
a plan sent him by the famous English agricul-
turist Arthur Young, but greatly improved by
him. . . .

"All is simple in the house of the general. His
table is good, without luxury; regularity is everywhere apparent in his domestic economy. Mrs.
Washington has her eye on everything, and joins
to the qualities of an excellent housekeeper the
simple dignity which befits a woman whose husband has played a great rôle. She adds to it
that amenity, those attentions toward strangers
which lend so much sweetness to hospitality.
The same virtues shine in her niece, so interesting, but who, unluckily, seems to be in a very
delicate state of health."

As for the general himself, "kindness appears
in his looks. His eyes have no longer that lustre
which his officers noticed when he was at the head
of his army, but they get enlivened in conversation. . . . Good sense is the dominant trait in
in all his answers, great discretion and diffidence
of himself goes with it, and at the same time a

firm and unshakable disposition when he has once
made up his mind."

His modesty is great: "He talks of the American
war as if he had not been the leader thereof, and
of his victories with an indifference which strangers
could not equal. . . . The divisions in his country break his heart; he feels the necessity of calling together all the friends of liberty around one
central point, the need of imparting energy to
the government. He is still ready to give up
that quiet which causes his happiness. . . . He
spoke to me of Mr. de Lafayette with emotion;
he considers him as his child."

Not only on agriculture and government, but
also on manners the future President gave his
visitor much information: "The general told me
that a great reform was going on among his compatriots; people drank much less; they no longer
forced their guests to drink; it had ceased to be
good form to send them home inebriated; those
noisy parties at taverns so frequent in former
times were not to be the fashion any more; dress
was becoming simpler."

On receiving news of the convocation of the
French States General, Brissot, who felt that this
was the beginning of immense changes, hastened
back to France and published an account of his
journey. He stated in his preface, written in
1790, why he had undertaken it, and what lessons

we might learn from our neighbors of over the sea:

"The object of this journey has not been to study antique statues, or to find unknown plants, but to observe men who had just conquered their liberty: to Frenchmen free men can no longer be strangers.

"We, too, have conquered our liberty. We have not to learn from Americans how to conquer it, but how to preserve it. This secret consists especially in morality. . . . What is liberty? It is the most perfect state of society, a state in which man depends only upon the laws made by himself;[1] and to make good ones, he must improve his reason; and to apply them he must again have recourse to his reason. . . . Morals are but reason applied to all the acts of life. . . . They are among free men what irons, whipping-posts, and gibbets are among peoples in slavery. . . . This journey will show you the wondrous effects of liberty on morals, on industry, and on the amelioration of men. . . . My desire has been to depict to my compatriots a people with whom it behooves, from every point of view, that they become intimately united."[2]

[1] "Under that name of liberty the Romans, as well as the Greeks, pictured to themselves a state where no one was subject save to the law, and where law was more powerful than men." (Bossuet.)

[2] *Nouveau Voyage dans les Etats Unis de l'Amérique Septentrionale*, Paris, 3 vols., April, 1791, but begun to be printed, as shown

by a note to the preface, in the spring of 1790. The work greatly
helped to make America better and very favorably known in Europe,
for it was translated into English, German, and Dutch. While
Brissot was returning to France (January, 1789), his brother-in-law,
François Dupont, was sailing for the United States, to settle there
among free men and, scarcely landed, was writing to a Swiss friend
of his, Jeanneret, who lived in Berlin, of his delight at having left
"a small continent like that of Europe, partitioned among a quantity of petty sovereigns bent upon capturing each other's possessions, causing their subjects to slaughter one another, in ceaseless
mutual fear, busy tightening their peoples' chains and impoverishing
them—and I am now on a continent which reaches from pole to
pole, with every kind of climate and of productions, among an independent nation which is now devising for itself, in the midst of
peace, the wisest of governments. We are not governed here by
a foolish or despotic sovereign. . . . Farmers, craftsmen, merchants,
and manufacturers are encouraged and honored; they are the true
nobles. . . . Between the man who sells his labor and the one
who buys it the agreement is between equals. The French are,
however, very popular in this country." Brissot, *Correspondance*,
ed. Perroud, pp. 218, 219.

IV

During the early stages of the French Revolution, Washington had followed with the keenest sympathy and anxiety the efforts of our ancestors, taking pride in the thought that the American example had something to do, as it undoubtedly had, with what was happening. "The young French nobility enrolled for the cause of [American] independence," wrote Talleyrand in his memoirs, "attached itself afterward to the principles it had gone to fight for." Pontgibaud, who remained a royalist, who hated the Revolution and became an *émigré*, observes the same fact, although deploring what occurred: "The officers of Count de Rochambeau had nothing better to do [after Yorktown], I believe, than to visit the country. When one thinks of the false ideas of government and philanthrophy with the virus of which these youths were infected in America, and which they were to enthusiastically propagate in France, with such lamentable success—since that mania for imitation has powerfully helped toward the Revolution, without being its unique cause—people will agree that all those red-heeled young philosophers had much better, for their sake and ours, have stayed at court. . . . Each of them fancied he would be called upon to play the part of Washington." Asked to join Lafayette and "his former brothers-in-arms of beyond the sea," he refused: "It has been justly said that in a revolution the difficulty lies not in doing one's duty, but in knowing where it is. I did mine because I knew where it was," and he joined the princes and emigrated.[1]

Of this American influence Washington was aware, and spoke, as may be surmised, in terms nearer those of Talleyrand than those of Pontgibaud. "I am glad to hear," he wrote to Jefferson, "that the *Assemblée des Notables* has been productive of good in France. . . . Indeed the rights of mankind, the privileges of the people, and the true principles of liberty seem to have been more generally discussed and better understood throughout Europe since the American Revolution than they were at any former period."[2]

Few of Washington's observations are a greater credit to him, as a statesman, than those concerning this extraordinary upheaval. From the first he felt that the change would not prove a merely local one, but would have world-wide consequences; that, in fact, a new era was beginning for mankind. "A spirit for political improve-

---

[1] *Mémoires du [Chevalier de Pontgibaud] Comte de Moré*, 1827, pp. 105, 132. Writing at that date, Lafayette's former companion thought that monarchy had been re-established in France forever.

[2] January 1, 1788.

ments seems to be rapidly and extensively spreading through the European countries," he wrote to La Luzerne. "I shall rejoice in seeing the condition of the human race happier than ever it has been." But let the people at the helm be careful not to make "more haste than good speed in their innovations."[1]

No less clearly did he foresee, long before the event, and when all was hope and rejoicing, that it was almost impossible to count upon a peaceful, gradual, and bloodless development where so many long-established, hatred-sowing abuses had to be corrected. This, however, was what, as a friend of France, he would have liked to see, and even before the Revolution had really started he had expressed to Lafayette, in striking words, his wish that it might prove a "tacit" one: "If I were to advise, I should say that great moderation should be used on both sides. . . . Such a spirit seems to be awakened in the kingdom as, if managed with extreme prudence, may produce a gradual and tacit revolution, much in favor of the subjects."[2]

The movement is started, the Bastile falls, and Lafayette sends the key thereof to his former chief. "It is a tribute," he wrote, "which I owe as a son to my adopted father, as an aide-de-camp to my general, as a missionary of liberty to

[1] New York, April 29, 1790.   [2] June 18, 1788.

its patriarch." Washington placed the key at Mount Vernon, where it is still, and returned thanks for this "token of victory gained by liberty over despotism." [1]

The beginnings were promising. The great leader was full of admiration, of awe, of apprehension. To Gouverneur Morris, then American minister to France, President Washington, as he now was, wrote on the 13th of October, 1789, in these prophetic terms: "The Revolution which has been effected in France is of so wonderful a nature that the mind can hardly realize the fact. If it ends as our last accounts to the 1st of August predict, that nation will be the most powerful and happy in Europe; but I fear, though it has gone triumphantly through the first paroxysm, it is not the last it has to encounter before matters are finally settled. In a word, the Revolution is of too great a magnitude to be effected in so short a space, and with the loss of so little blood. The mortification of the King, the intrigues of the Queen, and the discontent of the princes and the noblesse will foment divisions, if possible, in the National Assembly." The "licentiousness of the people" is not less to be feared. "To forbear running from one ex-

---

[1] March 17, 1790; August 11, 1790. The key is the one which gave access to the main entrance; those at the Carnavalet Museum in Paris opened the several towers.

treme to the other is no easy matter; and should this be the case, rocks and shoals, not visible at present, may wreck the vessel."[1]

The grandeur and importance of the change fills him, in the meanwhile, with wonder. In his before-quoted letter of April 29, 1790, to La Luzerne he said: "Indeed, the whole business is so extraordinary in its commencement, so wonderful in its progress, and may be so stupendous in its consequences that I am almost lost in the contemplation. Of one thing, however, you may rest perfectly assured, that nobody is more anxious for the happy issue of that business than I am, as nobody can wish more sincerely for the prosperity of the French nation than I do." To another correspondent, Mrs. Graham, he described "the renovation of the French Constitution," as "one of the most wonderful events in the history of mankind." So late as the 20th of October, 1792, he was writing to Gouverneur Morris: "We can only repeat the sincere wish that much happiness may arise to the French nation and to mankind in general out of the severe evils which are inseparable from so important a revolution."

[1] To this remarkable forecast of the Terror, and of the ruin of such great hopes, Jared Sparks, in his edition of the *Writings*, caused Washington to add a prophecy of Napoleon's rule, described as a "higher-toned despotism than the one which existed before." But this is one of the embellishments which Sparks, who prophesied *à coup sûr*, since he wrote after the events, thought he was free to introduce in the great man's letters.

Throughout the unparalleled crisis, the French friends of Washington kept him informed of events, of their hopes and fears. Lafayette's letters have been printed; those of Rochambeau, written in his own English, have not, and many of them are of great interest. The French general had early foreseen the necessity for profound changes, owing to abuses, to the excessive privileges of the few, the burdens of the many, the increasing maladministration, especially since Necker had been replaced by "a devil of fool named Calonne."[1] Maybe the States General will provide an adequate remedy, by devising a constitution: "I hope very much of this General States to restore our finances and to consolidate a good constitution."[2] But he has doubts as to what "aristocratical men" will do.

Himself a member of the Assembly, Rochambeau considers that there are not, in reality, three orders—the nobles, the clergy, and the third estate—but two: "the privileged people and the unprivileged." The vote being, in accordance with law and custom, taken per estate or order, the two privileged ones always vote in the same way and can ever prevail. Rochambeau informs Washington that, as for himself, he "voted in favor of the equal representation of the third

[1] Paris, May 12, 1787. Washington papers, Library of Congress.
[2] Calais, April 3, 1789.

order; your pupil Lafayette has voted for the
same opinion, as you may believe it; but we have
here a great number of aristocratical men that
are very interested to perpetuate the abuses." [1]

He agrees with Washington that, in order to
reach safe results, developments should be slowly
evolved; but the temper of the nation has been
wrought up, and it is, moreover, a fiery temper.
"Do you remember, my dear general," he writes,
"of the first repast that we have made together
at Rod-Island? I [made] you remark from the
soup the difference of character of our two nations, the French in burning their throat and all
the Americans waiting wisely [for] the time that
it was cooled. I believe, my dear general, you
have seen, since a year, that our nation has not
change[d] of character. We go very fast—God
will that we [reach] our aims." [2]

In his moments of deepest anxiety Rochambeau
is pleased, however, to remember "a word of the
late King of Prussia," Frederick II, who, considering what France was, what misfortunes and
dangers she had encountered, and what concealed
sources of strength were in her, once said to the
French minister accredited to him: "I have been
brought up in the middle of the unhappiness of
France; my cradle was surrounded with refugee

[1] Paris, July 31, 1789.
[2] "Rochambeau near Vendôme," April 11, 1790.

Protestants that, about the end of the reign of
Louis XIV and the beginning of the regency of
the Duc d'Orleans, told me that France was at
the agony and could not exist three years. I
[have] known in the course of my reign that
France has such a temper that there [is] no bad
minister nor bad generals [who] be able to kill it,
and that constitution has made it rise again of
all its crises, with strength and vigor. It wants
no other remedy but time and keep a strict course
of diet." [1]

Events followed their course, but, while everything else was changing in France, the feeling for
Washington and the United States remained the
same. The two countries felt nearer than before,
and showed it in many ways. At the death of
Franklin the National Assembly, on the proposal
of Mirabeau, went into mourning for three days;
our first Constitution, of 1791, was notified to
the American Government: "President Washington," the French minister informed his chief,
"received the King's letter with the tokens of
the greatest satisfaction; and in accordance with
your orders a copy of the Constitution and of
the King's letter to the National Assembly was
given to him as well as to Mr. Jefferson." [2] Tom

[1] Paris, May 12, 1787.
[2] Ternant to Montmorin, Philadelphia, March 13, 1792. *Correspondence of the French Ministers*, ed. Turner, Washington, 1904.

Paine, though an American, or rather because an American, was elected by several departments a member of the Convention, took his seat, but, as he knew no French, had his speeches translated and read for him; he played an important part in the drafting of our second Constitution, the republican one of 1793. As a sacred emblem of liberty, the American flag was displayed in the hall where the Convention held its sittings. A quite extraordinary decree was rendered by this body in the second year of the Republic, "after having heard the petition of American citizens," deciding, and this at a time when everybody was liable to arrest, that "the wives of American citizens, whatever the place of their birth, should be exempted from the law on the arrestation of foreigners."

The 14th of July was, in the meantime, celebrated in America, just as in France, as marking a new progress in the development of mankind. Our minister, Ternant, gave Dumouriez a glowing account of such a celebration: "It affords me great satisfaction to inform you that, in spite of the news received the day before of the bad success of our first military operations, the Americans have given, on the occasion of this anniversary, touching signs of their attachment for France and proof of the interest they take in the success of our arms. You will see by the

bulletins and newspapers accompanying this letter
that the same sentiments have been manifested
in almost all the cities which count in the Union,
and that the 14th has been celebrated with the
same ardor as the 4th, which is the anniversary
of American independence." [1]

For the person of the President French tokens
of veneration and friendship multiplied. In the
same year—year I of the Republic—the Convention had conferred on him the title of French
citizen, as being "one of the benefactors of
mankind." French officers had united to offer
Mrs. Washington a dinner service, each piece
ornamented with a star and her initials in the
centre, and the names of the States in medal-
lions around the border, the whole surrounded
by a serpent biting its tail, the emblem of per-
petuity.

French dramatists could not wait until the
great man should belong to the past to make of
him the hero of a tragedy in Alexandrine verse:
*Vashington ou la Liberté du Nouveau Monde, par
M. de Sauvigny*, performed for the first time in
the Theatre of the Nation (as the "Comédie Française" was then called), on the 13th of July, 1791,
and in which a nameless predecessor of mine,
"l'Ambassadeur de France," brought the play
to a conclusion with praise of Washington, of

[1] July 28, 1792.

Franklin, of Congress, and of the whole American people:

> Magistrats dont l'audace étonna l'univers,
> Calmes dans la tempête et grands dans les revers,
> Vous sûtes, par l'effet d'une sage harmonie,
> Enfanter des vertus, un peuple, une patrie.

And in a kind of postcript, the author, commenting on the events related in his play, observed with truth: "The great American Revolution has been the first result of one greater still which had taken place in the empire of opinion." Of any animosity against the English, the same comment offers no trace.

Gloomy days succeeded radiant ones. Past abuses, danger from abroad, general suffering, passions let loose, were not conducive to that coolness and moderation which Washington had recommended from the first. Ternant, had been succeeded as representative of France by that famous citizen Genet, who, in spite of his having some diplomatic experience gathered as Chargé d'Affaires in Russia, and being in a way a man of parts, an authority on Swedes and Finns, had his head turned the moment he landed, so completely, indeed, that it is impossible, in spite of the gravity of the consequences involved, not to smile when reading his high-flown, self-complacent, self-advertising, beaming despatches: "My journey (from

Charleston to Philadelphia) has been an uninter-
rupted succession of civic festivities, and my entry
in Philadelphia a triumph for liberty. True
Americans are at the height of joy."[1]

In his next letters he insists and gloats over
his own matchless deeds: "The whole of America
has risen to acknowledge in me the minister of
the French Republic. . . . I live in the midst
of perpetual feasts; I receive addresses from all
parts of the continent. I see with pleasure that
my way of negotiating pleases our American
brothers, and I am founded to believe, citizen
minister, that my mission will be a fortunate
one from every point of view. I include here-
with American gazettes in which I have marked
the articles concerning myself."

Encouraged by the Anti-Federalists, who
thought they could use him for their own purposes, Genet shows scant respect for "old Washington, who greatly differs from him whose name
has been engraved by history, and who does not
pardon me my successes"; a mere "Fayettist," he
disdainfully calls him elsewhere. But Genet will
have the better of any such opposition: "I am
in the meantime provisioning the West Indies, I
excite Canadians to break the British yoke, I
arm the Kentukois, and prepare a naval expedi-

[1] Philadelphia, May 18, 1793. *Correspondence of the French Ministers in the United States*, ed. Turner, Washington, 1904, p. 214.

tion which will facilitate their descent on New Orleans."[1]

He had, in fact, armed in American waters, quite a fleet of corsairs, revelling in the bestowal on them of such names as the *Sans-Culotte*, the *Anti-George*, the *Patriote Genet*, the *Vainqueur de la Bastille*, *La Petite Démocrate*.

His triumphs, his lustre, his listening to addresses in his own honor, and reading articles in his own praise, his being "clasped in the arms of a multitude which had rushed to meet him," his naval and military deeds were short-lived. Contrary to the current belief, the too well-founded indignation of "Fayettist" Washington had nothing to do with his catastrophe. On receipt of the very first letter of the citizen-diplomat, and by return of mail, the foreign minister of the French Republic took the initiative and wrote him:

"I see that you have been received by an hospitable and open-hearted people with all the manifestations of friendship of which your predecessors had also been the recipients. . . . You have fancied, thereupon, that it belonged to you to lead the political actions of this people and make them join our cause. Availing yourself of the flattering statements of the Charleston authorities, you have thought fit to arm corsairs, to or-

[1] May 31, June 19, 1793. *Ibid.*, pp. 216, 217.

ganize recruiting, to have prizes condemned, before even having been recognized by the American Government, before having its assent, nay, with the certitude of its disapproval. You invoke your instructions from the 'Conseil exécutif' of the Republic; but your instructions enjoin upon you quite the reverse: they order you to treat with the *government*, not with a *portion* of the people; to be for Congress the spokesman of the French Republic, and not the leader of an American party." The diplomat's relations with Washington are the opposite of what France desires: "You say that Washington *does not pardon you your successes, and that he hampers your moves in a thousand ways.* You are ordered to treat with the American Government; there only can you attain real successes; all the others are illusory and contrary to the interests of your country. Dazzled by a false popularity, you have estranged the only man who should represent for you the American people, and if your action is hampered, you have only yourself to blame." [1]

While this letter was slowly crossing the ocean, others from Genet were on the way to France, written in the same beaming style. He continued to gloat over his successes and mercilessly to abuse all Federalists, those confessed partisans of "monocracy."

[1] June 19, 1793. *Ibid.*, p. 230.

People were not for half-measures at Paris, in
those terrible days.   Instead of prolonging a useless epistolary correspondence, the Committee of
Public Safety rendered a decree providing that
a commission would be sent to Philadelphia, with
powers to disavow the "criminal conduct of
Genet," to disarm his *Sans-Culotte* and other corsairs, to revoke all consuls who had taken part in
such armaments, and, as for Genet himself, to
have him arrested and sent back to France.
What such an arrest meant was made evident by
the signatures at the foot of the decree: "Barère,
Hérault, Robespierre, Billaud-Varennes, Collot
d'Herbois, Saint-Just." [1]

Better than any one, Genet knew the meaning.
But that same government which he had abused
was generous and protected him.   "We wanted
his dismissal, not his punishment," said Secretary
of State Randolph, who refused to have him arrested.   Genet hastened to give up a country
so hard to please, he thought, as that of his birth,
became an American, and as, with all his faults,
he was not without some merits, being welcomed
in many families, and especially in the house of
"General Clinton, Governor," he wrote, "of the
State of New York, and chief of the Anti-Federal-
ist party," he married his daughter, and died at
Schodack, N. Y., a respected citizen and agricul-

[1] October 11, 1793.   *Ibid.*, p. 287.

turist, in 1834. His name has once more promi-
nently appeared, and in the most honorable
fashion, in those gazettes whose articles in his
favor pleased him so much: a descendant of his
has enlisted for the old country during the present
war, and has cast lustre on the name by his
bravery.

The last years of the former commander-in-
chief of the American and French armies were
saddened by difficulties, troubles, and quarrels
with American political parties and with the
French nation. The Jay treaty with England
(November 19, 1794) had raised a storm: "At
present the cry against the treaty is like that
against a mad dog; and every one in a manner
is running it down. . . . The string which is
most played on, because it strikes with most
force the popular ear, is the violation, as they
term it, of our engagements with France."[1] Anti-
Federalists were indignant; the French not at
all pleased, and their "captures and seizures,"
coupled with a desire to be allowed (which they
were not) to sell their prizes in American harbors,
increased the discontent. The opposition press
was unspeakably virulent, and the great man
sadly confessed he would never have believed that,
he said, "every act of his administration would
be tortured, and the grossest and most insidious

[1] Washington to Alexander Hamilton, July 29, 1795.

misrepresentations of them be made, by giving one side only of a subject, and that, too, in such exaggerated and indecent terms as could scarcely be applied to a Nero, a notorious defaulter, or even to a common pickpocket." [1]

The time came at last for his definitive retreat to Mount Vernon. He reached it a saddened, grand old man, longing to be at last an American farmer and nothing more, and never to go "beyond twenty miles" from his home. "To make and sell a little flour annually, to repair houses going fast to ruin, to build one for the security of my papers of a public nature, and to amuse myself in agricultural and rural pursuits, will constitute employment for the few years I have to remain on this terrestrial globe." [2]

His desire was to continue to the end in the regular occupations he describes to McHenry, in a letter giving us the best picture we have of everyday life at Mount Vernon. Wondering what he might say that would interest a secretary of war, he writes: "I might tell him that I begin my diurnal course with the sun; that if my hirelings are not at their places at that time I send them messages expressive of my sorrow for their indisposition; that, having put these wheels in motion, I examine the state of things further,

[1] To Jefferson, June 6, 1796.
[2] To Oliver Wolcott, May 15, 1797.

and the more they are probed, the deeper, I find, the wounds are which my buildings have sustained by an absence and neglect of eight years; by the time I have accomplished these matters, breakfast (a little after seven o'clock, about the time, I presume, you are taking leave of Mrs. McHenry) is ready; that, this being over, I mount my horse and ride round my farms, which employs me until it is time to dress for dinner, at which I rarely miss seeing strange faces, come, as they say, out of respect for me. Pray, would not the word curiosity answer as well? And how different this from having a few social friends at a cheerful board! The usual time of sitting at table, a walk, and tea brings me within the dawn of candle-light; previous to which, if not prevented by company, I resolve that as soon as the glimmering taper supplies the place of the great luminary, I will retire to my writing-table and acknowledge the letters I have received; but when the lights are brought I feel tired and disinclined to engage in this work, conceiving that the next night will do as well. The next comes and with it the same causes for postponement and effect, and so on. . . .

"It may strike you that in this detail no mention is made of any portion of time allotted for reading. The remark would be just, for I have not looked into a book since I came home; nor shall I be able to do it until I have discharged my workmen, probably not before nights grow longer, when possibly I may be looking in Doomesday Book." [1]

But in this calm retreat, described with a truth and charm almost reminding one of William Cowper's familiar letters, and where he was to spend such a small number of years, trouble, as previously, soon knocked at the door. It seemed at one time as if the former commander-in-chief of Franco-American armies would have to lead the Americans against the French. In spite of the preparations which he had himself to superintend, he refused to believe that war would really occur: "My mind never has been alarmed by any fears of a war with France." [2] But in his judgments of the French, as governed by the Directoire, Washington was gradually receding toward the time when he knew them only through Steele and Addison, and had, "in the *Spectator*, read to No. 143."

He died without knowing that the threatening clouds would soon be dispelled; that the next important event which would count in the annals of the United States and make their greatness secure would come from those same French people: the cession by them, unexpected and un-

[1] Mount Vernon, May 29, 1797.
[2] To T. Pickering, August 29, 1797.

asked-for, not of New Orleans, but of the immense territory then called Louisiana; and that, while his feelings toward the French had undergone changes, those of the French toward him had remained unaltered.

When the news came that on Saturday, 14th of December, 1799, the great leader had passed away,[1] the French Republic went into mourning; for ten days officers wore crape, flags were flown at half-mast, and the head of the state, young Bonaparte, issued an order in which he said: "Washington is dead. This great man fought tyranny. He established on a safe basis the liberty of his country. His memory will ever be dear to the French people as well as to all the free men of the two worlds, and especially to French soldiers, who, like himself and the American soldiers, fight now for equality and liberty."

An impressive and unparalleled ceremony thereupon took place at the Invalides, the Temple of Mars, as it was then called. Detachments from

---

[1] *"Nulli flebilior quam mihi,"* wrote Lafayette, in learning the news, to Crèvecœur, who had just dedicated to Washington his *Voyage dans la haute Pennsylvanie*, adorned, by way of frontispiece, with a portrait of Washington, "gravé d'après le camée peint par Madame Bréhan, à New York, en 1789." Crèvecœur wanted to offer a copy of his book to Bonaparte. "Send it," a friend of his who knew the young general told him; "it is a right you have as an associate member of the Institute; add a letter of two or three lines, mentioning in it the name of Washington." *St. John de Crèvecœur*, by Robert de Crèvecœur, 1883, p. 399.

the Paris garrison lined the aisles; all that counted in the Republic was present, Bonaparte included, and Fontanes, the most famous orator of the day, delivered the funeral eulogy on the departed leader: "Washington's work is scarcely perfected," he said, "and it is already surrounded by that veneration that is usually bestowed only on what has been consecrated by time. The American Revolution, of which we are contemporaries, seems now consolidated forever. Washington began it by his energy, and achieved it by his moderation. In rendering a public homage to Washington, France pays a debt due to him by the two worlds."

In one of the first sentences of the oration, England (with whom we were at war) was courteously associated to the homage rendered by us to the great man: "The very nation," said Fontanes, "that recently called Washington a rebel, now looks upon the emancipation of America as one of those events consecrated by the verdict of centuries and of history. Such is the privilege of great characters." [1]

In the centre of the nave stood the bust of Washington, wreathed in flags and laurels. Years before, in Independence Hall at Philadelphia, on

[1] "Eloge funèbre de Washington, prononcé dans le temple de Mars (Hôtel des Invalides) le 20 pluviose, an VIII (8 février, 1800)," in Œuvres de M. de Fontanes, recueillies pour la première fois, Paris, 1839, 2 vols., II, 147.

a spot now marked by an inscription, the flags taken at Yorktown had been laid at the feet of the President of Congress and of the minister from France, Gérard de Rayneval. Now General Lannes, the future marshal, came forth and with appropriate words laid before the image of the former commander ninety-six flags taken from the enemy by the troops of republican France.

A plan was formed thereupon, the realization of which troublous days did not allow, to erect a statue of Washington in Paris (he now has two there and one in Versailles, gratefully accepted gifts from America), and a decree was prepared by Talleyrand recalling, as a motive, the similitude of feelings between France and that "nation which is sure to be one day a great nation, and is even now the wisest and happiest in the world, and which mourns for the death of the man who did more than any, by his courage and genius, to break her shackles and raise her to the rank of independent peoples. . . . One of the noblest lives which have honored mankind has just passed into the domain of history. . . . Washington's fame is now imperishable; Fortune had consecrated his titles to it; and the posterity of a people which will rise later to the highest destinies continuously confirms and strengthens those titles by its very progress."

Châteaubriand, Lamartine, Guizot, Cornelis de

Witt, Laboulaye, Joseph Fabre, many other
French thinkers and writers, vied with each other
in their praise and admiration throughout the
century. Châteaubriand, who had seen the great
man at Philadelphia in 1791, inserted in his *Voyage en Amérique* his famous parallel between Bonaparte and Washington: "The republic of Washington subsists; the empire of Bonaparte is no
more; it came and went between the first and
second journey of a Frenchman[1] who has found a
grateful nation where he had fought for some
oppressed colonists. . . . The name of Washington will spread, with liberty, from age to age;
it will mark the beginning of a new era for mankind. . . . His fame rises like one of those
sanctuaries wherein flows a spring inexhaustible
for the people. . . . What would be the rank
of Bonaparte in the universe if he had added
magnanimity to what there was heroical in him,
and if, being at the same time Washington and
Bonaparte, he had appointed Liberty for the
heiress of his glory?"

Lamartine, receiving an Italian delegation in
1848, asked them to hate the memory of Machiavelli and bless that of Washington: "His name is
the symbol of modern liberty. The name of a
politician, the name of a conqueror is no longer
what is wanted by the world, but the name of

[1] Lafayette's journeys to America.

the most disinterested of men, and the most devoted to the people." Guizot published his noteworthy study on the first President of the United
States, and the American colony in Paris, to commemorate the event, had the portrait of the
French statesman painted by Healy in 1841, and
presented it to the city of Washington, where it
is preserved in the National Museum.

Publishing, during the early years of the Second
Empire, the series of lectures he had delivered
at the Collège de France during our Second
Republic, the great Liberal, Laboulaye, who did
so much to make America and the Americans
popular in France, wrote in his preface: "Washington has established a wise and well-ordered
republic, and he has left to after-times, not the
fatal example of crime triumphant, but a whole-
some example of patriotism and virtue. In less
than fifty years,[1] owing to the powerful sap of
liberty, we have seen an empire arise, having for
its base, not conquest, but peace and industry,
an empire which before the end of the century
will be the greatest state in the civilized world,
and which, if it remains faithful to the thought of
its founders, if ambition does not arrest the course
of its fortune, will offer to the world the prodigious
sight of a republic of one hundred million inhabitants, richer, happier, more brilliant than the

[1] An exact justification of Lacretelle's prediction; above, p. 94.

monarchies of the old world.   All this is Washington's work." [1]

Nearer our time, Joseph Fabre, the well-known historian of Joan of Arc, wrote: "This sage was a wonder of reasoned enthusiasm, of thoughtful intrepidity, of methodical tenacity, of circumspect boldness, facing from abroad oppression, at home anarchy, both vanquished by his calm genius." [2]

---

[1] *Histoire des Etats Unis*, 3 vols.; preface dated 1855; the lectures had been delivered in 1849. Washington is the hero of the work, which is carried on only to 1789.

[2] *Washington, libérateur de l'Amérique*, 1882, often reprinted, dedicated: "A la mémoire de Lazare Hoche, le soldat citoyen, qui aurait été notre Washington s'il eût vécu."

V

Once more now a republic has been established
in France, which, having, we hope, something of
the qualities of "coolness and moderation" that
Washington wanted us to possess, will, we trust,
prove perpetual. It has already lasted nearly
half a century: an unexampled phenomenon in
the history of Europe, no other republic of such
magnitude having thus survived in the old world
since the fall of the Roman one, twenty centuries
ago.

If the great man were to come again, we entertain a fond hope that he would deem us not un-
deserving now of the sympathies he bestowed on
our ancestors at the period when he was living
side by side with them. Most of the leading
ideas followed by him throughout life are those
which we try to put in practise. We have our
faults, to be sure; we know them, others know
them, too; it is not our custom to conceal them,
far from it; may this serve as an excuse for reviewing here by preference something else than
what might occasion blame.

That equality of chances for all, which caused
the admiration of the early French visitors to

this country, which was one of the chief things
for which Washington had fought, and continues
to be to-day one of the chief attractions offered
to the immigrant by these States, has been secured
in the French Republic, too, where no privileges
of any sort remain, the right to vote is refused to
none, taxation is the same for all, and military
service is expected from everybody.   No principle
had more importance in the eyes of Washington
than that of "equal liberty."   "What triumph
for our enemies to verify their predictions!"
Washington had written to John Jay, in a moment of depression, when he feared that what
Genet was to call "monocracy" was in the ascendant; "what triumph for the advocates of despotism to find that we are unable of governing
ourselves, and that systems founded on the
basis of equal liberty are merely ideal and falla-
cious." [1]

In France, as in the United States, the unique
source of power is the will of the people.   In our
search for the solution of the great problem which
now confronts the world, that of the relations
of capital and labor, we endeavor to practise the
admirable maxim of one of our statesmen of
to-day: "Capital must work, labor must possess."   And though we are still remote from this
goal, yet we have travelled so far toward it that,

[1] August 1, 1786.

at the present day, one out of every two electors in France is the possessor of his own house.[1]

The development of instruction was one of the most cherished ideas of Washington, as it is now of his descendants. "You will agree with me in opinion," he said in a speech to both houses of Congress in 1790, "that there is nothing that can better deserve your patronage than the promotion of science and literature. Knowledge is in every country the surest basis of happiness." Instruction has become, under the Republic, obligatory for all in France, and is given free of cost to all. Not a village, not a hamlet, lost in the recesses of valleys or mountains, that is without its school. The state expenditure for primary instruction during the Second Empire amounted only to twelve million francs; the mere salary of school-teachers alone is now twenty times greater. We try to live up to the old principle: three things should be given free to all—air, water, knowledge: and so it is that at the Sorbonne, the Collège de France, in the provincial universities, all one has to do in order to follow the best courses of lectures is to push open the door. The man in the street may come in if he chooses, just to warm himself in winter or to avoid a shower in summer. Let him; perhaps he will listen too.

[1] "It is estimated that there are more small holdings of land in France than in Germany, England, and Austria combined." *Report of the [U. S.] Commissioner of Education*, 1913, p. 714.

Very wisely, being, in many ways, very modern, Washington attached great importance to inventions. In a speech to Congress on January 9, 1790, he said: "I cannot forbear intimating to you the expediency of giving effectual encouragement as well to the introduction of new and useful inventions from abroad as to the exertions of skill and genius in producing them at home, and of facilitating the intercourse between the distant parts of our country by a due attention to the post-office and the post-roads."

Distances having immensely increased in America (as well as means to cover them), these latter remarks are certainly still of value. With a much less difficult problem to solve, we believe that, in the matter of post-roads, and with a system of rural delivery coextensive with the national territory, we would pass muster in the presence of the great man. As for inventions, we hope that even the compatriots of Franklin, Fulton, Whitney, Horace Wells, W. T. G. Morton, Morse, Bell, Edison, the Wright brothers, and many more. would consider that our show is a creditable one, with Jacquard's loom, the laws of Ampère on electricity, Séguin's tubular boilers, Sauvage's screw, Niepce and Daguerre's photography, Renard and Kreb's first dirigible, Lumière's cinematograph, Curie's radium, with the automobile, which is transforming our way of life (decentralizing

overcentralized countries) as much as the railroads
did in the last century; and, more than all, because so beneficent to all, with the discoveries
of Chevreul, Flourens, Claude Bernard, Laveran,
Berthelot, and especially Pasteur.

On the question of the preservation of natural
resources, to which, and not too soon, so much
attention has been paid of late, Washington had
settled ideas; so have we, ours being somewhat
radical, and embodying, for mines especially, the
French principle that "what belongs to nobody
belongs to everybody," and by everybody must
be understood the nation. Concerning this problem and the best way to solve it, Washington
sent once a powerful appeal to the President of
Congress, saying: "Would there be any impro-
priety, do you think, sir, in reserving for special
sale all mines, minerals, and salt springs, in the
general grants of land belonging to the United
States? The public, instead of the few knowing
ones, might in this case receive the benefits which
would result from the sale of them, without in-
fringing any rule of justice that is known to me." [1]

[1] To Richard H. Lee, December 14, 1784. On French exertions
in that line, Consul-General Skinner wrote: "If correspondents
could penetrate, as the writer has done, the almost inaccessible
mountain villages of this country, and there discover the enthusiastic
French forester at work, applying scientific methods to a work
which can not come to complete fruition before two or three hundred
years, they would retire full of admiration and surprise and carry the
lesson back to the United States." *Daily Consular Reports*, November 2, 1907.

One of the most memorable and striking things done by the French Republic is the building of a vast colonial empire, giving access to undeveloped, sometimes, as in Dahomey, barbaric and sanguinary races, still indulging in human sacrifices. Washington has laid down the rule of what should be done with respect to primitive races. "The basis of our proceedings with the Indian natives," he wrote to Lafayette, "has been and shall be justice, during the period in which I have anything to do with the administration of this government. Our negotiations and transactions, though many of them are on a small scale as to the objects, ought to be governed by the immutable principles of equality." And addressing the Catholic Archbishop of Baltimore, John Carroll, he again said: "The most effectual means of securing the permanent attachment of our savage neighbors is to convince them that we are just."

There is nothing we are ourselves more sincerely convinced of than that such principles are the right ones and should prevail. That we did not lose sight of them in the building of our colonial empire its very vastness testifies; using opposite means, with so many other tasks to attend to, we should have failed. The number of people living under the French flag is about one hundred million now. Judging from the testimony of independent witnesses,[1] it seems that, on this, too, we have acted in accordance with the views of the former commander-in-chief, who had written to Lafayette on August 15, 1786: "Let me ask you, my dear marquis, in such an enlightened, in such a liberal age, how is it possible that the great maritime powers of Europe should submit to pay an annual tribute to the little piratical states of Barbary? Would to Heaven we had a navy able to reform those enemies to mankind or crush them into non-existence." The "reform" was begun by Decatur in 1815, and perfected by Bourmont in 1830.

On one point Washington was very positive; this leader of men, this warrior, this winner of battles, loathed war. He wanted, of course, his nation, as we want ours, never to be without a military academy (our West Point is called Saint-

[1] "The story of French success in the exploration, the civilization, the administration, and the exploitation of Africa, is one of the wonder tales of history. That she has relied on the resources of science rather than those of militarism makes her achievement the more remarkable. . . . Look at Senegambia as it is now under French rule. . . . Contrast the modernized Dahomey of to-day with its railways, schools, and hospitals with the blood-soaked country of the early sixties; remember that Algeria has doubled in population since [the time of] the last Dey—and you will have a bird's-eye view, as it were, of what the French have accomplished in the colonizing field." E. Alexander Powell, *The Last Frontier*, New York, 1912, p. 25. Concerning the Arabs under French rule, Edgar A. Forbes writes: "The conquered race may thank the stars that its destiny rests in a hand that seldom wears the rough gauntlet." *The Land of the White Helmet*, New York, 1910, p. 94.

Cyr), and never to be without a solid, permanent army, for, as he said, in a speech to Congress in 1796: "However pacific the general policy of a nation may be, it ought never to be without an adequate stock of military knowledge for emergencies . . . war might often depend not upon its own choice." Of this we are only too well aware.

There is scarcely, however, a question that oftener recurs under his pen in his letters to his French friends than the care with which wars should be avoided, and no hopes were more fondly cherished by him than that, some day, human quarrels might be settled otherwise than by bloodshed. To Rochambeau, who had informed him that war-clouds which had recently appeared in Europe were dissipated (soon, it is true, to return more threatening), he expressed, in 1786, his joy at what he considered a proof that mankind was becoming "more enlightened and more humanized." To his friend David Humphreys he had written from Mount Vernon, July 25, 1785: "My first wish is to see this plague to mankind (war) banished from off the earth, and the sons and daughters of this world employed in more pleasing and innocent amusements than in preparing implements and exercising them for the destruction of mankind. Rather than quarrel about territory, let the poor, the needy, the oppressed of the earth, and those who want land, resort to the fertile plains of our Western country, the *second land of promise,* and there dwell in peace, fulfilling the first and great commandment." His dream was of mankind one day "connected like one great family in fraternal ties." [1]

On this matter, of such paramount importance to all the world, and in spite of so much, so very much remaining to be done, we may, I hope, consider in France that our Republic would deserve the approval of the departed leader. We have indeed vied with the United States (and praise be rendered to empires and kingdoms who have played also the part of realms of good-will), in an effort to find better means than wars for the settlement of human quarrels. Success could not be expected at once, but it is something to have honestly, earnestly tried. The great man would have judged failures with indulgence, for he well knew how others' dispositions are to be taken into account. "In vain," he had said, "is it to expect that our aim is to be accomplished by fond wishes for peace." [2]

And at the present hour, when it seems to the

[1] To Lafayette, Aug. 15, 1786. Cf. below, p. 347. Same views in Franklin, who had written to his friend David Hartley, one of the British plenipotentiaries for the peace: "What would you think of a proposition, if I should make it, of a family compact between England, France, and America? . . . What repeated follies are those repeated wars! You do not want to conquer and govern one another. Why, then, should you continually be employed in injuring and destroying one another?" Passy, Oct. 16, 1783.   [2] June 15, 1782.

author of these lines that, as he writes, his ears
are filled with the sound of guns, wafted by the
wind over the submarine-haunted ocean, what
would be the feeling of our former commander
if he saw what is taking place, and the stand made
by the descendants of those soldiers intrusted
years ago to his leadership? Perhaps he would
think, as he did, when told by Lafayette of a
recent visit to the battle-fields of Frederick II of
Prussia: "To view the several fields of battle over
which you passed could not, among other sensa-
tions, have failed to excite this thought: 'Here
have fallen thousands of gallant spirits to satisfy
the ambitions of their sovereign, or to support
them perhaps in acts of oppression and injustice.
Melancholy reflection! For what wise purpose
does Providence permit this?'"

Perhaps—who knows?—considering the silent
resolution, abnegation, and unanimity with which
the whole people, from the day when war was declared on them by a relentless enemy, tried to up-
hold the cause of independence and liberalism in
a world-wide conflict, the leader might be tempted
to write once more in the pages of his private
journal the three words he had written on May
1, 1781. Who knows? Of one thing we are sure,
no approval could please us more than that of
the commander-in-chief of former days.

IV

ABRAHAM LINCOLN

ABRAHAM LINCOLN

O N two tragic occasions, at a century's distance, the fate of the United States has trembled in the balance: would they be a free nation? Would they continue to be one nation? A leader was wanted on both occasions, a very different one in each case. This boon was granted to the American people, who had a Washington when a Washington was needed, and a Lincoln when a Lincoln could save them. Neither would have adequately performed the other's task.

A century of gradually increasing prosperity had elapsed when came the hour of the nation's second trial. Though it may seem to us small, compared with what we have seen in our days, the development had been considerable, the scattered colonies of yore had become one of the great Powers of the world, with domains reaching from one ocean to the other; the immense continent had been explored; new cities were dotting the wilderness of former days. When in 1803 France had, of her own will, ceded the Louisiana territories, which have been divided since into fourteen States, minds had been staggered; many in the Senate had shown themselves averse to the ratification of the treaty, thinking that it might prove rather a curse than a boon. "As to Louisiana, this new, immense, unbounded world," Senator White, of Delaware, had said, "if it should ever be incorporated into this Union . . . I believe it will be the greatest curse that could at present befall us; it may be productive of innumerable evils, and especially of one that I fear even to look upon."

What the senator feared to look upon was the possibility, awful and incredible as it might seem, of people being so rash as to go and live beyond the Mississippi. Attempts would, of course, be made, he thought, to prevent actions which would entail such grave responsibilities for the government; but those meritorious attempts on the part of the authorities would probably fail. "It would be as well to pretend to inhibit the fish from swimming in the sea. . . . To every man acquainted with the manner in which our Western country has been settled, such an idea must be chimerical." People will go, "that very population will go, that would otherwise occupy part of our present territory." The results will be unspeakable: "Our citizens will be removed to the immense distance of two or three thousand miles from the capital of the Union, where they will scarcely ever feel the rays of the general government; their affections will be alienated; they will gradually begin to view us as strangers; they will form other commercial connections, and our interests will become distinct."

The treaty had been ratified, however, and the prediction, not of Senator White, of Delaware, but of Senator Jackson, of Georgia, has proved true, the latter having stated in his answer that if they both could "return at the proper period," that is, "in a century," they would find that the region was not, as had been forecasted, "a howling wilderness," but "the seat of science and civilization."[1] The fact is that if the two senators had been able to return at the appointed date, they would have seen the exposition of St. Louis.

Progress had been constant; modern inventions

[1] *Debates and Proceedings in the Congress of the United States*, vol. XIII, col. 33 ff., November 2 and 3, 1803. Senator White had also objected that the price, of fifteen million dollars, was too high; while the French plenipotentiary, Barbé-Marbois, had observed that the lands still unoccupied, to be handed to the American Government "would have a value of several billions before a century had elapsed," in which he was no bad prophet. Marbois added: "Those who knew the importance of a perfect understanding between these two countries attached more value to the twenty million francs set apart for the American claims than to the sixty offered to France." In accordance again with Senator White, the deciding motive had not been that longing for "a perfect understanding" mentioned by Marbois, but a feeling that Louisiana would, at the next war, "inevitably fall into the hands of the British." "Of course, it would," future Marshal Berthier, who was averse to the cession, had observed when the point had been mentioned at the council held at the Tuileries, before the First Consul Bonaparte, on Easter Day, 1803, "but Hanover would just as soon be in our hands, and an exchange would take place at the peace. . . . Remember this: no navy without colonies; no colonies without a navy." Barbé-Marbois, *Histoire de la Louisiane*, Paris, 1829, pp. 295, 315, 330.

had brought the remotest parts of the country nearer together. The telegraph had enabled "the rays of the general government" to reach the farthest regions of the territory. That extraordinary attempt, the first transcontinental railroad, was soon to be begun (1863) and was to be finished six years later.

And now all seemed to be in doubt again; the nation was young, wealthy, powerful, prosperous; it had vast domains and resources, no enemies, and yet it looked as though her fate would parallel that of the old empires of which Tacitus speaks, and which, without foes, crumble to pieces under their own weight.

Within her frontiers elements of destruction or disruption had been growing; animosities were embittered among people equally brave, bold, and sure of their rights. The edifice raised by Washington was shaking on its base; a catastrophe was at hand, such a one as he had himself foreseen as possible from the first. Slavery, he had thought, should be gradually but thoroughly abolished. "Your late purchase," he had written to Lafayette, "of an estate in the colony of Cayenne, with a view of emancipating the slaves on it, is a generous and noble proof of humanity. Would to God a like spirit would diffuse itself generally into the minds of the people of this country, but I despair of seeing it." [1] And to John Francis

[1] May 10, 1786.

Mercer: "I never mean (unless some particular circumstance should compel me to it) to possess another slave by purchase, it being among my first wishes to see some plan adopted by which slavery in this country may be abolished by slow, sure, and imperceptible degrees."[1] For many reasons the steadiness of the new-born Union caused him anxiety. "We are known," he had written to Doctor W. Gordon, "by no other character among nations than as the United States. . . . When the bond of union gets once broken everything ruinous to our future prospects is to be apprehended. The best that can come of it, in my humble opinion, is that we shall sink into obscurity, unless our civil broils should keep us in remembrance and fill the page of history with the direful consequences of them."[2]

The dread hour had now struck, and civil broils meant to fill the page of history were at hand. Then it was that, in a middle-sized city of one hundred thousand inhabitants, not yet a world-famous one, Chicago by name, the Republican convention, assembled there for the first time, met to choose a candidate for the presidency, and on Friday, 18th of May, 1860, selected a man whom my predecessor of those days, announcing in an unprinted report the news to his government, described as "a man almost unknown, Mr. Abraham Lincoln." And so he was;

[1] September 9, 1786.   [2] July 8, 1783.

his own party had hesitated to nominate him;
only on the third ballot, after two others in which
he did not lead, the convention decided that the
fate of the party, of abolitionism, and of the
Union would be placed in the hands of that "man
almost unknown," Mr. Abraham Lincoln.

The search-light of history has since been
turned on the most obscure parts of his career;
every incident of it is known; many sayings of
his to which neither he nor his hearers attributed
any importance at the moment have become
household words. Biographies innumerable, in
pamphlet form or in many volumes, have told us
of the deeds of Abraham Lincoln, of his appearance, of his peculiarities, of his virtues, and of
the part he played in the history of the world,
not alone the world of his day, but that of after-
time. For not only the souvenir of his personality
and of his examples, and the consequences of
what he did, survive among us, but so do also a
number of his clean-cut, memorable, guiding sentences which continue alive and active among
men. His mind is still living.

Few suspected such a future at the time of his
election. "We all remember," wrote, years later,
the French Academician, Prévost-Paradol, "the
anxiety with which we awaited the first words of
that President then unknown, upon whom a
heavy task had fallen, and from whose advent to

power might be dated the ruin or regeneration of his country. All we knew was that he had sprung from the humblest walks of life; that his youth had been spent in manual labor; that he had then risen, by degrees, in his town, in his county, and in his State. What was this favorite of the people? Democratic societies are liable to errors which are fatal to them. But as soon as Mr. Lincoln arrived in Washington, as soon as he spoke, all our doubts and fears were dissipated, and it seemed to us that destiny itself had pronounced in favor of the good cause, since in such an emergency it had given to the country an honest man."

Well indeed might people have wondered and felt anxious when they remembered how little training in greatest affairs the new ruler had had, and the incredible difficulty of the problems he would have to solve: to solve, his heart bleeding at the very thought, for he had to fight, "not enemies, but friends. We must not be enemies!"

No romance of adventure reads more like a romance than the true story of Lincoln's youth and of the wanderings of his family, from Virginia to Kentucky, from Kentucky to Indiana, from Indiana to the newly-formed State of Illinois, having first to clear a part of the forest, then to build a doorless, windowless, floorless log cabin, with beds of leaves, and one room for all the uses of the nine inmates: Lincoln, the grandson of a man killed by the Indians, the son of a father who never succeeded in anything, and whose utmost literary accomplishment, taught him by his wife, and which he had in common with the father of Shakespeare, consisted in "bunglingly writing his own name," the whole family leading a life in comparison with which that of Robinson Crusoe was one of sybaritic enjoyment. That in those trackless, neighborless, bookless parts of the country the future President could learn and educate himself was the first great wonder of his life. His school-days, in schools as primitive as the rest of his surroundings, attended at spare moments, did not amount, put together, to so much as one year, during which he learned, as he stated afterward, how "to read, write, and cipher to the rule of three, but that was all . . . till within his twenty-third year, he was almost constantly handling that most useful instrument"—an axe, not a pen.[1] The event proved once more that learning does not so much depend upon the master's teaching as upon the pupil's desire. This desire never left him; as recorded by himself, he "nearly mastered the six books of Euclid since he was a member of Congress."

But no book, school, nor talk with refined men

---

[1] "Short Autobiography, written at the request of a friend," *Complete Works*, ed. Nicolay and Hay, 1905, pp. 26, 27.

would have taught him what this rough life did.
Confronted every day and every hour of the day
with problems which had to be solved, problems
of food, of clothing, of shelter, of escaping disease
—"ague and fever . . . by which they [the people
of the place] were greatly discouraged" [1]—of de-
veloping mind and body with scarcely any books
but those borrowed from distant neighbors, in
doubt most of the time as to what was going on
in the wide world, he got the habit of seeing, deciding, and acting for himself. Accustomed from
childhood to live surrounded by the unknown and
to meet the unexpected, in a region "with many
bears," he wrote later, "and other wild animals
still in the woods," his soul learned to be astonished at nothing and, instead of losing any time
in useless wondering, to seek at once the way
out of the difficulty. What the forest, what the
swamp, what the river taught Lincoln cannot be
overestimated. After long years of it, and shorter
years at now-vanished New Salem, then at Spring-
field, at Vandalia, the former capital of Illinois,
where he met some descendants of his precursors
in the forest, the French "coureurs de bois," [2]

---

[1] *Ibid.*, 28, 29.

[2] Some French settlements were still in existence in the region,
and were still French. "The French settlements about Kaskaskia
retained much of their national character, and the pioneers from the
South who visited them or settled among them never ceased to
wonder at their gayety, their peaceable industry, and their domestic
affection, which they did not care to dissemble and conceal like their

after years of political apprenticeship which had given him but a limited notoriety, almost suddenly he found himself transferred to the post of greatest honor and greatest danger. And what then would say the "man almost unknown," the backwoodsman of yesterday? What would he say? What did he say? The right thing.

He was accustomed not to be surprised, but to ponder, decide, and act. The pondering part was misunderstood by many who never ceased in his day to complain and remonstrate about his supposed hesitancy; many of Napoleon's generals, and for the same cause, spoke with disgust, at times, of their chief's hesitations, as if a weak will were one of his faults. Confronted with circumstances which were so extraordinary as to be new to all, Lincoln was the man least astonished in the government. His rough and shrewd instinct proved of better avail than the clever minds of his more-refined and better-instructed seconds. It was Lincoln's instinct which checked Seward's complicated schemes and dangerous calculations. Lincoln could not calculate so cleverly, but he could guess better.

shy and reticent neighbors. It was a daily spectacle which never lost its strangeness for the Tennesseeans and Kentuckians to see the Frenchman returning from his work greeted by his wife and children with embraces of welcome 'at the gate of his dooryard, and in view of all the villagers.' The natural and kindly fraternization of the Frenchmen with the Indians was also a cause of wonder." Nicolay and Hay, *Abraham Lincoln*, 1904, I, 58.

In writing the words quoted above, Prévost-Paradol was alluding to the now famous first inaugural address. But even before Lincoln had reached Washington he had, so to say, given his measure. Passing through Philadelphia on his way to the capital, he had been entertained at Independence Hall and, addressing the audience gathered there, had told how he had often meditated on the virtues and dangers of the men who used to meet within those walls in the days when the existence of the nation was at stake, and on the famous Declaration signed there by them. The purport of it, said the new President, is "that in due time the weights should be lifted from the shoulders of all men, and that all should have an equal chance." And he added: "Now, my friends, can this country be saved on that basis? If it can, I will consider myself one of the happiest of men in the world if I can help to save it. . . . If it cannot be saved upon that principle . . . I would rather be assassinated on this spot than to surrender it."[1]

France was then an empire, governed by Napoleon III. During the great struggle of four years, part of the French people were for the North, and part for the South; they should not be blamed: it was the same in America.

But, to a man, the increasing numbers of French

[1] February 22, 1861.

Liberals, making ready for a definitive attempt at a republican form of government in their own land, were for the abolition of slavery and the maintenance of the Union. The American example was the great one which gave heart to our most progressive men. Americans had proved that republican government was possible in a great modern country by having one. If it broke to pieces, so would break the hopes of those among us who trusted that one day we would have one, too—as we have. These men followed with dire anxiety the events in America.

They had all known Lafayette, who died only in 1834, a lifelong apostle of liberty and of the American cause. The tradition left by him had been continued by the best thinkers and the most enlightened and generous minds France had produced in the course of the century, such men as Tocqueville, Laboulaye, Gasparin, Pelletan, and many others. Constant friends of the United States, and stanch supporters of the liberal principles, they had, so to say, taken the torch from the hands of dying Lafayette and passed it on to the new generation. Tocqueville, who was not to see the great crisis, had published in 1835, with extraordinary success, his work on American democracy, showing that individual liberty, equality for all, and decentralization were the goal toward which mankind was steadily moving, and that such a system, with all its defects, was better than autocratic government with all its guarantees. Although living under a monarchy, he could not help sneering at the kindness of those omnipotent governments who, in their paternal desire to spare the people they govern all trouble, would like to spare them even the "trouble of thinking."

Those who felt like him eloquently defended in their books, pamphlets, and articles, when the crisis came, the cause of the Union, and strongly influenced public opinion in European countries. Such was the case, for example, with the *America before Europe* of Agénor de Gasparin, full of enthusiasm for the States, and of confidence in the ultimate issue. "No," said the author in the conclusion of his work, published early in 1862, "the sixteenth President of the Union will not be its last; no, the eighty-fifth year of that nation will not prove her last; her flag will come out of the war, rent by bullets, blackened by powder, but more glorious than ever, and without having dropped in the storm any of its thirty-four stars."[1]

To Gasparin Lincoln wrote thereupon: "You are much admired in America for the ability of your writings, and much loved for your generosity to us and your devotion to liberal principles generally. . . . I am very happy to know that

[1] *L'Amérique devant l'Europe*, Paris, 1862; conclusion.

my course has not conflicted with your judgment of propriety and policy. I can only say that I have acted upon my best convictions without selfishness or malice, and that, by the help of God, I shall continue to do so."[1]

But there were, withal, men among us who, remembering the trials of our revolutionary years, the most terrible any nation had gone through, inclined to consider that, as Tocqueville had said, "to think" was indeed a real trouble, and that thinkers might prove very troublesome people. Those men, too, watched with care what was going on in America; the quiet development of the country under democratic institutions caused them little enough joy, as being the actual condemnation of their most cherished theories. They kept saying: the country has no neighbors, it is exposed to no storm; any system is good enough under such exceptional conditions. If there was any storm, the worthlessness of such institutions would soon be obvious. And it had come to pass that the storm had arisen, and that a man "almost unknown" had been placed at the helm.

Then developed that famous struggle between equally brave opponents, with its various fortunes, its miseries, its hecatombs, and the coming of days so dark that it often seemed as though there remained little chance for the survival of

[1] Washington, August, 4, 1862.

one great, powerful, united nation: the hatreds
were so deep, the losses so immense. One of the
generals who served the cause of the Union was
French, and as a colonel first commanded a regiment, the 55th New York, otherwise called the
Lafayette Guards, in which French blood predominated, and who wore the red trousers, red
képi, and blue coats of the French army. It was
before the war one of those regiments whose functions, owing to the prevalençe of peace, had for
a long time been of the least warlike, mainly
consisting in parades and banquets, so much so
that, with that tendency to irony rarely lacking
in Gauls, those Gardes Lafayette had nicknamed
themselves "Gardes La fourchette."[1] War came,
the country was changed, a new spirit pervaded
the nation, and the Gardes La fourchette became
Lafayette again, and worthy of the name.

General de Trobriand has left a captivating
account of the campaign[2] and of what his first
regiment did in it, beginning with military in-

[1] "L'esprit Gaulois, toujours moqueur, avait saisi le côté plaisant
de cet inutile étalage d'épaulettes et de tambours, et les officiers du
55ᵉ New York qui, à l'heure du danger, prodiguèrent pour leur
nouvelle patrie le sang français sous la direction d'un chef habile et
vaillant, M. de Trobriand, s'étaient donnés à eux-mêmes, dans l'un
des repas de corps qui terminent toujours ces cérémonies, le titre
joyeux de 'Gardes La fourchette.'" Comte de Paris, *Histoire de la
Guerre civile en Amérique*, 1874, I, 311.
[2] *Quatre ans de campagnes à l'armée du Potomac, par Régis de
Trobriand, ex-Major Général au service volontaire des Etats Unis*

struction hastily imparted before the start by French sergeants, "some of whom had made war in Algeria, others in the Crimea or Italy, familiar, all of them, with field service"; then the coming of his soldiers to Washington, as yet a small, sparsely peopled city, with "Pennsylvania Avenue for its principal artery"; their following Rock Creek, not yet a public park, "cadencing their march by singing the *Marseillaise* or the *Chant des Girondins*, hymns unknown to the echoes of the region, which repeated them for the first time, perhaps the last," and crossing Chain Bridge to camp beyond the Potomac.

On one memorable day, in the winter of 1862, the regiment, encamped then at Tennallytown, entertained Lincoln himself. The occasion was the presentation to it by the hands of the President of two flags, a French and an American one. The day chosen had been the 8th of January, as being the anniversary of the battle of New Orleans, won by Andrew Jackson, some of whose

d'Amérique, Paris, 1867, 2 vols. As is well known, two French princes took part in the war as staff-officers in the Army of the Potomac, the Comte de Paris and the Duc de Chartres. An American officer who was present told me that, whether on foot or on horseback, the Comte de Paris had the habit of stooping. During a severe engagement he was asked to carry an order across an open field, quite exposed to the enemy's fire. He took the order, straightened on his saddle, crossed the field quite erect, fulfilled his mission, recrossed the field, keeping perfectly straight, and when back in the lines, stooped again.

troops were French creoles, who, they too, had fought to the sound of the *Marseillaise*.

Mrs. Lincoln had accompanied the President. There was a banquet which the regiment had had cooked by its own soldier-cooks, who surpassed themselves. "The President heartily partook of the meal. Never, was he pleased to say, had he eaten so well since he had entered the White House. He wanted to taste of everything, and his gayety and good humor showed well enough how much he enjoyed this diversion in the midst of the anxious cares with which he was oppressed at that moment."[1]

There were toasts, of course; the then Colonel de Trobriand drank to the "prompt re-establishment of the Union, not so prompt, however, that the 55th may not first have time to do something for it on the battlefield." President Lincoln answered good-humoredly: "Since the Union is not to be re-established before the 55th has had its battle, I drink to the battle of the 55th, and wish that it may take place as soon as possible."

The 55th had its battle, and many others, too; the beautiful American flag handed to it on the 8th of January was torn to shreds by grape-shot; at Fredericksburg only the staff was left; during the course of that terrible day even the staff was broken, and that was the end of it. It was also

[1] *Quatre ans de campagnes*, I, 131.

the end of the 55th: reduced to 210 men, it was merged into the 33d.

Lincoln's instinct, his good sense, his personal disinterestedness, his warmth of heart for friend or foe, his high aims, led him through the awful years of anguish and bloodshed during which, ceaselessly, increased the number of fields dotted with tombs, and no one knew, so great were the odds, whether there would be one powerful nation or two less powerful, inimical to one another. They led him through the worst and through the best hours; and that of triumph found him none other than what he had ever been before, a shrewd man of sense, a convinced man of duty, the devoted servant of his country, but with deeper furrows on his face and more melancholy in his heart. "We must not be enemies."

A French traveller who saw him at his second inauguration has thus described him: "I shall never forget the deep impression I felt when I saw come on to the platform the strange-looking great man to whom the American people had been so happy as to intrust their destinies. The gait was heavy, slow, irregular; the body long, lean, over six feet, with stooping shoulders, the long arms of a boatman, the large hands of a carpenter, extraordinary hands, with feet in proportion. . . . The turned-down shirt-collar uncovered the protruding muscles of a yellow neck, above which

shot forth a mass of black hair, thick, and bris-
tling as a bunch of pine-boughs; a face of irresistible attraction.

"From this coarse bark emerged a forehead
and eyes belonging to a superior nature. In this
body was sheathed a soul wondrous by its greatness and moral beauty. On the brow, deep-fur-
rowed with lines, could be detected the thoughts
and anxieties of the statesman; and in the large
black eyes, deep and penetrating, whose dominant
expression was good-will and kindness mixed
with melancholy, one discovered an inexhaustible
charity, giving to the word its highest meaning,
that is, perfect love for mankind."[1]

The nation was saved, and when the work was
done Lincoln went to his doom and fell, as he had
long foreseen, a victim to the cause for which he
had fought.

When the news of his tragic death reached

---

[1] *Abraham Lincoln*, by Alphonse Jouault. The work was begun
in Washington at the time of Lincoln's assassination, which the
author witnessed, but printed only in 1875. The text of the second
inaugural address had been read in France with great admiration.
The famous bishop of Orleans, Dupanloup, wrote concerning it to
Augustin Cochin: "Mr. Lincoln expresses with solemn and touching gravity the feelings which, I am sure, pervade superior souls
in the North as in the South. . . . I thank you for having made
me read this beautiful page of the history of great men, and I beg
you to tell Mr. Bigelow of my sympathetic sentiments. I would
hold it an honor if he were so good as to convey an expression of
them to Mr. Lincoln." Orleans, April 2, 1865; an appendix to
Montalembert's *Victoire du Nord*, Paris, 1865.

France, the emotion was intense; party lines at that solemn hour disappeared for a moment, and the country was unanimous in the expression of her horror. The Emperor and Empress telegraphed their condolences to Mrs. Lincoln; the Senate and Chamber voted addresses of sympathy; M. Rouher, the premier, interrupted by applause at every word, expressed himself as follows in proposing the vote: "Mr. Abraham Lincoln has displayed in the afflicting struggle which convulses his country that calm firmness which is a necessary condition for the accomplishment of great duties. After victory he had shown himself generous, moderate, and conciliatory." Then followed these remarkable words: "The first chastisement that Providence inflicts on crime is to render it powerless to retard the march of good. . . . The work of appeasement commenced by a great citizen will be completed by the national will."

Addressing the Chamber in the same strain, its President, Mr. Schneider, said: "That execrable crime has revolted all that is noble in the heart of France. Nowhere has more profound or more universal emotion been felt than in our country. . . . After having shown his immovable firmness in the struggle, Mr. Lincoln, by the wisdom of his language and of his views, seemed destined to bring about a fruitful and durable reconciliation between the sons of America. . . . France ardently desires the re-establishment of peace in the midst of that great nation, her ally and her friend."

But more noteworthy than all was the feeling of unofficial France, that of the whole people. Trying to describe it, the American minister to France, but recently taken from among us, Mr. Bigelow, wrote home: "The press of the metropolis shows sufficiently how overwhelming is the public sentiment"; and sending, only as samples, a number of testimonials of sympathy received by him, he added: "They will suffice to show not only how profoundly the nation was shocked by the dreadful crime which terminated President Lincoln's earthly career, but how deep a hold he had taken upon the respect and affections of the French people."

Once more, owing to the death of a great American, the whole nation had been moved. From thirty-one French cities came addresses of condolence; students held meetings, unfavorably seen by the imperial police, little pleased to find how closely associated in the sentiments expressed therein were admiration for Lincoln's work and the longing for a republic similar to that over which he had presided. The youthful president of such a meeting thus conveyed to Mr. Bigelow the expression of what was felt by "the young men of the schools": "In President Lincoln we mourn a fellow citizen; for no country is now inaccessible, and we consider as ours that country where there are neither masters nor slaves, where every man is free or is fighting to become free.

"We are the fellow citizens of John Brown, of Abraham Lincoln, and of Mr. Seward. We young people, to whom the future belongs, must have the courage to found a true democracy, and we will have to look beyond the ocean to learn how a people who have made themselves free can preserve their freedom. . . .

"The President of the great republic is dead, but the republic itself shall live forever."

Deputations flocked to the American legation, "so demonstrative" that the police more than once interfered, as if to remind the delegates that they were not living as yet in a land of liberty. "I have been occupied most of the afternoon," Bigelow wrote to Seward, "in receiving deputations of students and others who have called to testify their sorrow and sympathy. Unfortunately, their feelings were so demonstrative in some instances as to provoke the intervention of the police, who would only allow them in very limited numbers through the streets. . . . I am sorry to hear that some have been sent to prison in consequence of an intemperate expression of their feelings. I can now count sixteen policemen from my window patrolling about in the neighborhood, who occasionally stop persons calling to see me, and in some instances, I am told, send them away."[1]

A unique thing happened, unparalleled anywhere else. A subscription was opened to offer a commemorative medal in gold to the unfortunate widow, and this again did not overplease the police. The idea had occurred to a provincial paper, the *Phare de la Loire;* its success was immediate. All the great names in the Liberal party appeared on the list of the committee, Victor Hugo's conspicuous among them, and with his those of Etienne Arago, Louis Blanc, Littré, Michelet, Pelletan, Edgar Quinet, and others. In order to allow the poorer classes to take part, and so as to show that the offering was a truly national one, the maximum for each subscriber was limited to two cents.

The poorer classes took part, indeed, with alacrity; the necessary sum was promptly collected; the medal was struck, and it was presented by Eugene Pelletan to Mr. Bigelow, with these words: "Tell Mrs. Lincoln that in this little box is the heart of France." The inscription, in French, is an excellent summing up of

---

[1] April 28, 1865. Text as well as that of the documents just quoted in *The Assassination of President Lincoln*. *Appendix to Diplomatic Correspondence of 1865*, Government Printing Office, 1866.

Lincoln's character and career: "Dedicated by French Democracy to Lincoln, President, twice elected, of the United States—Lincoln, honest man, who abolished slavery, re-established the Union, saved the Republic, without veiling the statue of liberty."[1]

The French press had been unanimous; from the Royalist *Gazette de France* to the Liberal *Journal des Débats* came expressions of admiration and sorrow, by the writers of greatest repute, present or future members, in many cases, of the French Academy, Prévost-Paradol, John Lemoine, Emile de Girardin, the historian Henri Martin, the publicist and future member of the National Assembly of 1871, Peyrat, and with them some ardent Catholics, like Montalembert.

"Who among us," said the *Gazette de France*, "would think of pitying Lincoln? A public man, he enters by the death which he has received in the midst of the work of pacification after victory into that body of the *élite* of the historic army which Mr. Guizot once called the battalion of Plutarch. A Christian, he has just ascended before the throne of the final Judge, accompanied by the souls of four million slaves created, like

[1] "Dédié par la Démocratie Française à Lincoln, Président deux fois élu des Etats Unis—Lincoln, honnête homme, abolit l'esclavage, rétablit l'union, sauva la République, sans voiler la statue de la liberté." The medal is now the property of the President's son, Mr. Robert T. Lincoln.

ours, in the image of God, and who by a word from him have been endowed with freedom."[1]

In his *La Victoire du Nord aux Etats Unis*, Montalembert expressed, with his usual eloquence and warmth of heart, the same sorrow at Lincoln's death, and the same joy also at the "success of a good cause served by honorable means and won by honest people. . . . God is to be thanked because, according to the surest accounts, victory has remained pure, unsullied by crimes or excesses. . . . That nation rises now to the first rank among the great peoples of the world. . . . Some used to say: Don't talk to us of your America with its slavery. She is now without slaves; let us talk of her."

But happy as he was at the results, Montalembert rendered, nevertheless, full justice to the South and its great leaders: "The two parties, the two camps, have shown an equal courage, the same indomitable tenacity, the same wonderful energy . . . the same spirit of sacrifice. All our sympathies are for the North, but they in no way diminish our admiration for the South. . . . How not to admire the Southerners, while regretting that such rare and high qualities had not been dedicated to an irreproachable cause! What men, and also, and especially, what women! Daughters, wives, mothers, those women of the South

[1] A very long article by L. de Gaillard, April 30, 1868.

have revived, in the midst of the nineteenth century, the patriotism, devotion, abnegation of the Roman ones in the heyday of the republic. Clelia, Cornelia, Portia have found their equals in many a hamlet, many a plantation of Louisiana or Virginia."[1]

Many among the Liberals seized this opportunity to praise the American system of government as opposed to European ones: "Democracy," said Peyrat, "is not incompatible with great extent of territory or the power and duration of a great government. This has been demonstrated on the other side of the Atlantic, and that is the service which the United States have rendered to liberty.

"They have rendered another, equally important to human dignity, in showing that the citizen has become among them great and powerful, precisely because he has been little governed; they have proved that the real grandeur of the state depends upon the high personal qualities of the individuals. In our old societies, power put man into tutelage, or rather, man put himself in that position at the hands of the government, to which he looked for everything he wanted in life and for solutions which no government, whether monarchical or republican, could give.

"The United States, on the contrary, have

[1] *La Victoire du Nord*, Paris, 1865, pp. 7, 11, 20, 23.

granted to public power just what it is fit that that power should possess, neither more nor less."[1]

In the *Journal des Débats*, Prévost-Paradol, one of the best writers of the day, said: "The political instinct which caused enlightened Frenchmen to be interested in the maintenance of American power, more and more necessary to the equilibrium of the world, the desire to see a great democratic state surmount terrible trials and continue to give an example of the most perfect liberty united with the most absolute equality, assured to the cause of the North a number of friends among us. . . . Lincoln was indeed an honest man, if we give to the word its full meaning, or rather, the sublime sense which belongs to it when honesty has to contend with the severest trials which can agitate states and with events which have an influence on the fate of the world. .˙. . Mr. Lincoln had but one object in view from the day of his election to that of his death, namely, the fulfilment of his duty, and his imagination never carried him beyond it. He has fallen at the very foot of the altar, covering it with his blood. But his work was done, and the spectacle of a rescued republic was what he could look upon with consolation when his eyes were closing in death. Moreover, he has not lived for his country alone, since he leaves to every one in the

[1] In the *Avenir National*, May 3, 1865.

world to whom liberty and justice are dear a
great remembrance and a great example."[1]

Accounts of Lincoln's career multiplied in order
to answer popular demand. The earliest one, by
Achille Arnaud, was printed immediately after
his death, and concluded thus: "There is in him
a more august character than even that of the
statesman and reformer, namely that of the man
of duty. He lived by duty and for duty. . . .
No mistake is possible; what Europe honors in
Lincoln, whether or not she is aware of it, is
duty. She thus affirms that there are not two
morals, one for the masters, the other for the
slaves; one for men in public life, the other for
obscure citizens; that there is only one way to
be great: never to lie to oneself, nor to others,
and to be just."[2]

Régis de Trobriand, whose loyalty to Lincoln
never wavered, and who had believed in him even
in the darkest hours, well saw the importance for
the whole world of the issue of the great conflict,
and justly stated that, though more directly concerning the United States, the fight had been for
"those grand principles of progress and liberty
toward which modern societies naturally tend,
and to which civilized nations legitimately aspire.

[1] April 29, 1865.
[2] *Abraham Lincoln, sa naissance, sa vie, sa mort, par Achille Arnaud,
Rédacteur à " l'Opinion Nationale."* Paris, 1865, p. 96.

Such a cause is worth every sacrifice. By defending it at all costs the United States have done more than fulfil a task worthy of their power and patriotism, for their triumph is a victory for mankind."

Lectures were delivered in France on Lincoln and America, one, under the chairmanship of Laboulaye, by Augustin Cochin, a member of the Institute, showing that Lincoln was "not only a superior type of the American race, but one of the highest and most respected of the human race," something more than a great man: a great honest man.[1]

As a sort of pendant and counterpart for the funeral ceremony held in the Invalides at the death of Washington, the French Academy gave as the subject of its grand prize in poetry: *La mort du Président Lincoln*. Selected in the year following the event, the subject excited immense interest; almost a hundred poets (some of whom, truth to say, were only would-be poets) took part in the competition, which was decided in 1867; several of the productions proved of great literary merit. The prize went to a former secretary of embassy, Edouard Grenier, who had already made his mark as a gifted literary artist, and whom many of us still remember: a lovable old man, of

[1] *Bibliothèque Libérale—Abraham Lincoln*, by Augustin Cochin, Paris, 1869.

upright ideas, a model of courtesy, counting only friends in the very large circle of his acquaintances. He ended with these admirable lines:

> Tous ces fléaux célestes,
> Ces ravageurs d'États dont les pieds triomphants
> Sur les pères broyés écrasent les enfants,
> Grâce à toi, désormais, pâliront dans l'histoire. . .
> L'humanité te doit l'esclavage aboli . . .
> L'Amérique sa force et la paix revenue,
> L'Europe un idéal de grandeur inconnue,
> Et l'avenir mettra ton image et ton nom
> Plus haut que les Césars—auprès de Washington.

When, in a log cabin of Kentucky, over a century ago, that child was born who was named after his grandfather killed by the Indians, Abraham Lincoln, Napoleon I swayed Europe, Jefferson was President of the United States, and the second War of Independence had not yet come to pass. It seems all very remote. But the memory of the great man to whom these lines are dedicated is as fresh in everybody's mind as if he had only just left us; more people, indeed, know of him now than was the case in his own day. "It is," says Plutarch, "the fortune of all good men that their virtue rises in glory after their death, and that the envy which any evil man may have conceived against them never survives the envious." Such was the fate of Lincoln.

V

THE FRANKLIN MEDAL

PHILADELPHIA, APRIL 20, 1906

THE FRANKLIN MEDAL

O
N the occasion of the second centennial of Franklin's birth, a solemn celebration, lasting several days, was held in Philadelphia, under the auspices of the American Philosophical Society, founded by himself more than a century and a half before.

Many Americans of fame took part in the celebration, such men as the Secretary of State Elihu Root, Senator Lodge, Horace H. Furness, former Ambassador Joseph Choate, the President (not yet emeritus) of Harvard, Charles W. Eliot, Doctor Weir Mitchell, and many others. Several foreign nations were represented; England notably by one of her sons who has succeeded in the difficult task of adding lustre to the name he bears, Sir George Darwin.

In accordance with a law passed by Congress two years before, a commemorative medal was, on that occasion, offered to France. The speech of acceptance is here reproduced solely to have a pretext for reprinting the generous and memorable address of presentation by the then Secretary of State, Mr. Elihu Root; and also in order to help in better preserving the souvenir of a more than graceful act of the United States toward France.

Speech by the Secretary of State Presenting the Medal

Excellency: On the 27th of April, 1904, the Congress of the United States provided by statute that the Secretary of State should cause to be struck a medal to commemorate the two-hundredth anniversary of the birth of Benjamin Franklin, and that one single impression on gold should be presented, under the direction of the President of the United States, to the Republic of France.

Under the direction of the President I now execute this law by delivering the medal to you as the representative of the Republic of France. This medal is the work of fraternal collaboration by two artists whose citizenship Americans prize highly, Louis and Augustus Saint-Gaudens. The name indicates that they may have inherited some of the fine artistic sense which makes France pre-eminent in the exquisite art of the medallist.

On one side of the medal you will find the wise, benign, and spirited face of Franklin. On the other side literature, science, and philosophy attend, while history makes her record. The material of the medal is American gold, as was Franklin.

For itself this would be but a small dividend upon the investments which the ardent Beaumarchais made for the mythical firm of Hortalez and Company. It would be but scanty interest on the never-ending loans yielded by the steady friendship of de Vergennes to the distressed appeals of Franklin. It is not appreciable even as a gift when one recalls what Lafayette, Rochambeau, de Grasse, and their gallant comrades were to us, and what they did for us; when one sees in historical perspective the great share of France in securing American independence, looming always larger from our own point of view, in comparison with what we did for ourselves.

But take it for your country as a token that with all the changing manners of the passing years, with all the vast and welcome influx of new citizens from all the countries of the earth, Americans have not forgotten their fathers and their fathers' friends.

Know by it that we have in America a sentiment for France; and a sentiment, enduring among a people, is a great and substantial fact to be reckoned with.

We feel a little closer to you of France because of what you were to Franklin. Before the resplendence and charm of your country's history

—when all the world does homage to your literature, your art, your exact science, your philosophic thought—we smile with pleasure, for we feel, if we do not say: "Yes, these are old friends of ours; they were very fond of our Ben Franklin and he of them."

Made more appreciative, perhaps, by what France did for us when this old philosopher came to you, a stranger, bearing the burdens of our early poverty and distress, we feel that the enormous value of France to civilization should lead every lover of mankind, in whatever land, earnestly to desire the peace, the prosperity, the permanence, and the unchecked development of your national life.

We, at least, can not feel otherwise; for what you were to Franklin we would be—we are—to you: always true and loyal friends.

The French Ambassador's Answer

On behalf of the French Republic, with feelings of gratitude, I receive the gift offered to my country, this masterful portrait of Franklin, which a law of Congress ordered to be made, and which is signed with the name, twice famous, of Saint-Gaudens.

Everything in such a present powerfully appeals to a French heart. It represents a man ever venerated and admired in my country—the

scientist, the philosopher, the inventor, the leader
of men, the one who gave to France her first notion of what true Americans really were. "When
you were in France," Chastellux wrote to Franklin, "there was no need to praise the Americans.
We had only to say: Look; here is their representative."

The gift is offered in this town of Philadelphia
where there exists a hall the very name of which
is dear to every American and every French heart
—the Hall of Independence—and at a gathering
of a society founded "for promoting useful knowledge," which has remained true to its principle,
worthy of its founder, and which numbers many
whose fame is equally great on both sides of the
ocean.

I receive it at the hands of one of the best
servants of the state which this country ever produced, no less admired at the head of her diplomacy now than he was lately at the head of her
army, one of those rare men who prove the right
man, whatever be the place. You have listened
to his words, and you will agree with me when I
say that I shall have two golden gifts to forward
to my government: the medal and Secretary
Root's speech.

The work of art offered by America to France
will be sent to Paris to be harbored in that unique
museum, her Museum of Medals, where her his-

tory is, so to say, written in gold and bronze, from the fifteenth century up to now, without any ruler, any great event, being omitted. Some of the American past is also written there—that period so glorious when French and American history were the same history, when first rose a nation that has never since ceased to rise.

There, awaiting your gift, are preserved medals struck in France at the very time of the events, in honor of Washington, to commemorate the relief of Boston in 1776; a medal of John Paul Jones in honor of his naval campaign of 1779; another medal representing W. Washington, and one representing General Howard, to commemorate the battle of Cowpens in 1781; one to celebrate the peace of 1783 and the freedom of the thirteen States; one of Lafayette; one of Suffren, who fought so valiantly on distant seas for the same cause as Washington; one, lastly, of Franklin himself, dated 1784, bearing the famous inscription composed in honor of the great man by Turgot: "Eripuit cælo fulmen, sceptrumque tyrannis." [1]

My earnest hope is that one of the next medals

[1] An official note informed the Secretary of State, in the following December, of the arrangements made by the French Republic for the preservation, among proper surroundings, of the Franklin medal: "In the centre of the Hall of Honor in the Museum of Medals at the Paris Mint, stand four ancient show-cases of the time of Louis XVI. One of these has been selected for the Franklin medal, which has been surrounded with the medals herein below enumerated, which were deemed the fittest to make up a worthy retinue, if the phrase

to be struck and added to the series will be one
to commemorate the resurrection of that great
city which now, at this present hour, agonizes
by the shores of the Pacific. The disaster of
San Francisco has awakened a feeling of deepest
grief in every French heart, and a feeling of admiration, too, for the manliness displayed by the
population during this awful trial. So that what
will be commemorated will not be only the
American nation's sorrow, but her unfailing hero-
ism and energy.

Now your gift will be added to the collection
in Paris; it will be there in its proper place.
The thousands who visit this museum will be reminded by it that the ties happily formed long
ago are neither broken nor distended, and they
will contemplate with a veneration equal to that
of their ancestors the features of one whom Mirabeau justly called one of the heroes of mankind.

The Franklin ceremony had occurred at the
time of the San Francisco catastrophe, at a moment when, communication having been cut,
anxiety was intense.

be permissible." There follows a description of sixteen medals com-
memorative of Franco-American history, placed in the same case.
"House of Representatives," 59th Congress, 2d session, Document
No. 416.

I had spoken without instructions, but the French Government took their representative's words to the letter. The medal was ordered, and was for Bottée, the artist, a former recipient of the "Grand Prix de Rome," a work of love. It shows on one side the city rising from its ruins, surrounded with emblems of recovered youth and prosperity. On the other side the image of the French Republic is seen offering from over the sea a twig of laurel to America.

One single copy in gold was struck, and the presentation took place in rebuilt San Francisco, in 1909, the medal being received by the statesman and poet, the translator of the sonnets of Heredia, Edward Robeson Taylor, then mayor of the city.

VI

HORACE HOWARD FURNESS

AN ADDRESS DELIVERED IN THE NAME OF THE
AMERICAN PHILOSOPHICAL SOCIETY, PHILADEL-
PHIA, JANUARY 17, 1913

HORACE HOWARD FURNESS

WE meet on a solemn occasion.

One has recently disappeared from our midst whose work was a model; whose life, too, was a model; whose benign influence, exerted for many years from the seclusion of a quiet retreat, was felt far beyond the limits of his own country; whose views, always expressed in the gentlest terms, will outlive the thunder of many a noisy writer, as ever-renewing flowers survive earthquakes.

A member of the American Philosophical Society, founded in his own city by Franklin "to promote useful knowledge," Furness was true to the motto of the society and lived the life of a true philosopher. I call him Furness, without Doctor or any other title, not because he is no more, but to obey a request of his. "I do not like titles in the republic of letters," he wrote me in the early times of our acquaintance; "if you will drop all to me, I will do the same to you. One touch of Shakespeare makes the whole world kin."

All those whom the spirit of philosophy has penetrated and who stanchly adhere to its ideal count among the noblest types of humanity and, whatever their rank in life or the period when they lived, resemble each other. When Furness died numerous eulogies, biographies, and portraits of him, penned, many of them, by the hands of masters, were published. I wonder if any better resembled him than this one:

"Remember his constancy in the fulfilling of the dictates of reason, the evenness of his humor at all junctures, the serenity of his face, his extreme gentleness, his scorn for vainglory, his application to penetrate the meaning of things. He never dismissed any point without having first well examined and well understood it. He bore unjust reproaches without acrimony. He did nothing with undue haste. . . . A foe to slander, he was neither hypercritical, nor suspicious, nor sophistical. He was pleased with little, modest in his house, his clothing, his food. He loved work, ate soberly, and thus was able to busy himself, for the whole day, with the same problems. Let us remember how constant and equable was his friendship, with what open mind he accepted a frank contradiction of his own views, with what joy he received advice that proved better than his own, and the kind of piety, free from all superstition, that was his. Do as he did, and your last hour will be comforted, as his was, by the conscience of the good accomplished."

In those higher regions where true philosophers

live, equality reigns; they resemble each other by their virtues; this portrait, which, to my mind, gives such a vivid idea of the life Furness led at Wallingford, near Philadelphia, was drawn eighteen centuries ago, by that noblest of antique minds, Emperor Marcus Aurelius, describing his predecessor, the first of the Antonines, he who, on the last night of his life, being asked for the password, had answered: "Æquanimitas."

After studies at Harvard and Philadelphia and a visit to Europe and the Levant, having taken such part in the Civil War as his infirmity allowed him, a happy husband, a happy father, Horace Howard Furness decided to devote his life to the "promotion of useful knowledge." He withdrew, in a way, from the world, settling in a quiet retreat, and started on his life's work with the equipment of a modern scientist and the silent enthusiasm, the indefatigable energy of mediæval thinkers, the compilers of *Summæ* of times gone, regretting nothing, happy with his lot, at one with that master mind of old English literature, the author of *Piers Plowman*. "For," said centuries ago the man "robed in russet,"

"If heaven be on this erthe · and ese to any soule,
  It is in cloistre or in scole · be many skilles I finde;
  For in cloistre cometh no man to chide ne to fihte,
  But all is buxomnesse there and bokes · to rede and to
    lerne."

Such a cloister, with ease to his soul, with buxomness, with books to read and learn, was for our departed friend his house in Wallingford, where he lived surrounded by that extraordinarily gifted family of his: a wife to whom we owe the Concordance to the poems of Shakespeare, a sister who translated for him the German critics, sons and a daughter and a sister's relative[1] who have all made their mark in their country's literature. There, for years, he toiled, never thinking of self nor of fame, busy with his task, and even in his seclusion, with his tenderness of heart and ample sympathies, listening to

> The still sad music of humanity.

What that task was all the world now knows. A passionate admirer of Shakespeare, he wanted to make accessible to all every criticism, information, comment, explanation concerning the poet which had appeared anywhere at any time. Each volume was to be a complete encyclopædia of all that concerned each play. The first appeared in 1871, the sixteenth is the last he will have put his hand to.

In the introduction to each volume, his purposes and methods are explained, and never has any writer more completely and more unwittingly allowed us to look into his own character than

[1] Owen Wister.

Furness when writing what he must have considered his very impersonal statements. What
strikes the reader, before all, is the philosophical
spirit which pervades the whole work. A worthy
member of the American Philosophical Society,
he wanted to be "useful." Lives are and will be
more and more encumbered; the acquisition of
knowledge should, therefore, be made more and
more easy of reach. "To abridge the labor and
to save the time of others" was, said he in his
first volume, what impelled him to write. No
pains of his were spared to lessen those of others.
And all specialists know the extraordinary relia-
bility of his texts and statements. "Nowhere,
perhaps," Sir Sidney Lee wrote in his *Life of
Shakespeare*, "has more labor been devoted to
the study of the works of the poet than that given
by Mr. H. H. Furness, of Philadelphia, to the
preparation of the new Variorum edition."

The labor was one of love, and a lover naturally
forgets himself for the beloved one. Furness tried
not to show the ardor of his sentiments; but it
now and then appears, usually in small details
when he would, more naturally, be off his guard.
Shakespeare calls Cæsar's Ambassador Thidias,
and not Thyreus, as the later-day editors do,
under pretense that it was the real name. They
are wrong: "Shakespeare in his nomenclature
was, as in all things, exquisite. . . . For certain

reasons (did he ever do anything without reason ?)
he chose the name of Thidias. . . ."

In the privacy of intimate correspondence Furness would be more outspoken, being not restrained
by the thought that he would be imposing his
own views upon the mass of readers. On Cleopatra, about whom I had risked opinions somewhat
different from his, he wrote me—it seems it was
yesterday: "Of course, Shakespeare's Cleopatra
is not history. But who cares for history? Of
this be assured, that, if you had lived with her as
I have for two years, you would adore her as
deeply as I do."

The truth is that, as he said, he actually *lived*
with the personages of the plays, and he raptur-
ously listened to those far-off voices, which came
clearer to his infirm ears than to those of any one
of us, meant only for commonplace uses. He had
a better right than any to form an opinion, but
was ever afraid to seem to force it on others. Of
his edition itself he had written: "I do not flatter
myself that this is an *enjoyable* edition of Shakespeare. I regard it rather as a necessary evil."[1]
On another occasion, having been criticised about
a certain statement of his, he wrote: "I now wish
to state that my critic was entirely right and I
entirely wrong." His work was a work of love,
but it was also a work of reason, as befits a phi-

[1] Introduction to *Hamlet*.

losopher. He leaned throughout toward conservative methods, which have doubtless the fault of attracting less tumultuous attention to the worker: a great fault in the eyes of the many, a great quality in Furness's own.

His shrewd good sense, seconded by a no less enjoyable good humor, never failed him. When he began, one important question had first to be decided: would he admit in his work only textual and philological criticisms or also æsthetic criticism, mere poetry, sheer literature? To many the temptation would have been great to exclude the latter, the fashion being among the most haughty, if not the most learned, of the learned to doubt the seriousness, laboriousness, usefulness of any who can enjoy, in a play of Shakespeare's, something else than doubtful readings and misprints. This school is less new than is generally believed, and in his *Temple du Goût* Voltaire had already represented the superb critics of the matter-of-fact school answering those who asked them whether they would not visit the temple:

"Nous, Messieurs, point du tout.
Ce n'est pas là, grâce à Dieu, notre étude;
Le goût n'est rien, nous avons l'habitude
De rédiger au long, de point en point,
Ce qu'on pensa, mais nous ne pensons point."

The fact is that, as Furness well perceived from the first, the two elements should no more be separated than soul from body. Without accuracy, literary criticism is mere trumpery; without a sense of the beautiful, mere accuracy is death-like. Much so-called æsthetic criticism, wrote Furness, "is flat, stale, unprofitable. . . . But shall we ignore the possible existence of a keener insight than our own? . . . Are we not to listen eagerly and reverently when Coleridge or Goethe talks about Shakespeare?"

With such a rule in mind he made his selections, pruning what he deemed should be pruned: "*rejectiones et exclusiones debitas*," as Bacon would have said. But one more kind of thing he excluded, and this is an eminently characteristic trait of his. His gentleness (not a weak, but a manly one) rebelled at others' acerbity, and when he saw appear that unwelcome and somewhat abundant element in modern criticism, he simply left it out: no admittance for any such thing within the covers of a gentleman-scholar's gentlemanly and scholarly work. True it is that, while Shakespeare is the author most read—after the Bible, it is also the one about which the most furious and unchristian disputes have been waged —after the Bible. The Philadelphia scholar wanted all the critics admitted within his fold to keep the peace there, and he adopted the following rule: "First, all unfavorable criticism of fellow critics is excluded as much as possible. . . .

To confound Goethe, Schlegel, or Tieck is one
thing, to elucidate Shakespeare is another." He
went even further, and since he could not quote
whole books and had to select, "the endeavor,"
he said, "in all honesty has been to select from
every author the passages wherein he appears to
best advantage." What critic, then, can be
imagined so blind to the service rendered, so
much in love with his own harshness, that would
not feel toward Furness as Queen Katharine
toward Griffith:

> After my death I wish no other herald,
> No other speaker of my living actions,
> To keep mine honor from corruption,
> But such an honest chronicler as—*Furness*.

His friendly appreciation of French critics (who,
with all they lacked in early days, were, after all,
the first to form, outside of England, an opinion
on Shakespeare, the oldest one being of about
1680) cannot but touch a French heart. "It has
given me especial pleasure," he said in the Introduction to his first volume, "to lay before the
English reader the extracts from the French; it is
but little known, in this country at least, outside
the ranks of Shakespeare students, how great is
the influence which Shakespeare at this hour is
exerting on French literature, and how many and
how ardent are his admirers in this nation." He

had even, at a later date, a good word for poor
Ducis and his Hamlet, a Hamlet truly Ducis's
own.

Nor shall I ever forget in what tones, amidst
friendly applause, the great scholar spoke of
France in his own city of Philadelphia, at the
memorable gathering of April 20, 1906, when, in
accordance with the will of the nation as expressed
by Congress, a medal was offered to my country
to commemorate her reception of Franklin at the
hour when the fate of the States was still weighing in the balance.

In the early years of manhood one sees, far
ahead on the road, those great thinkers, scientists, master men, tall, powerful, visible from a
distance, ready to help the passer-by, like great
oaks offering their shade. They seem so strong,
so far above the common that the thought never
occurs that we of the frailer sort may see the day
when they will be no more. Who was ever present at the death of an oak? Whoever thought
that he could see the day when he would accompany Robert Browning's remains to Westminster
or mourn for the disappearance of Taine or Gaston
Paris? The feeling I had for them I had for
Furness, too. Was it possible to think that this
solid oak would fall?

He himself, however, had misgivings, and it
seemed, of late years, as if the dear ones who had

gone before were beckoning to him. "Do you remember," he wrote me in 1909, "my sister, Mrs. Wister, to whom I had the pleasure of introducing you at the Franklin celebration? I am now living under the black and heavy shadow of her loss. She left me last November, solitary and alone, aching for the 'sound of a voice that is silent.'" And at a more recent date: "I have been so shattered by the blows of fate that I doubt you'll ever again receive a printed forget-me-not from me."

And now, in our turn, members of the American Philosophical Society, members of the Shakespeare Societies of the world, members innumerable of the republic of letters, we too ache for "the sound of a voice that is silent." On the signet with which he used to seal his letters, Furness had engraved a motto, which is the best summing up of Emperor Marcus Aurelius's firm and resigned philosophy: "This, too, will pass away."

For him, too, the august sad hour struck. But so far as anything in this fleeting world may be held to remain, so long as mankind shall be able to appreciate honest work honestly done, the name of Furness will not pass away, but live enshrined in every scholar's grateful memory.

VII

FROM WAR TO PEACE

AN ADDRESS DELIVERED BEFORE THE AMERICAN
SOCIETY FOR THE JUDICIAL SETTLEMENT OF IN-
TERNATIONAL DISPUTES, DECEMBER 17, 1910

FROM WAR TO PEACE[1]

DOES peace mean progress? Is the disappearance of war a sign of improvement or of decay? At a yet recent date learned men, their eyes to their microscopes, were teaching us that among the various kinds of living creatures they had studied, war was the rule; that where struggle ceased, life ceased; and that, since more beings came into the world than the world could feed, the destruction of the weakest was both a necessity and a condition of progress. Struggle, war, violence meant development; peace meant decay. And a bold generalization applied to reasoning man the fate and conditions of unreasoning vermin. Since it was fate, why resist the inevitable and what could be the good of peace debates?

But the stumbling-block that Science had placed on the road to better days has been removed by Science herself. The sweeping conclusions attributed to that great man Darwin by pupils less great have been scrutinized; other experiments, such as he would have conducted him-

[1] The text of this address is reproduced exactly as it was delivered, December 17, 1910, only a few notes and references being added.

333

self had he been living, were tried, and their results added to our book of knowledge. Great
results, indeed, and notable ones; it turned out
that the explanation of transformism, of progress,
of survival, was not to be found in a ceaseless war
insuring the predominance of the fittest, but in
quiet and peaceful adaptation to environment, to
climate, and to circumstances. And we French
are excusably proud to see that, for having un-
folded those truths years before Darwin wrote,
due honor is now rendered almost everywhere, and
especially in America, to Jean Baptiste de Lamarck, author of the long obscure and now famous
Philosophie Zoologique, 1809.

As for the undue multiplication of individuals,
statistics unknown to Darwin have since shown
that, whatever may be the case with beetles or
fishes (and let them work out their own problems
according to their own laws), there is, for man at
least, no need of self-destruction to ward off such
a peril: the general decrease of the rate of re-
production, so striking throughout the world, is
all that is wanted, and in some cases is even
more than is wanted.

War, therefore, is not our unavoidable fate, and
that much of the road has been cleared: a long
road followed amid terrible sufferings by mankind
through centuries. The chief danger in times
past, and partly still in our own, does not result

from an ineluctable fate, but from the private
disposition of men and of their leaders. And we
know what for ages those dispositions were.
Former-day chroniclers are wont to mention, as
a matter of course, that "the king went to the
wars in the season," as he would have gone a-fish-
ing. People at large saw not only beauty in war
(as there is in a just war, and of the highest order,
exactly as there is in every duty fulfilled), but they
saw in it an unmixed beauty. Men and nations
would take pride in their mercilessness, and they
were apt to find in the sufferings of an enemy an
unalloyed pleasure.

Such were the feelings of the time. To none
of the master artists who represented the day of
judgment on the walls of Rome, Orvieto, or Padua,
or on the portals of our northern cathedrals, did
the thought occur to place among his fierce angels
driving the guilty to their doom, one with a tear
on his face: a tear that would have made the
artist more famous than all his art; a tear, not
because the tortures could be supposed to be unjust or the men sinless, but because they were
tortures and because the men had been sinful.
Dies iræ!

Artists belonged to their time and expressed
their time's thought. The teaching of saints and
of thinkers long remained of little avail. War,
that "human malady," as Montaigne said, was

considered as impossible to heal as rabies was—
until the day when a Pasteur came. Yet protests
began to be more perceptibly heard as men better
understood what they themselves were and commenced to suspect that the time might come
when all would be equal before the law. Nothing,
Tocqueville has observed, is so conducive to
mercy as equality.[1]

All those who, in the course of centuries, led
men to the conquest of their rights can be truly
claimed as the intellectual ancestors of the present
promoters of a sane international peace: men like
our Jean Bodin, who, while upholding, as was
unavoidable in his day, the principle of autocracy,
yet based his study of the government of nations
on the general interests of the commonwealth,
and who, in opposition to Machiavelli, who had
called his book *The Prince*, called his *The Republic*.
To Bodin, who protests against the so-called

---

[1] On this he is very insistent. He speaks of "cette disposition à
la pitié que l'égalité inspire." According to him, "les passions
guerrières deviendront plus rares et moins vives, à mesure que les
conditions seront plus égales," and elsewhere: "Lorsque le principe
de l'égalité ne se développe pas seulement chez une nation, mais en
même temps chez plusieurs peuples voisins . . . ils conçoivent
pour la paix un même amour . . . et finissent par considérer la
guerre comme une calamité presque aussi grande pour le vainqueur
que pour le vaincu." But this goal has not yet been reached, and
in the meantime, "quel que soit le goût que ces nations aient pour la
paix, il faut bien qu'elles se tiennent prêtes à repousser la guerre ou,
en d'autres termes, qu'elles aient une armée." *Démocratie en Amérique*, 14th ed., 1865, III, 444, 445, 473, 474.

right of the strongest, have been traced some of the principles embodied much later in the American and in the French "Declaration of the Rights of Man."[1]

Such thinkers truly deserve the name of forerunners; such men as that great Hugo Grotius, whose ever-living fame was not without influence on the selection of his own country as the seat of the peace conferences of our day, and who, being then settled in France, near Senlis, dedicated to

[1] *Les six livres de la République de Jean Bodin, Angevin*, Paris, 1576; innumerable editions, so great was the success. The work is expressly written in opposition to that of Machiavelli, "this procurer of tyrants." Kings may be a necessity, yet the thing of the state is not theirs, but is the common property of the citizens, *res publica*. No one on board the ship can play the part of an onlooker, especially in stormy weather; all on board must bestir themselves and bring such help as they can: "Depuis que l'orage impétueux a tourmenté le vaisseau de nostre République avec telle violence que le Patron mesme et les pilotes sont comme las et recreus (worn out) d'un travail continuel, il faut bien que les passagers y prestent la main, qui aux voiles, qui aux cordages, qui à l'ancre, et ceux à qui la force manquera, qu'ils donnent quelque bon advertissement, ou qu'ils présentent leurs vœux et prières à Celuy qui peut commander aux vents et appaiser les tempestes, puisque tous ensemble courent un mesme danger." (Preface, to the magistrate and poet, the friend of Ronsard, Guy du Faur de Pibrac.) For Bodin, peace is the ideal; yet "war must be waged to repel violence, in case of necessity. . . . The frontier of a well-ordered republic is justice, and not the point of the lance." ("La frontière d'une république bien ordonnée est la justice . . . et non pas la pointe de la lance.") Such is the ideal, but since it has not been reached yet, the keeping up of a permanent military force is a necessity, "and to bestow on it a third of the revenue is not too much," especially when you have warlike neighbors, which is the case of "peoples living in fertile and temperate regions, like France." Bk. V, chap. 5.

King Louis XIII his famous work on war and
peace, so memorable for its denunciation of frivo-
lous wars and wanton cruelties.[1]

Soon the names of those to be honored for the
same cause became legion: men like Pascal,
Saint-Pierre, the Encyclopedists, Kant, Bentham,
Tocqueville, and many others.

Among Pascal's *Thoughts* is this memorable one,
which forecasts and sums up much of what has
since been or will be done: "When it is a question of deciding whether war should be waged,
of sentencing so many Spaniards to death, one
man only decides, and one who is interested.
The decision ought to rest with an impartial third
party."

A little later, that strange Abbé de Saint-Pierre
was writing those works considered as so many
wild dreams in his day and no longer read at all
in ours.   But if he were to return now, he would,
according to one of his latest critics, feel not at
all dismayed, but say: "This is all for the best;
you need not study my works, since you have
put in practise nearly all my ideas; there remains
only my *Perpetual Peace;*[2] but, like the others,
its turn will come."

---

[1] *De Jure Belli ac Pacis Libri III*, Paris, 1625.

[2] *Projet pour rendre la paix perpétuelle en Europe*, 1713–17, 3
vols.   The abbé dreamed of a league of all governments in favor of
peace; any of them breaking the pledge, to be attacked by the others.
Differences between states should be arbitrated.   A French prede-

If its turn has not come yet, great practical steps have surely been taken toward it, chief among them that move, so unexpected a few years ago, so dubiously wondered at when it occurred, and now so thoroughly accepted, that, as in the case of all great inventions, one wonders how things could go on before it existed: the calling of the first conference at The Hague by the Emperor of Russia, Nicholas II.

"The maintenance of general peace," read the Russian circular of August, 1898, "and a possible reduction of the excessive armaments which weigh upon all nations, present themselves in the actual situation of the world, as the ideal toward which should tend the efforts of all governments. . . . The ever-increasing financial expense touches public prosperity at its very source; the intellectual and physical powers of peoples, labor and capital, are, most of it, turned aside from their natural functions and consumed unproductively. . . .

cessor of the abbé had been Emeric Crucé, whose *Nouveau Cynée ou Discours d'Estat représentant les occasions et moyens d'establir une paix générale et la liberté du commerce par tout le monde*, was published in Paris, 1623 (modern edition, with an English translation by T. W. Balch, Philadelphia, 1909). Crucé was in favor of the establishment at Venice of a Supreme Court of Arbitration, in which every sovereign would have had his representative: "If any one rebelled against the decree of so notable a company, he would receive the disgrace of all other princes, who would find means to bring him to reason" (Balch's ed., p. 104)—a plan which, in fact, is still under discussion.

In connection with the works of these theorists should be read *e. g.*, Alberico Gentili's *De Jure Belli*, 1588-98.

To put an end to those ceaseless armaments and to find means for preventing the calamities which threaten the entire world, such is the supreme duty which to-day lies upon all states."

When one man, then another, then another, had come and said: I can draw the lightning from the clouds; I can rise in the air; I can flash your words and thoughts to any distance you please; I can cure rabies by inoculating rabies; I can make you talk with your friend miles away; I can navigate a boat under the sea, scepticism had scarcely been greater than when the circular took the world by surprise. The issue seemed more than doubtful; many among the most sanguine barely hoped to succeed in preventing the absolute failure that would have killed such a project for generations.

Shortly afterward I happened to be in St. Petersburg and had the honor of being received by the Emperor. The conversation fell on the "Great Design," to give it the name used for the very different plan (implying coercion) attributed two centuries before to the French King Henry IV. I was struck by the quiet conviction of the originator of the new movement as to its ultimate results, and his disposition not to give up the plan if at first it met with difficulties and delays. Emperor Nicholas summed up his views with the remark: "One must wait longer when planting an oak than when planting a flower."

Longer, indeed, yet not so very long, after all.
The first conference took place, and in it, I may
say, the delegations of our two Republics presided
over by such statesmen and thinkers as Andrew
D. White and Léon Bourgeois, failed not to fulfill
the part assigned to our democracies by their
ideals and traditions. In spite of scepticism, that
first conference reached an unexpected measure
of success. Eight years later a second one was
convened on the felicitous suggestion of President
Roosevelt, and now the supposedly useless mechanism from dreamland has been so heartily
accepted by mankind at large, all over the globe,
that the approximate date for a third one has
already been selected. Governments at first
doubted that one would be of any use; now they
want more.

The word had been spoken indeed at the proper
moment. The teachings of philosophers and of
experience, the outcome of revolutions, a more
vivid sense of equality among men imbuing them
with mercy, according to Tocqueville, had caused
the seed to fall on prepared ground. We scarcely
realize, looking at it from so near, how great the
movement thus started has already become. The
practical ideas put forth less than a dozen years
ago have progressed so much that more treaties
of arbitration have been signed between the first
Hague Conference and now than between the
day of creation and that conference. I take, if

I may be permitted to allude to my own feelings, no small pride in having concluded the first one, duly ratified by both countries, ever signed by the United States with any European Power, and I was glad to thus continue an old-established tradition, since, in the matter of treaties with the United States, be they treaties of commerce, alliance, or amity, France has been accustomed to take the lead among nations.[1]

Quicker, indeed, than was anticipated by the sower himself, the oak has grown and the nations can rest under its shade. Several important appeals have been made to the court of The Hague, the United States taking the lead and giving to all the best example. Those experiments, which most of the great Powers have already tried, have had manifold advantages: they have shown that dangerous quarrels *could* thus be honorably settled; they have shown also that defects in the working of the court exist and should be remedied.

Public utterances and circulars from Presidents Roosevelt and Taft and from Secretaries of State Root and Knox have pointed out the importance of trying to establish a permanent court, with judges ever present, paid by the associated nations,

---

[1] First (and only) treaty of alliance, 1778; first treaty of amity and commerce, 1778; first consular convention, 1788; first treaty for the aggrandizement of the territory of the United States, 1803. The only example lacking, and for good reasons, is that of a treaty of peace following a war.

selected from among men of such a high moral standing as to be above influence of creed or nationality, true citizens of the world, fit magistrates to judge the world.

In these views, the future realization of which the second conference has insured, France heartily concurred, having indeed, during the first conference, initiated an early preliminary move toward continuity and permanence.

Given these more and more enlightened dispositions among governments, it may seem that the work of a private society like this must needs be of comparatively little import. The reverse is the truth. It has an immense power for good, for it can act directly on the lever that moves the world: public opinion. So powerful is such a lever that even in the past, in times when men were not their own masters, public opinion had to be reckoned with; such imperious leaders of men as a Richelieu or a Napoleon knew it better than any one. *Opinio veritate major*, had even cynically said the great philosopher Francis Bacon. But if opinion can occasionally defeat truth, much better can it defend truth. With the spreading of instruction and with an easier access to men's minds through books, journals, public meetings, and free discussion, its power against truth has been considerably diminished and its power for good increased and purified.

You know this and act accordingly. Though doing so in your private capacity, you conform in fact to the instructions drawn by a masterly hand for the American delegates at the second conference at The Hague. In these instructions Secretary Root told the delegates never to forget that "the object of the conference was agreement, not compulsion," and that the agreements reached should be "genuine and not reluctant."

This is, undoubtedly, the road to follow, a road not yet smooth, nor cleared of its rocks and pitfalls. The dangers continue to be many. One of the dangers is of asking too much too soon and of causing nations to fear that, if they make any little concession, they will be led by degrees to a point where, being peacefully disarmed, their continuance as a nation will depend upon the will, the good faith and the excellent virtues of some one else. Another is to describe war as being such an abominable thing in itself, whatever be its occasion, as to cause that public opinion on which so much depends to rebel against the preacher and his whole doctrine.

Let us not forget that, even in the land of "Utopia," the country of Nowhere, in which every virtue of good citizenship was practised, and war held as a monstrosity, *rem plane beluinam*, all wars had not been abolished. Sir Thomas More informs us that Utopians make war for two causes and keep, therefore, well drilled. The causes are: First, "to defend their own country"; second, "to drive out of their friends' land the enemies that have invaded it."[1] We have waged in the past such wars and cannot pretend to feel repentant.

Such wars continue to be unavoidable to-day, and to deny this is only to increase the danger of a revulsion of feeling among well-disposed nations. What we may hope and must strive for is that, with the development of mankind, a better knowledge of our neighbors, an understanding that a difference is not necessarily a vice, nor a criticism a threat, with that better instruction which a society like this one is giving to the many, a time may come when that same public opinion will render impossible the two sorts of *casus belli* for which More deems war to be not only necessary but noble and virtuous.

No less dangerous is it to load war with all the sins in Israel, thus running the same risk of mak-

---

[1] "Thoughe they do daylie practise and exercise themselves in the discipline of warre, and not onelie the men but also the women upon certen appointed daies, lest they should be to seke (*inhabiles* in the Latin) in the feate of armes, if nede should require, yet they never go to battell, but either in defence of their owne countrey, or to drive out of their frendes lande the enemies that have invaded it, or by their power to deliver from the yocke and bondage of tirannye some people, that be therewith oppressed. Which thing they do of meere pitie and compassion." Ralph Robinson's translation, 1st ed., 1551; ed. Arber, p. 132.

ing people rebel not only against the preacher but against his very creed. When we are told by the pacifist that, owing to the wars of the early nineteenth century, only inferior people were left in France to perpetuate the race, we wonder how it is that she got a Victor Hugo, an Alexandre Dumas, a Louis Pasteur, sons of soldiers of Napoleon, all three. We wonder how, in spite of this supposed survival of "the weakest," that country got so many thinkers, philosophers, poets, artists, soldiers, explorers; how the venturous spirit of the former "coureurs de bois" awoke again in our days with such notable results in Asia, Africa, and elsewhere; how birth was given in our land to the inventors of the dirigible, the automobile, the submarine, photography, and radium; how the love of sport in the race has reappeared of late, as active as it had ever been in the remote times when football and cricket found in France their rough-hewn cradle.

Exaggeration will not help, but on the contrary surely hurt. Truth, if we follow her, is certain to lead to better times. She has already. Wars in former centuries lasted a hundred years, then they lasted thirty years, then seven years; and now, as disastrous as ever, it is true, but separated by longer intervals, they last one year.[1] You are

---

[1] Most of them much less. In this, however, as in so many other respects, the present war, declared by Germany against Russia,

about to celebrate a hundred years' peace with
England; so are we.

That move toward truer, longer, perhaps one
day definitive peace, has been prophesied long before our time, not merely by a dreamer like Abbé
de Saint-Pierre, but by one who had a rare experience of men, of war, and of peace, and who, considering especially the influence of trade on nations, once said:

"Although I pretend to no peculiar information respecting commercial affairs, nor any foresight into the scenes of futurity, yet as the member of an infant empire, as a philanthropist by
character, and (if I may be allowed the expression)
as a citizen of the great republic of humanity at
large, I cannot help turning my attention sometimes to this subject. I would be understood to
mean that I cannot help reflecting with pleasure
on the probable influence that commerce may
hereafter have on human manners and society in
general. On these occasions I consider how mankind may be connected like one great family in
fraternal ties. I indulge a fond, perhaps an enthusiastic idea that, as the world is evidently
less barbarous than it has been, its amelioration
must still be progressive; that nations are be-

August 1, 1914 (five days before Austria could be persuaded to act
likewise), against France the 3d, against Belgium the 4th, which
was tantamount to declaring it on England too, is an exception.

coming more humanized in their policy, that the
subjects of ambition and causes for hostility are
daily diminishing; and in fine that the period is
not very remote when the benefits of a liberal
and free commerce will pretty generally succeed
to the devastations and horrors of war."

Thus wrote to Lafayette, on the 15th of August,
1786, that "citizen of the great republic of humanity," George Washington.[1]

That practical results have been secured is certain; that better ones are in store, if we act wisely,
is no less certain. Mankind longs for less troubled
days, and moves toward this not inaccessible
goal. Such is the truth; and we may feel confident that, according to the oft-quoted word of
dying Wyclif, "Truth shall conquer."

[1] In connection with Washington's views, those of Franklin concerning amicable relations between great countries may appropri-
ately be quoted. He wrote from Passy, on October 16, 1783, to his
friend David Hartley, one of the British plenipotentiaries for the
peace: "What would you think of a proposition, if I sh'd make it
of a family compact between England, France, and America? America would be as happy as the Sabine girls if she could be the means
of uniting in perpetual peace her father and her husband. What repeated follies are those repeated wars! You do not want to conquer and govern one another. Why, then, should you continually
be employed in injuring and destroying one another? How many
excellent things might have been done to promote the internal welfare of each country; what bridges, roads, canals, and other public
works and institutions tending to the common felicity, might have
been made and established with the money and men foolishly spent
during the last seven centuries by our mad wars in doing one another
mischief!" *Works*, ed. Smythe, IX, 107.

A POSTSCRIPT

A few years after this address had been delivered threatening clouds began to gather. Germany, who had prevented, at the first conference
of The Hague, anything being done toward a
limitation of armaments as proposed by Russia,[1]
suddenly, in full peace, when other nations were
inclined to think that they were rather too much
armed than not enough, passed a law increasing,
in a prodigious degree, her military forces.

On this move of hers, on what peace-loving
democracies ought to do in the presence of such
an unexpected event, on the future of the peace
and arbitration ideas, after such a blow, the
former president of the French delegation at The
Hague, Mr. Léon Bourgeois, wrote in May, 1913,
little more than a year before the present war, a
noteworthy letter,[2] in which we read:

"One fact strikes us most painfully and might
at first disturb our minds. The bills presently
submitted to the Reichstag are going to increase
in a formidable manner the armaments of Germany, and to necessitate on the part of France an

---

[1] "Notwithstanding the support given to the Russian proposition
by France, one of the most martial of the nations, and by various
other governments, the objections voiced by the German delegates
were too serious to be overcome." John W. Foster, *Arbitration and
The Hague Court*, Boston, 1904, p. 32.

[2] Text, *e. g.*, in the *Temps*, May 12, 1913.

extraordinary effort, and sacrifices to which **we** must manfully and promptly consent. . . .

"No one more than myself deplores that folly of armaments to which Europe is yielding, and I do not forget that it was I who, in 1899, at the first Hague Conference, drew up and defended the resolution in favor of a limitation of the military load weighing on the world. But I do not forget either what I said before the Senate, in 1907, after the second conference: 'As for us, confirmed partisans of arbitration and peace, *disarmament is a consequence, not a preparation.* For disarmament to be possible, one must first feel that one's right is secure. The security of right is what must be organized first of all. Behind that rampart alone, nations will be able to lay down their arms. . . .

"Let us be pacific, but let us be strong. And let us know how to wait. The very excess of the load weighing on Europe will originate, sooner than is sometimes believed, that irresistible movement of opinion which will cause a policy of wisdom, mutual respect, and real security, to become an unavoidable necessity."

The chief factor will be public opinion. Present events will, one may hope, have served to educate public opinion throughout the world.